# THE BRAZEN ALTAR

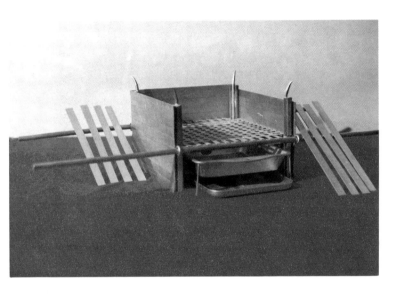

## "HOLLOW WITH BOARDS SHALT THOU MAKE IT"
(Exod. 27.8)

The boards one one side have been removed and laid against the carrying staves, thus showing the ease with which the priest could attend to the sacrifices and the perpetual fire. Note also the "pan to receive his ashes" and the "firepan". (Exod. 27.3).

# THE TENT

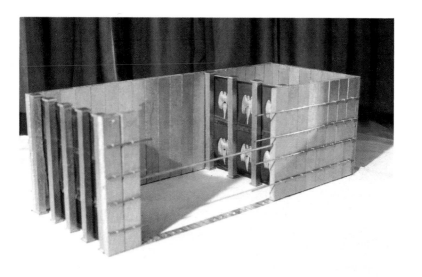

"AND THOU SHALT MAKE BOARDS FOR THE
TABERNACLE OF SHITTIM WOOD STANDING UP"
(Exod. 26.15)

Ten boards have been removed from the front of the model and
four of the bars cut away to show "the middle bar in the midst of
the boards" reaching "from end to end" (Exod. 26.28). Note also
the five pillars supporting the entrance curtain, the four pillars
suporting the cherubim embroidered vail and the sockets of
silver waiting to receive the ten boards that have been removed.

# THE CURTAINS

"TEN CURTAINS OF FINE TWINED LINEN, AND BLUE AND
PURPLE AND SCARLET; WITH CHERUBIM OF CUNNING WORK
SHALT THOU MAKE THEM." (Exod. 26.1).
Represented by the coloured curtain.

AND THOU SHALT MAKE CURTAINS OF GOATS' HAIR TO BE
A COVERING UPON THE TABERNACLE ... AND THOU SHALT
DOUBLE THE SIXTH CURTAIN IN THE FOREFRONT OF THE
TABERNACLE." (Exod. 26.7-9).

One corner of the goats' hair curtain has been folded back to
reveal the inner curtain. Note the goats' hair curtain folded back
at the front of the tabernacle.

# GOD'S SANCTUARY

TABERNACLE
MEDITATIONS

*by*

C. H. RAVEN

PUBLISHED BY
JOHN RITCHIE LTD.
KILMARNOCK, SCOTLAND

"LET THEM MAKE ME A SANCTUARY THAT I MAY
DWELL AMONG THEM."                    *(Exod. 25.8)*

## DEDICATION
This book is dedicated to all the saints who through the years
have enjoyed fellowship at Park Road Hall, Crouch End, London,
for they have helped to fund this publication.

# Contents

*v*

# CONTENTS

# SUGGESTED PLAN OF THE TABERNACLE

## (2mm = 1 Cubit)

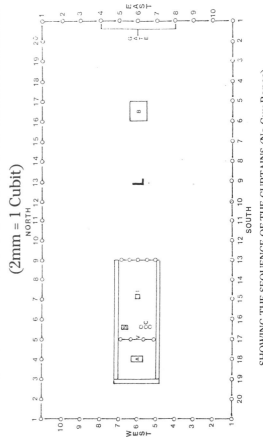

SHOWING THE SEQUENCE OF THE CURTAINS (No Guy Ropes)

A = ARK; V = VEIL; C = CANDLESTICK; S = TABLE OF SHEWBREAD;
I = ALTAR OF INCENSE; L = LAVER (shapeless); B = BRAZEN ALTAR

NO CLAIM IS MADE FOR THE EXACT LOCATION OF THESE ARTEFACTS, THE PLAN SIMPLY SHOWS THEIR RELATIVE POSITIONS.

# Preface

Well might the reader of these pages ask himself, "Who is this man, what arrogance is this that he should write of such sacred things?" If such be the question that arises in your mind then read on. If there be no such question then ignore this chapter for its purport is not egotistical but rather to satisfy your curiosity.

First of all let me make it abundantly clear that when I refer to "man" or "mankind" in the following pages I usually use these in the fullest and broadest sense so that man means man and woman, and mankind means mankind and womankind. The difficulties that we experience in ordinary secular writing still exist when we write about the Word of God. In everyday parlance we find difficulty in describing a "manhole" as a "personhole" or even a "chairman" as a "chairperson". Perhaps it is through ignorance or bias that these difficulties arise for one of the meanings of "man" is "man and woman" and of "mankind" is "mankind and womankind".

Since childhood I was brought up in the assemblies. Over the years I have kicked and rebelled but in spite of my waywardness the Lord has graciously brought me back and kept me.

I can claim no great scholarship in the schools of men but the lessons that I have learned in God's school have often been sharp and severe, and none the worse for that. I have studied the tabernacle for over sixty years, not continuously of course, but constantly returning to it and pondering its lessons. My interest was first aroused by my old Bible Class teacher, Mr Alexis Jacob of Highbury, North London, to whom I owe so much. By the time I was fifteen I knew it all and would argue and dogmatise on most of the tabernacle's items – such is youth. I have learned since that so numerous and varied are the tabernacle lessons that the dogmatist is a fool. No, perhaps that is too harsh, rather brand him as immature even as I was at fifteen. From this do not assume that now, at seventy-five years of age, I consider myself fully mature, far from it, but if we are willing we can, over the years, learn many important lessons and not the least that learned by the "noblemen" of Berea.

Mayhap you will not agree with all the thoughts expressed, don't dismiss them unless you have another solution that you feel better fits the type. If you reject any thought or reason let it exercise you and strengthen you in your own understanding so that even my weaknesses may serve to establish you. If there be some new thought that fills you with wonder, then praise the Lord and rejoice therein, but brand me not as a heretic because at times I do not see things exactly as they have been taught before.

I have read and considered many, many works on the tabernacle including Soltau, Scott, Pollock, Newberry, Jacob and a host of others. I am deeply indebted to all of them for exercising my mind to think on these things. Had I nothing to add then the following pages would be worthless.

At a bank managers' business dinner some years ago at which I was the "guest of honour" (how empty), my own bank manager introduced me as an inventor who actually makes his inventions pay. Perhaps he knew more than I did. Sufficient to say that I have an inventor's mind, a warped mind if you so wish to call it, but I must be able to visualise every description as it is given and it has to make sense, hence the understanding of the peripheral curtains and the boards and covers. Maybe your mind is more practical than mine and you have greater insight, may the Lord bless you in it, but because of the puzzles and complexities of the tabernacle a little text from Isaiah chapter one, although perhaps taken out of context, assumes a wonderful significance, "Come now, and let us reason together, saith the Lord". (Isa. 1 v 18). Ah! that reasoning together, how precious. It has taken many hours to actually write this book, but these hours are as nothing compared to the hours of reasoning, pondering, asking for guidance, lying awake at night for hours while the Holy Spirit slowly opened a dull mind to the glories of the Word of God. Presumptuous! did you say? Oh my brother, my sister, read the fourteenth chapter of John's gospel where the Lord promises the gift of the Holy Spirit. "For He shall . . . be in you". "He shall teach you all things". Maybe there are those who require the evidence of healings, or of tongues, who express the presence of the Spirit by clapping and shouting and dancing – who am I to condemn? but give me those quiet hours with a difficult problem from the Word of God, insoluble problems (even for an inventor), a constant prayer for understanding and a cry of "Teach me thy way", and when an answer comes, as it surely will, the wonder, the glory, the praise - none can describe it for His ways are past finding out unless He reveals them to us.

This book is far from exhaustive. Volumes could be written on the tabernacle. Sometimes in sheer weariness of mind and hand I have laid aside my pen and said in my heart that my reader will surely see such and such a point for himself, and he will, if he reads these pages in conjunction with a far more important book, the Word of God.

I have not endeavoured to write a stolid, stuffy theological treatise. Maybe at times you will condemn my style (please remember that love suffereth long and is kind) but I have approached this subject as a Bible Class leader might chat to his students, that they might enter into these wonders, not just as theological truths but as spiritual experiences to be appreciated and enjoyed.

So read these pages, not as dogmatic statements, but rather as furnishing keys that may be used to unlock those treasure chests from which may be brought forth "out of His treasure, things new and old" (Matt. 13 v 52). The natural man may not appreciate them so pray the prayer of a hymn that we often sang in Bible Class;

> *Open my eyes that I may see*
> *Glimpses of truth thou has for me,*
> *Place in my hands the wonderful key*
> *That shall unclasp and set me free.*

Now read on.

C.H. Raven,
"Sarepta",
Crossmichael,
Castle Douglas,
Scotland,
DG7 3BD.

# Foreword

In Stephens address to the Jewish council, he stated that "our fathers had the tabernacle of witness in the wilderness, as He had appointed, speaking unto Moses, that he should make it according to the fashion that he had seen" (Acts 7:44). Since it was "the tabernacle of witness", there could be no inaccuracy in its construction, and no innovation on the part of Moses. If otherwise, the witness would be imperfect. Hence the command, "See, saith He, that thou make all things according to the pattern shewed thee in the mount." Heb 8:5, citing Exod. 25:40.

But how was it, "the tabernacle of witness?" In what way was it, "the example (representation) and shadow of heavenly things?" This book often addresses these questions in an unusual way. It is thoroughly non-standard in approach. It is refreshingly unorthodox, whilst remaining undeviatingly orthodox in handling "those things which are most surely believed among us." The reader must be prepared for some surprises. How many of us thought that the ark could have been carried in any other way but by staves running parallel to the long sides? The reader must also be prepared for close and thought-provoking attention to detail. How many of us have noticed, let alone understood, the fact that in Heb. 9, the ark is said to be "overlaid round about with gold" (v4), whereas Exod. 25:11 states that it was overlaid "with pure gold", but the surrounding crown was just "gold?".

Bob Raven has made a life-long study of this subject and during the last thirty years, I have enjoyed and profited from his 'Tabernacle' ministry, together with teaching from all parts of Holy Scripture. The ultimate test of all teaching, whether written or oral, is its ability to warm our hearts and to engage us with Christ. This book meets those criteria. May the Lord use these studies to promote the spiritual well-being of His people.

*John Riddle*
*Cheshunt*

# The Tabernacle

CHAPTER ONE

## Introduction

Woe betide the man who handles the Word of God lightly or deceitfully. It is the most powerful force in the world today "for the word of God is quick and powerful, and sharper than any two-edged sword, piercing even to the dividing asunder of soul and spirit, and of the joints and marrow, and is a discerner of the thoughts and intents of the heart." (Heb. 4 v 12). In it there are the ways of life and death and these are taken to the extreme for it deals with eternal life and eternal death. Not only does it concern itself with profound subjects such as these but, in some mysterious way, known only to those who have experienced it, it gives a divine power that makes possible things that to the natural man are outside his experience and understanding. Superficially the Old Testament deals with the history of a nation; the biographical accounts of certain men connected with that nation; a fair amount of poetry and predictions as to the future. What then makes it so potent? Simply this, that its prophecies are centred, not only in a nation, but more essentially in a Messiah. There is an historic or prophetic account but hidden underneath in every page there is a typography concerning Him, so much so that when the unrecognised Messiah, after His resurrection from among the dead, walked with two of His unbelieving disciples "beginning at Moses and all the prophets, He expounded unto them in all the scriptures the things concerning Himself". (Luke 24 v 27), obviously dealing with Abraham and Isaac and the sacrificial lamb, yes obviously so, but do not let us gloss over the import of those words "Moses and ALL the prophets . . . And in ALL the scriptures". Now, how far can we take this? Does not the apostle

Paul tell us in 1 Cor. 10 vv 1-4? The crossing of the Red Sea was a picture, yes that's easy, but, says Paul, guided by the Holy Spirit, even the very rocks of the desert speak of Him for, "that rock was Christ".

Handle God's book with care. It is not ordinary literature, it is part of God. That is worth repeating, and let it sear into our hearts and minds, it is not ordinary literature, it is part of God, with the power of God behind it. How do we dare to make such a statement? John begins his gospel "In the beginning was the Word, and the Word was with God, and the Word was God.", and as we read down the chapter we find that the Lord Jesus, God's only begotten Son, is synonymous with the written and spoken word.

Dare any man then seek to unravel type and picture as displayed in the Old Testament? Not with man's wisdom for 1 Cor. 2 v 11 tells us that "the things of God knoweth no man, but the Spirit of God" and goes on more explicitly to say that "the natural man receiveth not the things of the Spirit of God . . . neither can he know them, because they are spiritually discerned". Ah! here's the secret. The Lord Jesus made a promise before He left His disciples, "but the Comforter, which is the Holy Ghost, whom the Father will send in my name, he shall teach you all things." (Jno. 14 v 26). Teaching is a slow process, it is a continuing thing and we never know it all. It is the elder who must be apt to teach, not the novice.

How then are we to understand all the types and pictures of the Old Testament? In John's gospel chapter five and verse thirty-nine, the Lord Jesus is speaking to the Jews who sought to kill Him (v 18) and says, "Search the scriptures; for in them ye think ye have eternal life; and they are they which testify of me." So that the Lord himself tells us that the Old Testament is all about Him and not only about Himself as a person, although this is of prime importance, but also, as in the scripture quoted earlier, "the things concerning Himself" (Luke 24 v 27). This is illustrated in one of the first types that we have in the Old Testament, God's first created man, Adam. Now we can be in no doubt that Adam was a picture of the Lord for the apostle Paul refers to Him as "the last Adam" in that glorious resurrection chapter, 1 Cor. 15 v 45, here we have Adam as a type of the Lord himself, the first Adam in the Old Testament, the last Adam in the New. But the apostle also states in verse twenty-two "For as in Adam all die, even so in Christ shall all be made alive." This concerns the children of Adam and the children of the Christ, here it is not so much His person but "the things concerning Himself." This is amplified in the pictures that we have of the children of Israel, and Paul says that we should understand these as types (1 Cor. 10 v 11) for here we have, not only a revelation of the perfect qualities of the Saviour as exemplified by "that rock was Christ", the one from whom the life-giving water emanates (Jno. 4 v 10), but also a wonderful series of events showing God's dealings with His earthly people but enshrined therein an understanding of the Lord's dealings with His heavenly people in their pathway down here. Surely "the things concerning Himself".

We feel this explanation to be necessary for some would see in the tabernacle an exclusive picture of the Lord himself. May we submit that this is a limited view of this most expressive type, for consider its purpose, "Let them make me a sanctuary; that I may dwell among them." (Exod. 25 v 8). This is a picture of God coming down to earth and dwelling among His people. Two components are necessary to understand the tabernacle. First and foremost, God manifest in the flesh, the Lord Jesus. Second, those among whom the Lord came to dwell, His people.

If the Old Testament is entirely about the Lord Jesus and the things pertaining to him, both in picture and prophecy, then there can be only one source of information to throw light on these ancient God-breathed writings, that is, the New Testament. Luke commences his gospel, "Forasmuch as many have taken in hand to set forth in order a declaration of those things which are most surely believed among us." If many have taken this project in hand why have we only four gospels and scarcely a mention of the Lord Jesus in ordinary secular history? One reason is obvious, although there may be others. Surely God intended that the sole source of knowledge concerning His Son should be enshrined in the God-breathed New Testament, for this must be the sole guide book when looking at types and pictures of the Old Testament. It follows therefore that every interpretation of any portion of the Old Testament that fails to comply with the revelation and teaching of the New Testament must be erroneous and therefore to be avoided.

Examples of error that have their origin in misapplied Old Testament types abound. The High Priest and his sons had glorious and distinctive dress, all of which, even although they be inanimate things even as the rock in the wilderness, speak of the person of our great High Priest and the things pertaining to him. For us to understand from this that there should be a priestly class with an archbishop or pope sumptuously attired to pontificate and rule over the church is entirely contrary to New Testament teaching. We will deal with this more fully in the chapter headed "THE PRIESTHOOD".

It is universally agreed in Christendom that we no longer have animal sacrifices, for there has been one sacrifice for sins for ever (Heb. 10 v 12). Then why do we need an altar? – a man-made innovation with no New Testament backing. A legacy from the Old Testament.

In the old Jewish economy the sabbath was the prominent day, the last day of the week, but when we come to the New Testament we find that the emphasis is laid on the first day of the week, the resurrection day. The binding shackles of the Mosaic law are no longer relevant. Sacrifices, new moons, ordinances and sabbaths have fulfilled their purpose in speaking of Him and the things pertaining to Him. Therefore the rise of various sects with a sabbatarian bias is an understanding of the Old Testament without reference to the New.

A more insidious error is to interpret half of an incident in New Testament terms and then to superimpose upon it some Old Testament activity. There is, in some sections of the church, an almost phrenetic phenomenon where the congregation is exhorted to participate in the worship by clapping, swaying and dancing to the rhythm of accentuated beat music. The justi-fication for these antics is based upon such scriptures at 2 Sam. 6 vv 11-23 where King David brings up the ark of God from the house of Obed-edom and on its arrival at Jerusalem, David "danced before the Lord with all his might". (v 14). The interpretation given to this passage is that the ark represents the presence of God and when that is experienced by the Lord's people they should follow David's example and dance with shouting and the sound of the trumpet. The interpretation begins well. The ark of God is surely a picture of the presence of God among His people. No one suggests that a physical ark should be constructed but rather that the presence of God is experienced among His people by the action of the Holy Spirit. So far, so good. Now these charismatic brethren leave the guide book, the New Testament, and revert to the Old Testament even as the saints in Galatia did, so that Paul writes to them, "O foolish Galatians, who hath bewitched you, that ye should not obey the truth, before whose eyes Jesus Christ hath been evidently set forth, crucified among you? This only would I learn of you, Received ye the spirit by the works of the law, or by the hearing of faith? Are ye so foolish? having begun in the Spirit, are ye now made perfect by the flesh?". (Gal. 3 vv 1-3). What is our justification for saying this? Let us analyse the interpretation in detail. The ark of God being the Lord's presence among His people presents no difficulty. David attempted to bring up the ark on a new cart. What is wrong with that, it's a very good cart and brand new? It was the Philistines' way of carrying the ark even although it was accompanied by music "on all manner of instruments made of fir wood, even on harps, and on psalteries, and on timbrels, and on cornets, and on cymbals". (2 Sam. 6 v 5). Quite a pop concert! and because it was man's way of approach, man's way of obtaining the presence of the Lord, very popular, very exciting, but because it was not God's way it failed and a man died. David found this a hard lesson to learn (vv 8-11) but he did learn it for in verse 13 on his second attempt we read, "they that bare the ark". This was the way that the ark was to be carried, on the shoulders of the Levites. Lesson one, make sure that the presence of the Lord is with His people in the way that He has appointed, not in any way that seems good to men.

Lesson two concerns the musical instruments and dancing. Although we do not find the musical instruments specifically detailed in David's second attempt to bring up the ark, nevertheless we do have the "sound of the trumpet" (v 15).

Turn to your guide book, the New Testament. Neither the Lord, nor the apostles, nor any of His disciples are recorded as playing a musical instrument. Almost the only mention that we have of them in the New Testament is when the children piped and no one danced (do not use this as a justification for music and dancing for the complaint continues that the children have mourned and you have not wept.), the harps played in heaven, and the trumpets of judgement in the Revelation. We have a reference to a trumpet sounding an uncertain note in the Corinthian epistle and also a reference to the last trump, but nowhere is a musical instrument connected with worship. Indeed the trumpet is usually connected with warning of impending events. The musical instrument was the invention and device of Jubal and he was a direct descendant of Cain, the man who brought the fruits of the field as a sacrifice.

Very good fruit no doubt, possibly the best, but it was the natural man's conception of worship. Perhaps it would be too harsh to condemn all musical instruments out of hand, but they must never dominate. Why ever not? Because the New Testament tells us how we should react if we are filled with the Spirit. Look at Ephesians 5 vv 18-20 ". . . be filled with the spirit; speaking TO YOURSELVES in psalms and hymns and spiritual songs, singing and making melody IN YOUR HEART to the Lord; giving thanks always for all things unto God and the Father in the name of our Lord Jesus Christ". Firstly we should speak TO OURSELVES "in psalms and hymns and spiritual songs". Not a course of action approved by the natural man, speaking to ourselves is deprecated by him, but the Spirit of God does not obey the natural man for the natural man cannot understand the things of the Spirit. This melody may not even be audible for verse nineteen tells us that it is to be the melody of the heart. Secondly we should give thanks to God the Father in the name of our Lord Jesus Christ (v 20). How is this to be done? We should obviously thank Him for creature benefits, nothing spiritual about this for how often we hear unconverted men "thanking God" for this, that and the other, but the spiritually minded man goes further, much further, into a realm unknown by the natural man, for Paul at the outset of this epistle to the Ephesians details how we should give thanks saying "Blessed be the God and Father of our Lord Jesus Christ, who hath blessed us with all spiritual blessings in heavenly places in Christ . . ." (Eph. 1 v 3), and he continues in this strain almost to the end of the letter, certainly until chapter 2 v 10. Nowhere is a musical instrument involved, nowhere is an emotional outburst of clapping or rhythmic dancing suggested. Why ever not? Surely it involves everyone in the worship, it is a medium that even the youngest can understand, true, very true. It is the medium that the natural man can appreciate, a rival of the pop concert or the last night at the proms, a carnal experience lacking spirituality, the Philistines' way of carrying the ark, a wonderful new cart, but man's way of approach and not God's.

We may well ask why all this preamble before any consideration of the tabernacle proper. Because in the tabernacle we have the initiation of collective public worship on the pattern laid down by the Holy Spirit. The previous manifestation of public worship had been that of the golden calf and on that occasion Aaron had not presented the golden calf to the people as an idol but as an embodiment of Jehovah saying to the Israelites, "These be thy gods, O Israel, which brought thee up out of the land of Egypt . . . Tomorrow is a feast to the Lord" and the people offered burnt offerings and peace offerings (Exod. 32 v 4-6) and the people sang and danced and rose up to play. Man's approach to God, something visible, something tangible, singing, dancing, community participation. Did God appreciate such worship? Read in chapter 32 from verse 7 onwards

Now God institutes HIS way of public worship in the tabernacle. No music, except perhaps the occasional use of a trumpet (even as David did in 2 Sam. 6 v 15), no dancing, just an overwhelming sense that God was in the midst.

Before leaving the question of singing and dancing it may be well to mention what is perhaps the greatest example of singing in the New Testament. In Acts 16 vv 22-25 Paul and Silas had been thrown into prison after many stripes were laid upon them and at midnight Paul and Silas first of all prayed, then they sang praises unto God. This was the object of their singing, not to whip up a frenzy, but because that singing had been engendered by prayer, so that even in these adverse circumstances they could praise God who had counted them worthy to suffer for the Lord, and as an incidental the prisoners heard them. So we should never conduct our praise and our worship expressly for the benefit of the congregation, our praise and our worship should be to God. Should others happen to observe it, well and good, but we must not put on an exhibition for man's benefit.

In verse 24 of Acts chapter 16 we read that the jailor thrust Paul and Silas into the inner prison. As safe as man could make them, there was no chance of escape. Wonder why the Holy Spirit also records "and made their feet fast in the stocks." Doubtless to show that even although they were in the inner prison, their escape was made so absolutely impossible that the jailor, who knew that he guarded the prison with his life, could settle down to sleep. Is this the only lesson that we can learn from Paul and Silas having their feet fast in the stocks? Could it not also show that although these two godly men could sing praises to God in their affliction they were barred from jigging about and dancing? Is it possible that the Holy Spirit knew in advance that singing was going to be associated with dancing some two thousand years later and therefore He clearly indicated that these two saints were fast in the stocks? Just a thought!

# CHAPTER TWO

# The Priesthood

A further word of explanation is needed before we embark on the tabernacle proper. As the thoughts expressed in this chapter do not necessarily follow traditional lines parts will occasionally be repeated under various headings as the practical applications come before us. We trust that the repetition will be forgiven.

On the subject of the priesthood many of us have been so concerned that we must not introduce any form of sacerdotalism into our church life that we have failed to appreciate the true priestly role of the believer.

That there must not be a two tier format in the church is clear in the New Testament. The deeds of the Nicolaitans are mentioned twice in the book of the Revelation, once in the letter to the church at Ephesus (Rev. 2 v 6) and once in the letter to Pergamos (Rev. 2 v 15) and on both occasions the Lord denounces them as something that He hates. For a thing to be mentioned twice in scripture denotes its importance and there seems to be no other understanding of the "Nicolaitans" than the meaning of the name which implies "those who exalt themselves above the laity".

There is no room in the New Testament for a division between the amateur and the professional Christian, between the knowledgeable and the ignorant, between the believer with half of the alphabet behind his name and the saints who are to be marvelled at as Peter and John were in Acts 4 v 13 because they are accounted as "unlearned and ignorant men" yet speak with a wisdom not of this world. Worse still, there must be no differentiation between men who claim unscriptural titles before their names giving them a god-like status of being revered.

On the other hand the Church is not a democracy. Democracy is man's answer to theocracy, which is God's government. Democracy is anti-god. It was democracy that crucified the Lord. Pilate, the voice of authority, would have released Him but the people, democracy, cried, "Crucify, crucify". God's law demands the death penalty, not only on the basis of an eye for an eye but primarily because man was made in the image of God. (Gen. 9 v 6). Man knows better and we are now experiencing a crime rate that makes apparent the evil that is in man's heart. God's law condemns homosexuality, democracy tolerates or even advocates it and the scourge of AIDS sweeps through the world. Need we go on into co-habiting, divorce, illegitimacy, abortion, drugs and drunkenness.

This is democracy and the Church must not be contaminated by it. If then the Church is not a democracy and is also not to be organised into appointments of archbishops, bishops, canons, cardinals, popes and reverends, what then is it and how does it function? The New Testament pattern appears to be the formation of local churches or assemblies each one of which is autonomous but they are all bound together into one unique and living whole. The introduction to the first epistle to the Corinthians illustrates this structure, "unto the church of God which is at Corinth, to them that are sanctified in Christ Jesus, called saints (local assembly) with all that in every place call upon the name of Jesus Christ our Lord, both theirs and ours (church universal)." (1 Cor. 1 v 2).

That the local church is autonomous is evidenced by the letters to the seven churches in Revelation chapters two and three. Each local church is addressed individually and is held directly responsible to the Lord. No assembly is given authority to control or judge another even when it is a question of holding false doctrine as in Pergamos (Rev. 2 v 14) and Thyatira (Rev. 2 vv 20-23). Yet it appears that the whole church is to profit by the mistakes and shortcomings of each assembly for John is instructed to write all these things in a book and send it to the seven churches. (Rev. 1 v 11).

It is important to note that the Lord alone must always be the head, not the Archbishop of Canterbury, or the Moderator of the Church of Scotland or even the Pope. It is as though there is a common pattern widening out like the ripples from a stone thrown into a pond. We have physical bodies and the Lord must be head of those. There is the local body of believers and the Lord must be head of that, then there is the great church composed of every saint who is alive today and who has ever lived since Pentecost and the Lord is the head of that.

Yet in all this great company all do not function uniformly. This is most clearly shown in the local assembly.

The twelfth chapter of the first epistle to the Corinthians seems to put things very clearly. That this chapter has an application to the universal church is undoubtedly correct, but would the Corinthian saints have understood it as such? In modern times, with the advent of the car, the railway, the aeroplane, and electronic communication the world has shrunk. We can know and understand what is happening in assemblies all over the world but in A.D. 60 it was not so. The Corinthian saints would have had the greatest difficulty in visualising say, the eye of the Church being in Jerusalem, the ear being in Antioch, the nose in Rome and the feet in Ephesus and each member being able to communicate and talk to each other as in verses 14-21. Surely they would have understood that the apostle was also referring to the local assembly for it is in the local assembly that relationships must exist. Always remember that no matter how great and knowledgeable a saint is he has no jurisdiction in the universal church, this is the Lord's domain, it is only in the local assembly that an elder can endeavour to guide and control.

How beautiful is the picture given by the apostle of a corporate body. A body in which the smallest member is important. How many assemblies have been split by knowledgeable brethren riding their own particular hobby-horses and pontificating and dogmatising, wretched men. How many assemblies have been strengthened by the solitary sisters, never taking vocal part yet never missing a meeting, "upon these we bestow more abundant honour" (1 Cor. 12 v 23).

Not only are there diversities of gifts and manifestations of the Spirit but there are also elders and deacons manifest in the local church, but the elder must not act as though he were lord over God's heritage (1 Pet. 5 v 3), yet on the other hand an elder that rules well should be honoured especially if he labours in the word and doctrine. So that the church whether local or universal must function as a body with Christ as the head, not forgetting that the saints are exhorted to covet earnestly the best gifts (1 Cor. 12 v 31) and to desire the recognition of being an elder (1 Tim. 3 v 1) but the whole must be steeped and swamped in love. (1 Cor. 13).

Now look at this question of priests. There is a priestly order in the church, an order in which every saint should endeavour to rise and achieve, not from the point of view of exercising dominion but because of a desire to know, serve and worship Him.

A verse that throws much light on the priesthood of believers is 1 Pet. 2 v 9, "But ye are a chosen generation, a royal priesthood, an holy nation, a peculiar people; that ye should show forth the praises of Him who hath called you out of darkness into His marvellous light". First of all note the purpose of priesthood, not to create a separate class, not to exalt one brother above another but to show forth the praises of the Lord. This scripture in Peter is an Old Testament quotation and comes from Exod. 19 v 6. Jehovah is about to give His law to Moses telling him that if the people would obey His voice and keep His commandments then the blessings of being a peculiar treasure and a kingdom of priests would be their portion. This promise was made to the whole nation, not just the tribe of Levi, the Levites had not yet been appointed, and in any case the Levites were identified with all of the tribes by linking them with the firstborn in Numbers 3 vv 39-end.

We dismiss the scripture in Exodus referring to the Jews as obviously being future. The people did not obey Jehovah's voice and therefore their priesthood is postponed until that day when ten men will hang on to the skirt of one Jew. (Zech 8 v 23). If we adopt this approach then we must do the same with Peter's exhortation for we do not see all Christians functioning as priests whereas we are told in Rev. 5 v 10 that when we get home in glory our song will be ". . . and hast made us unto our

God a kingdom of priests" (margin). Dare we suggest that we have not interpreted the type correctly and that perhaps, if we do, we shall understand 1 Peter 2 v 9 a little better.

Bear in mind the purpose of priesthood, "that ye should show forth the praises of Him . . ." Now look at Isaiah 43 v 21. "This people have I formed for myself; They shall show forth my praise." May we ask the obvious question, "To whom?" The answer is equally obvious, to the gentile nations.

There is no question that Israel was stiffnecked and rebellious, and so are we. But if there was one thing that they achieved more than anything else it was their separation from the nations round about (see Numbers 14 vv 13-17.) It is true that they had their lapses, as in Exod. 32 v 25 where we read "For Aaron had made them naked unto their shame among their enemies." The priestly testimony was damaged but the Jew has gone down in history as a peculiar people, arrogant, separate, the chosen nation of Jehovah. Hated, despised, persecuted because he would not amalgamate with the Gentile; even under the power of Rome the Jew would not bow the knee and still today they are known as "the chosen people". No other nation claims so blatantly that God has specifically given them their land.

From this we can see that although their obedience was incomplete yet nonetheless they have borne a constant witness to the fact that Jehovah is God and they are His people. Was this not part of the purpose of the sabbath, when in the wilderness the camp slept as it were, one day in seven? No work, no games, no journeys. You nations round about take note, these are the people of Jehovah, bearing witness to the fact that in six days the Lord made heaven and earth and rested the seventh day.

When the tabernacle was erected the various tribes took their stations and set their tents and standards in strict order around this small sanctuary. Constantly the sacrifice was burning in the centre. The people would not move unless the cloud or pillar of fire led them. Moabite, Girgashite, Jebusite and every other tribe and nation take note, these people are showing forth the praises of Jehovah, functioning as a nation of priests. It is surely a lesson that we should observe and note today. Israel as a nation has been reformed within a lifetime. Unique, separate from all nations, claiming their land as God-given, telling the world that Jehovah is not dead as some would suggest, telling the nations that the purposes of God are sure and certain. Unbelieving, rebellious, having rejected their Messiah yet still fulfilling Deuteronomy 28 v 10 "And all people of the earth shall see that thou art called by the name of the Lord; and they shall be afraid of thee." So that as a nation and perhaps unwittingly and unwillingly the nation of Israel has functioned and is still functioning as a kingdom or nation of priests, unique, no other nation like it, a peculiar people.

In interpreting and understanding the Old Testament types we must be careful not to limit them to our particular church persuasion, these divisions are of men. That does not mean that we should cease to emulate the pattern and teaching of the New Testament with regard to the local assembly but what it does mean is that although a believer may not belong to a New Testament local church yet nevertheless he belongs to that great body the Lord loved and gave Himself for. Every believer, no matter how weak and faltering, who names the Lord as Saviour or who conducts himself as a follower of Him, bears visible and silent witness that God has been manifest in the flesh, that the Lord has died and because He lives a generation is born again. We may hold up our hands in horror at the mass evangelism of America with its immorality and law suits, with every Tom, Dick, Harry and even Ronalds and Georges claiming to be born again but with all its imperfections and obscenities it functions to tell the world that there is a God of creation and redemption, "telling forth the praises of Him" – a royal priesthood. For this reason it is perhaps commendable to treat the first day of the week, the Lord's day, as something special, not as being under any law (except the law of love) but testifying to Him by keeping this day special that the world may see that we do not work either at our places of business or about our homes or gardens, that we avoid travel for work or holidays, that we do not use this day for recreation or joy-riding but keep it holy to the Lord for a testimony that all may see that we live to the praise of His glory, a kingdom of priests. Apart from being called to be a nation of priests, that is, evidencing the glory and power of Jehovah to the peoples round about, Israel had an internal priesthood designed with the same objective, to show forth Jehovah but this time in a fuller and deeper sense to the people themselves, as Moses himself put it when blessing the tribes in Deut. 33 v 10 referring to Levi, "They shall teach Jacob thy judgments, and Israel thy law".

The role of the priest, even in heathen religions, was twofold. First and foremost there was his service to his deity, often involving strange rites to which others were not a party. Secondly the priest, whether intentionally or not, conveyed the image or character of his deity to people round about. This is the general function of priesthood, it has a dual aspect, the godward responsibility and the manward revelation or demonstration. Israel was no exception to this generalisation. As a nation they showed forth and evidenced the fact that they were chosen by Jehovah and by the keeping of the sabbath they proclaimed, silently perhaps, yet nonetheless very eloquently, that in six days the Lord made heaven and earth and rested on the seventh day. As a nation, Israel fulfilled this role, maybe unwittingly, maybe even unwillingly, yet nonetheless very effectively.

Our priesthood is exactly the same today. We must ever remember that the Church Universal, as distinct from the local church, is composed of everyone who since Pentecost has accepted salvation by believing on the Lord Jesus Christ. Much of this church has already passed from this scene. Those of us who remain are scattered among practically every denomination and sect that man has ever invented and many of the saints in the systems, especially in sacerdotal Rome or the established churches would refute any suggestion that they were priests. Yet they are, for by their profession and by their mode of life they testify, maybe unwittingly and even unwillingly, to the facts that Jesus Christ came to earth as a man, suffered on Calvary, was raised from among the dead and is alive today.

The second role of Israel as a kingdom of priests is a little more difficult to appreciate. The tribe of Levi was originally chosen to be the priests within Israel. On the surface this may appear to be the setting up of a special religious class among God's people. If we look carefully at the appointment of the

Levites we shall find that God took meticulous care to identify the Levites with the firstborn of Israel, even to the extent of balancing the difference by a silver levy (Num. 3 vv 40-51). It would have been impractical to have called every firstborn Israelite to function as a priest within the nation. The firstborn would have had children and presumably the firstborn of these would be priests but what of the other children, would they have reverted to their original tribe? The subsequent firstborn of the tribes after the original appointment – were they to be counted as priests and removed from the parent tribe? It is obvious that such an arrangement would lead to the breakdown of the tribal system and also to that of the family unit, both of which institutions were an important part of Israel's economy. The tithe system, which was the portion of the priests would also have been impossible to operate. Instead, God identifies each tribe, each family and indeed each individual Israelite, with the Levites by matching Levite with firstborn from every tribe and family in Israel. The rest of the tribes of Israel were further linked with the Levites by the introduction of tithes.

The Levitical system itself worked in a twofold way. From among the sons of Levi, Aaron and his sons were set apart not only to form a continuance of the office of high priest which was handed down from father to son but these priests were the only ones allowed to touch the brazen altar and the other holy artifacts of the tabernacle (Num. 4 v 15). These few were the only ones, out of the thousands of Levites, who entered the Holy Place. Here it was that the blazing sun of the desert never shone, the only light was the lampstand. Here it was that the priests ate special food from the table of shewbread, not the manna that fell daily for the people. Here it was that the fragrance of the incense ascended night and morning.

Perhaps it would have been more exact to have said that Israel's priesthood was expressed in three aspects instead of two. There were the people themselves who witnessed to a creative God, the manward aspect of their priesthood. There were the priests, Aaron's sons, who served in the holy things and in the sanctuary, the Godward aspect of Israel's priesthood. Finally there were the Levites who formed a link between these two, helping the people with their sacrifices on the one hand and assisting Aaron's sons in the service of the tabernacle.

Every believer is called to be a priest. Every believer, whether he recognises it or not, is a priest "showing forth the praises of him who hath called you out of darkness into his marvellous light:" (1 Pet. 2 v 9), but the calling of every believer is to be a complete priest, that is not only to witness to his God but to serve Him by ministry to his fellow believers and in the service of the assembly generally (the Levites) and then go on in the deep things of Christ, entering into that Holy Place where the world and its legitimate things are excluded, where the only light goes beyond the generality of the Lord being the Light of the world. Instead we see the "light of the knowledge of the glory of God in the face of Jesus Christ" (2 Cor. 4 v 6), where our food is not just God's daily provision for the journey, great though that is, but to feed on the perfections of Christ typified by the shewbread and to be so occupied with Him, entering into that yearning expression of Paul, "That I may know him, and the power of his resurrection, and the fellowship of his sufferings" (Phil. 3 v 10) and yielding ourselves as a willing, living sacrifice of praise upon that altar of incense. This is the complete priest that we are called to emulate. How few believers make the full grade, washing their hands and their feet at the laver and entering into that sanctuary where the Father who alone knows the Son reveals something of His glory to them (Matt. 11 v 27).

How many believers are content just to be saved. Indeed how many believers are taught that this is the end all and be all of their salvation, the great weakness of mass evangelism. Let us endeavour to be good complete priests, going on to serve our brethren and the assembly and in the process learning more about God's Son until we can enter into that sanctuary where we are occupied alone with Him.

There is a marked progression in the internal priesthood that is within the nation of Israel as distinct from its priesthood nationally before the Gentile nations. The ten and two half tribes, other than Levi, are not counted as priests, but the Levites, although separate, are not exalted above the children of Israel but are regarded as representative of them (they took the place of the firstborn in Num. 3 vv 40-41) and also as servants to Aaron and the tabernacle. Twenty-one times over in Numbers chapter four where the role of the Levites is detailed, we have the word "service", in much the same way that we have all of the writers of the epistles referring to themselves as "bond servants". Any respect or dignity conferred upon these men resulted from their being the servants of Jehovah in ministry to His people.

Although the children of Israel were a redeemed people and had all sheltered beneath the blood, had all left Egypt, crossed the Red Sea and Jordan, yet they were not all counted as priests among the twelve tribes. Indeed the number of Levites, although running into thousands, was comparatively few when compared to the millions who journeyed in the wilderness. Is it not the same today? Millions of Christians in the world but comparatively few going on as priests. As already stated, the Levites were representative of every tribe, they were taken in place of the firstborn, teaching us that it is possible for any believer to go forward as a Levite, but how few do.

The Levites alone were allowed to camp near the tabernacle (Num. 18 v 22 and Num. 3) and Aaron's sons are distinguished even from the Levites (Num. 18 v 3). Aaron and his sons camped by the gate, the rest of the Levites camped on the other three sides of the tabernacle. Outside of these came the rest of the tribes according to their specific stations.

This demarcation was very strong indeed. We sometimes imagine that the Israelites could gather inside the court of the tabernacle but this was not so. The tabernacle was too small for such gatherings being little larger than a tennis court and it served perhaps 3,000,000 people. In addition Numbers 18 vv 22 and 23 states "Neither must the children of Israel henceforth come nigh the tabernacle of the congregation lest they bear sin, and die. But the Levites shall do the service of the tabernacle of the congregation". So that the children of Israel had to keep their distance from the tabernacle and only the Levites could go into the courtyard. The Levites themselves were not allowed to look upon the holy things of the sanctuary (Num. 4 v 20) so that the only Israelites to go into the Holy Place were the priests, the sons of Aaron. This seems to be borne out in Solomon's temple for the Holy Place is referred to as the Priests' Court (2 Chron. 4 v 9) and if the reconstructions of Herod's temple are anything to go by the Priests' Court was immediately in front of the Holy of Holies and it appears that the Lord himself was not allowed here as He was not of Levi's tribe but He always gathered in the outer court. This would mean that when the veil of the temple was rent in twain from the top to the bottom the only people who would have access to the Holy of Holies were the priests. Revolutionary? Yes. Heretical? We trust not as we shall seek to explain.

In Numbers chapter four we are told over and over again that the service of the Levites was from thirty years old until fifty, but in Numbers 8 vv 23-26 the Lord tells Moses that the Levites "shall go in and wait upon the service of the tabernacle of the congregation" from twenty and five years old, but they must cease "waiting upon the service thereof and shall serve no more" after reaching the age of fifty. These superannuated priests were to "minister with their brethren in the tabernacle of the congregation, to keep the charge, and shall do no service". It would appear therefore that the five years between twenty-five and thirty was an instruction period during which the priests who had finished their service could watch over and teach the young Levite so that on attaining the age of thirty he would be fully fledged in his duties and no novice.

The number of Levites who finished their service in the wilderness must have been minimal. A man just born when the priesthood was instituted would spend his first thirty years in the wilderness before being appointed to the priesthood when he would only have ten years of service before reaching the promised land. From this we can deduce that only Levites who were between eleven and forty-nine when the children of Israel left Egypt could have retired in the wilderness and these were possibly decimated for no man who was over twenty at the time of the Exodus reached Canaan.

Even among the comparatively small number that were allowed inside the tabernacle there were those who were barred from service. Any man that had a blemish could not approach and some of these blemishes are listed, "A blind man, or a lame, or he that hath a flat nose, or anything superfluous, or a man that is brokenfooted, or brokenhanded, or crookbackt, or a dwarf, or he that hath a blemish in the eye, or be scurvy, or scabbed, or hath his stones broken, no man that hath a blemish of the seed of Aaron shall come nigh". (Lev. 21 vv 17-21). How stringent, how unfair, democracy would cry, but God says that these things must be for He would teach His people, not just of the Jewish economy, but us today, the lessons of holiness and sanctity. The natural man who is already "dead in trespasses and sins" (Eph. 2 v 1) is of little account when it comes to the spiritual lessons that God would teach His people. In 1 Cor. 10 vv 1-12 the apostle Paul points out that twenty-three thousand died in one day and "all these things happened unto them for ensamples (types)". How important these lessons must be.

Are all of these things just idle observations or have they a strict import for us today? Remember that when Moses was commissioned by Jehovah to build the tabernacle He was insistent that every detail must be observed. We must do the same. If our understanding of a type is correct the anti-type will fit perfectly.

We have little patience with brethren who tell us that we must not push the gospel parables too far. These parables are perfect, they are the words of the Lord himself and we suggest that before these brethren say that the Lord's words should be limited they should examine their own interpretation of the parable and fit their finite understanding into the perfect structure of the parables of the Lord.

We have already shown that Israel fulfilled God's purpose in making them a kingdom of priests among the nations. That this was a national project is evidenced by the precise words "an holy nation", and it is equally true that the universal Church functions in the same way among those who do not know the Lord whether as nations or individuals.

Now look at the internal priesthood. The majority of the children of Israel were not priests. They were redeemed, they were in the wilderness. Although they lusted after the things of Egypt they could not enjoy them. God fed them, often they rejected Jehovah's provision, their souls loathing the light food of the manna and at almost every opportunity they departed from God's law. Look around Christendom today. Is not the picture the same? Most of those who cry and sing aloud "Jesus is Lord" have not progressed further than the brazen altar. Oh, herein is salvation, the Lord has died, "I'm on the rock, hallelujah!". We would not detract from these glorious truths for one moment, the trouble is we get bogged down by half truths. Ever remember that one of Satan's guises is as an angel of light. This was how he appeared to Eve, presenting her with a half truth and thereby blinding her eyes. Beware of catch phrases and clichés, they are so nice and concise but are fraught with danger. How often do we hear saints declaring that if such and such a church is evangelical it must be alright. Some evangelicals do not belong to a local church, they do not know the meaning of the words and in any event a church that is not evangelical is not a church. To every church in Revelation chapters two and three the Lord says, "I know thy works but . . .". This makes us look twice at the cliché "Saved to serve" – a half truth. The saint is saved to worship. His service and his giving should be part of his worship. The great apostle Paul was more evengelical than most yet he puts as his target "that I might know Him, and the power of His resurrection and the fellowship of His suffering". (Phil. 3 v 10). Yes, but Paul, you are so much in advance of us, you had direct revelations from the Lord, you wrote best part of the New Testament, you must know it all. No, says Paul in verse twelve, "Not as though I had already attained, either were already perfect; but I follow after, if that I may apprehend that for which also I am apprehended of Christ Jesus". How then do we do this? Peter helps us here, "that ye should show forth the praises of Him who hath called you out of darkness into His marvellous light" (1 Pet 2 v 9). Yes, but Peter, how? Says Peter, I've just told you, by being a "royal priesthood". (1 Pet. 2 v 9).

The Levites were the first order of priests. They had to be born of the high priest's family. A priest was ordained primarily to serve Aaron and the tabernacle. Before we can be priests we must be born into the family of the last Adam. By nature we are born into the family of the first Adam. By the Spirit we must be born again before we can be priests. Have a brief look at this question of being born again. The difficulties were certainly enough to puzzle Nicodemus for he asks, "How can a man be born when he is old? Can he enter the second time into his mother's womb and be born?" (Jno. 3 v4) and even after the Lord had elaborated on the Spirit's activities Nicodemus was still puzzled, and understandably so, for he answers the Lord by saying, "How can these things be?"

Perhaps we assume that we have a greater insight and understanding than this "master of Israel" and being born a second time presents no difficulties, or maybe we have not really considered the problem. In what way could we find an answer to the query of Nicodemus, "How can these things be?", bearing in mind two important points. First of all that the statement, "Ye must be born again" did not come from any disciple or apostle but from the Lord himself. There can be no two ways about this dictate, it is a compulsion and therefore vitally important. Secondly our only reference must be to the Word of God for this is the way in which the Lord answered Nicodemus, challenging him with his knowledge of the scriptures to furnish the answer, "Art thou a master of Israel, and knowest not these things?" Nicodemus, with your understanding of the sacred writings, you should be able to comprehend what the Lord is saying.

What part did we have in our natural birth? Did we choose our father or mother? Did we decide into which country we should be born, whether we should be black, yellow or white and a thousand other points? We just were not consulted. Here we are, born into a sin stained world. If we believe in a God and in eternity we cannot get off, we cannot escape, we must all appear before the God who made us. These are inescapable facts, epitomised in the texts, "It is appointed unto man once to die, but after this the judgment" (Heb. 9 v 27) and "As in Adam all die" (1 Cor. 15 v 22). How wonderful that in both quotations there follows the God-given remedy for sin. In Hebrews the apostle continues, "so Christ was once offered to bear the sins of many" and in the Corinthian epistle he adds ". . . even so in Christ shall all be made alive".

The problem is, how can we get from the family of the first Adam where all die into the family of the second Adam where all live? The Lord says that the answer is straightforward. As we have been born into the family of the first Adam so a new birth is necessary in order that we can be born into the family of the second Adam, the Lord himself, our great High Priest. Surely we must be just as puzzled as Nicodemus was and realising that this must be the way of eternal life, we join that teacher and say "How can these things be?"

From what has been written we can understand that as far as we are concerned our case is hopeless. We could not give ourselves natural life, neither can we give ourselves spiritual life. God must be the author. If this be true then we are helpless, we can only sit back and wait, longing to see whether a capricious God will, as it were, draw our number out of the hat. God would be perfectly entitled to do this if He wished. Each one of us has proved ourselves to be sinners by disobeying God and therefore any mercy that is extended to us is purely gratuitous and the chance of being chosen by this all powerful God is better than no chance at all. Does this argument ring true to you? If so, why did God have to send His Son to die? Why did the Lord Jesus turn round to Nicodemus and put the key into his hand by saying that "As Moses lifted up the serpent in the wilderness even so must the Son of Man be lifted up; that whosoever believeth in Him should not perish, but have eternal life" (Jno. 3 v 14)?

It is perfectly true that we cannot have natural life unless God gives it to us, and it is also true that we cannot obtain spiritual life unless God gives it to us. How were we born naturally? A tiny seed was sown, a seed so small that the human eye cannot see it, and from this seed there grew a man or a woman, an Einstein or a Napoleon! A Madam Curie or the Queen of England! We often talk of great oaks growing from little acorns. Surely a bigger contrast is that the greatest of men and women develop from a minuscule sperm seed. Rather humbling isn't it?

The New Birth is just as insignificant in its conception, a seed, that the natural man cannot see, is sown, and the Bible says "The seed is the word of God" (Luke 8 v 11). Quick, powerful, the greatest force in the world today. Listen to the way in which the apostle John begins his gospel. After describing the Lord as the Word he goes on to write "As many as received Him, to them gave He power to become the sons of God, even to them that believe on his name: which were born, not of blood, nor of the will of the flesh, nor of the will of man, but of God". Here it is again, three chapters earlier than the interview with Nicodemus. If a man is to be born again there is nothing that he can do about it for his new birth is "not of blood, nor of the will of the flesh, nor of the will of man, but of God". Are we that helpless?

Is this the God that the Lord Jesus came to manifest in the flesh? No! This is only half of the truth. It is true that God exercises His sovereignty and chooses some men in spite of themselves. The apostle Paul is a notable example. He was "a chosen vessel". God chose him. Paul just had to believe. The Lord stopped him dead in his tracks, spoke to him directly, blinded him for three days, told him where to go to receive his sight. Short of killing Paul there was not much more that the Lord could do. God laid his hand upon him and claimed him for His own. Maybe our experience has been similar to that of Paul. It is not to be supposed that we were on a journey to Damascus and were stopped in our tracks but it is quite possible that the Lord laid His hand upon us and claimed us for His own, that He so overruled our lives and led in such a pathway that we were brought face to face with the risen Lord and bowed in obedience.

How about the rest, those who can see others with this life? Must they just sit back and wait? No, for one of the essential features of the tabernacle is that the gate is far too wide for all practical purposes, teaching us this important lesson that entrance is for "whosoever will". Can it still be possible for us to be born again even although our experience is not parallel with that of the apostle Paul? Yes, it is gloriously possible. To use a contemporary phrase, "the ball is firmly in our court". How so? God makes repeated promises in the New Testament, simple promises but very profound. Here are a couple, "him that cometh to Me I will in no wise cast out" (Jno. 6 v 37); "Ask, and ye shall receive" (Jno. 16 v 24). Some may contend that we have taken these scriptures out of context. This may be true, but it is equally true that they summarise the Lord's attitude to sinful men. No one ever came to the Lord when He was upon earth and asked for a blessing but went away often with more than he asked. You and I cannot give ourselves new birth but we can turn to God and ask, saying in our hearts, "Oh God, give me life, eternal life in your Son". God is pledged to answer such a prayer.

While it is true that "None can by any means redeem his brother, nor give to God a ransom for him" (Psa. 49 v 7), yet call to mind the number of women who prayed for a son, that the giver of life might visit them in this way. Remember Sarah, Manoah's wife, Samuel's mother and others that you will find in the scriptures. Although we must be careful not to dictate to God and tell him who is to be saved yet, nevertheless, God does listen to and answer our prayers so do not cease to pray for that mother, that father, that son, that daughter or friend. God does listen. God can be entreated but our prayers must always be subject to His will.

How real is our new birth? We must bear in mind when seeking to understand the scriptures that the translation that we use must bear a part of the theological thinking of the translator. This is perhaps shown to the full in the translation that is used by the Jehovah's Witnesses. Slight deviations are made, many of which could possibly be allowable, that alter the whole meaning of a passage. This is why, when meditating on the scriptures we should consult various translators in order to arrive at what we consider to be the exact meaning. In this work scriptural quotations are often from J.N. Darby or Thomas Newberry, not that the A.V. is unreliable. In our opinion it is much to be preferred to most modern translations, but there are certain points that other translators make more clear and the question of sonship is one of them.

That we must be born again is undeniable. The Lord has said it. The apostle John tells us that this is not something for the future but is for the here and now, "Beloved, now are we the sons of God" (1 Jno. 3 v 2) presumably because we have been born into His family. There are at least three texts in the A.V. that appear to contradict this. Rom. 8 v 15 says "Ye have received the Spirit of adoption, whereby we say, Abba, Father" from which we conclude that we do not call God Father because we have been born into His family but because we have been adopted. Galatians 4 vv 5 & 6 support this thought, "That we might receive the adoption of sons, and because ye are sons, God hath sent forth the Spirit of His Son into your hearts, crying, "Abba Father". Ephesians 1 v 5 seems to put the matter beyond doubt, "Having predestinated us unto the adoption of children by Jesus Christ to Himself, according to the good pleasure of His will".

Many long and detailed addresses have been spoken and many exhaustive articles have been written on our being adopted sons. Scofield's note on Ephesians chapter one is a good summary. We quote this, not in any wise to pillory Dr. Scofield but as a concise example of the theory of adoption. "Adoption (huiothesia, 'placing as a son') is not so much a word of relationship as of position". (We may not agree with this dogmatism, "placing as a son" seems to savour more of relationship than position, but, to continue,) "The believer's relation to God as a child results from the new birth" (Amen to that) "whereas adoption is the act of God whereby one already a child is, through redemption from the law, placed in the position of an adult son". (So that God now adopts His own sons. If we are sons we do not need adoption. Even if we are babes now we shall ultimately grow into adults.) "The indwelling Spirit gives the realisation of this in the believer's present experience; but the full manifestation of the believer's sonship awaits the resurrection change, and translation of saints, which is called "the redemption of the body". This seems a little difficult when the apostle John has already told us that "NOW are we the sons of God" (1 Jno. 3 v 2).

Quite a problem, until we look at Newberry's marginal translation. In all cases where adoption is used in this sense T.N. gives a marginal note "sonship" or an equivalent term and you will observe that Dr. Schofield in his note gives the meaning of "HUIOTHESIA" as "placing as a son". Neither is Newberry alone in this. The R.S.V. gives "sonship" in Romans and Ephesians, the N.E.B. gives "sonship" in all three cases, the N.I.V. gives "sonship" in Romans and Galatians, Moffat gives "sonship" in all three cases, and J.N.D. even gives "sonship" in Galatians. What difference does it make if we use "sonship" in the scriptures quoted? Romans 8 v 15 now reads, "Ye have received the Spirit of sonship, whereby we cry, Abba Father". Galatians 4 vv 5 & 6 reads, "That we might receive the position of sons, and because ye are sons, God hath sent forth the Spirit of His son into your hearts, crying Abba, Father". Finally Ephesians 1 v 5 "Having predestinated us unto the position of sons by Jesus Christ to Himself according to the good pleasure of His will".

How do we feel about this? Do we still wish to be adopted sons? After all, an adopted son does not really know who his father is. Or do we call God "Abba, Father" because we have been born into His family? Should you decide on the former I will still call you my brother for I know who your father is even if you do not. Selah!

Thus we see that the initial requirement of the Levite was his birth. He must be of the tribe of Levi. This in itself made the Levite a priest manward. Whatever else happened he was always entitled to eat of the priests' food (Lev. 21 v 22). This was barred to the other twelve tribes (Ephraim and Manasseh counting as two separate tribes). This man was called to be a priest by birth. The ground must now be clear for him to begin the sacerdotal training in order that he might serve Aaron and the tabernacle. Not quite! The service of Jehovah requires perfection in man and beast. The Passover Lamb had to be without spot or blemish. The picture is obvious. "Christ our passover is sacrificed for us" (1 Cor. 5 v 7). Jehovah says, "Behold my servant" (Isa. 52 v 13). Pilate echoes, "Behold the man" (Jno. 19 v 5). The dying thief says, "This man hath done nothing amiss" (Luke 23 v 41). Whether it be godward or manward He is perfect. Not necessarily so with our Levite. May we quote Leviticus 21 vv 17-21 again? "A blind man, or a lame, or he that hath a flat nose, or anything superfluous, or a man that is brokenfooted, or brokenhanded, or crookbackt, or a dwarf, or he that hath a blemish in the eye, or be scurvy, or scabbed, or hath his stones broken; no man that hath a blemish of the seed of Aaron the priest shall come nigh." How would we qualify physically as a Levite? More important still, how do we qualify spiritually to serve as a priest godward?

Let us look at some of these imperfections. One or two are obvious. The blind man cannot see where he is going. He cannot see that highway of holiness that he has to tread. The lame man can see but his walk is such as not to be commended to his fellows. How about the man that "hath a flat nose"? Perhaps it is not by accident that one of the chief characteristics of the Jew, even today, is his nose. Two lessons here. First of all do we look like the people of God? If we do not then our priesthood is forfeit. There is a cult among certain young people that they must liken themselves to the man and woman of the world in order to reach them with the gospel; young men growing their hair long in defiance of the Word of God (1 Cor. 11 v 14), adorning themselves with earrings, which are a doubtful acquisition even for the young ladies (1 Tim. 2 vv 9 & 10, 1 Pet. 3 v 3) in order that they might look like the world. Does this commend the gospel of Christ? My brother, my sister, you do not even look like one of God's people, your nose is as flat as a pancake. Separate yourselves from the world is the injunction of scripture, not become part of it. (1 Cor. 6 vv 16 & 17).

The second lesson must be that a flat nose impedes a man's breathing and therefore his sense of smell. A priest who cannot smell is no good to Aaron. What a drawback a flat nose would be to one of Aaron's sons, unable to smell the fragrance of the incense in the Holy Place. Any other Levite, had he a flat nose, would be unable to smell the evening and morning sacrifice as the odour of the burning lamb permeated the tabernacle confines. Once again the antitype is fairly obvious. If our breathing, as it were our intake of the Holy Spirit, is restricted then we cannot worship in the Holy Place neither can we appreciate to any full degree the sacrifice of Calvary.

Maybe we should add a third lesson. If, as priests, we have not a sensitive sense of smell our priesthood will be marred. How so? As he walks among God's people the priest with the sensitive spiritual nose will smell many odours. Some will bring joy to his heart as, in moving round the camp he hears believers singing,

*"Thy name blessed Lord is as ointment poured forth*
*And e'en as we utter it fragrance doth rise."*

Other smells he finds sad and depressing. The stench of un-cleanness among the Lord's people. Yet again, as he pursues his pathway there is a smell that he cannot clearly identify, a sickly smell, sweetish yet nauseating. The priestly nose twitches. The smell seems alright yet there is something wrong. Perhaps the help of another more experienced priest is needed, certainly not one with a flat nose, that together they might decide whether the odour is an asset or a liability in the camp. How essential it is that the modern priest has not a flat nose. 1 Corinthians 14 vv 8-10 tells us that there are many voices in the world often with uncertain sounds. It is equally true that among the Lord's people there are many odours, some good, some bad and some indefinable. The priest sniffs the air, there is something there that stinks. His knowledge, his skill, his care and above all his love are called upon as he serves his High Priest and His tabernacle.

We cannot dwell upon all of these priestly imperfections. In any event we should not consider them primarily in order to fault our fellow priests but rather as a help in perfecting ourselves. We might wonder what essential difference there is between one man being lame and another brokenfooted. A man can be brokenfooted and hide the fact with his shoe. Similarly a man can have "a blemish in the eye" without necessarily being blind. Maybe he is the only one who knows that he has not twenty-twenty vision. Once again the lesson is patent to all. Our walk as priests before God is not only governed by what our fellows can see but also by those blemishes known only to the priest and his God. Ever remember that it is "the little foxes that spoil the vines" (Cant. 2 v 15).

One last defect, then we must leave the rest to private study and meditation. Consider the man that is crookbackt. He cannot, or does not, lift his eyes godward. His gaze is ever upon the ground. Such were those in Phil. 3 v 19 who minded earthly things. Follow not their example, but walking humbly before your God, stand tall, clothed with the righteousness of Christ. Another aspect of the perimeter curtains.

CHAPTER THREE

# The Setting

"Let them make me a sanctuary; that I may dwell among them" (Exod. 25 v 8). Such was the divine edict delivered through Moses. This was indeed an edict even although it was presented to Moses as a request, for in the previous chapter it is recorded twice over that the children of Israel had promised, "All that the Lord hath said will we do, and be obedient." (Exod. 24 vv 3 & 7). Every wish of the deity then becomes a command. There is no room here for human intrusion or invention, the requirement is strict and precise, "According to all that I show thee, after the pattern of the tabernacle, and the pattern of all the instruments thereof, even so shall ye make it." (Exod. 25 v 9). How faithful was Moses in the execution of these instructions, so that the Holy Spirit could say of him in the last chapter of Exodus, "Thus did Moses: according to all that the Lord commanded him, so did he" (v 16). And this is not just a broad survey of the work but it applies to every little detail, for seven times over in this last chapter we read these words, "as the Lord commanded Moses" (vv 19, 21, 23, 25, 27, 29, & 32).

Why was Moses so faithful in even the smallest detail of the tabernacle? It is true that Moses spent forty years in Egypt learning to be something. He spent forty years in the backside of the desert learning to be nothing. Finally he spent forty years leading the children of Israel through the wilderness and learning that God was everything. Were these broad experiences the only things that made Moses so obedient? Consider his brother Aaron. Aaron was not a faithful high priest. Perhaps this is why he is not singled out for mention in the eleventh chapter of Hebrews. Aaron led the people to worship the golden calf

(Exod. 32 vv 1-6). Aaron was slack in supervising his sons when they offered strange fire before the Lord (Lev. 10 vv 1 & 2). Aaron seemed slow to learn his lessons. When Moses is told to give Aaron details concerning the Day of Atonement, God prefixes His instructions with "And the Lord spake unto Moses after the death of the two sons of Aaron, when they offered before the Lord, and died;" (Lev. 16 v 1). Perhaps a gentle yet poignant reminder that if Aaron put one foot wrong his own life would be forfeit. This is borne out by the description given concerning the High Priest's garments. A bell and a pomegranate were to alternate round the hem of the blue robe of the ephod, and the reason, "his sound shall be heard when he goeth in unto the holy place before the Lord, and when he cometh out, that he die not" (Exod. 28 v 35). How about Moses, have we any indication that God taught him a specific lesson of obedience?

Consider one or two cryptic verses in Exodus chapter four. Moses is on his way to Egypt to perform one of the greatest missions of his life, to confront Pharaoh with God's ultimatum that he was to, "Let my people go". On the way he stopped at a caravanserai with Zipporah his wife and his young son. During their stay at the inn God threatened to kill Moses and the patriarch's life is only saved through Zipporah circumcising their son. What can we understand from this? Moses was obviously at fault for not circumcising his son on the eighth day according to the explicit instruction given by Jehovah to Abraham. (Gen. 17 vv 9-14). Disobedience spelt death. How would we have stood under the law? Let us make sure that we do not abuse the grace of God. Moses is saved by his wife making good his shortcomings and Moses learns his lesson that complete obedience is imperative if he is to lead the people of God. The lessons of God are useless unless we apply them to ourselves. Are we, in any way, a leader or an example to God's people? A leader of God's people must be obedient and must count this as more important than life itself.

Just a word about Zipporah. There is not much said about her in scripture but here she was obviously instrumental in saving Moses from God's judgement. You wives have an important part to play among the people and assemblies of God. You can influence your husband for good or for ill. Instances of both abound in the scriptures. Do they abound in our assemblies? We'll go no further. Selah! Sufficient to say that Moses knew that he had to be meticulous in obeying the word of God and a similar requirement rests upon us.

On the night of His betrayal the Lord Jesus made a request of His disciples. As He broke the bread and passed the cup to those who ate that last passover supper with Him, He asked that they should do this in remembrance of Him. A simple request, rather like Jehovah saying to Moses, "Let them make me a sanctuary" and in the same way that this latter request became a binding edict for Moses who must ensure that it was obeyed to the letter, so the request of the Lord becomes a binding edict upon those who hear His voice. Already the cry goes up, "We are under grace, not under the law". How very true. The believer is free from the shackles of the Mosaic law, that law of sin and death, but he finds himself captivated by another law, the law of love. The law of Moses revealed sin and punished with death. The law of love reveals righteousness and imposes no penalties other than the fear of disrupting the enjoyment of that divine love. When the Lord instituted that last supper He did not tell His disciples that if they constantly remembered Him they would receive a special reward, neither did he tell them that if they never remembered Him in this way a dire punishment would befall them. Rather does it work on the principle 'If ye love Me, keep my commandments." It is worthy of note that at that last supper the Lord gathered His DISCIPLES to Him, not just believers, but DISCIPLES, those who were close followers of Him. Is there a difference? Have a look at John 2 v 23, "many believed in His name, when they saw the miracles which He did," These men believed in his name, they were believers, "But Jesus did not commit himself unto them." (v. 24). How different was the Lord's attitude to His disciples. Right from the commencement of His ministry in Matt. 5 vv 1 & 2 we read, "and when He was set, His disciples came unto Him: and he opened His mouth and taught them." and so till the time of His decease when the son of perdition had gone out into the darkness of the night, He turns to his disciples and indeed commits himself to them from John chapter 13 right through till the end of chapter 16. With whom do we choose to break bread and drink of the cup, with believers or disciples? A disciple is baptised to his Lord, baptism in this sense is a sign of obedience and that is the prime requirement of a disciple as is the question of head coverings and long or short hair in both men and women, and the silence of sisters in the church.

The children of Israel had been in Egypt for many, many, long years. Much of the time they had been slaves, serving cruel and harsh taskmasters. During that period many of them had been occupied in making brick and hewing stone for the temples and tombs of Egypt. Now the people are free. In front of them is a journey. Had the people known that the journey would last forty long years doubtless they would have fainted at the prospect. Moses' request to Pharaoh had been that he might lead the children of Israel into the desert for three days (Exod. 8 v 27) and it is highly probable that Jacob's descendants visualised their wanderings in terms of days rather than years. What must have been the reaction of the people when Moses announced that Jehovah wanted them to build a sanctuary that He might dwell among them. Temples! ornate brick! "No" say Moses, "No brick". Finely wrought stone then? "No, no stone, just curtains and pillars". But the children of Israel had no skills in working with the materials that God required. "And the Lord spake unto Moses, saying, "See, I have called by name Bezaleel the son of Uri, the son of Hur, of the tribe of Judah: and I have filled him with the spirit of God, in wisdom, and in understanding, and in knowledge, and in all manner of workmanship, . . . all that I have commanded thee shall they do". (Exod. 31 vv 1-11). God gave the instructions, instructions that may have seemed impossible to the Israelites, but not only did God give the instructions, but He gave the power and the skills necessary to implement those instructions. God does not change, He turns to simple fisherfolk and the like and tells them to go into all the world and make disciples for an absent Lord. What a commission! Little education, practically no capital, no premises. Even for a business-conscious Jew the prospect must have been daunting and so it proved until the Lord implemented the rest of His statement "And lo, I am with you alway, even unto the end of the world." (Matt. 28 v 20). The Lord not only gave instructions but He gave the power to implement those instructions, for when the Holy Spirit came at Pentecost, in one morning the civilised world was turned upside down. The Hebrew epistle states that the Lord is the same "yesterday", He gave power for an impossible task to the disciples, and "today", He'll give that same power for the impossible tasks with which we are faced, and that power will not fail for He is the same "for ever". (Heb. 13 v 8).

Learn another lesson. God does not use the skills of Egypt to build His house. The apostle Paul in the first epistle to the Corinthians and chapters two and three condemns and sets aside the wisdom of this world, summarising it in verse 19 of chapter 3, "For the wisdom of this world is foolishness with God". How often do we hear such expressions as "sanctified common sense". Common sense cannot be sanctified, it belongs to Egypt. What we need is spiritual insight for, "the things of God knoweth no man, but the Spirit of God . . . not the spirit of the world, but the spirit which is of God;" (1 Cor. 2 vv 11 & 12). Similarly there is no such thing as "sacred music". Music as such belongs to Egypt. It was Cain's descendant who was skilled therein (Gen. 4 v 21). The disciple's music is not a cleaned up or modified wordly skill but the spiritual music of the heart, however that may be expressed.

"That I may dwell among them", this is the key to the tabernacle. It accounts for the gate, for the brazen altar, the laver, the lampstand, the table of shewbread, the altar of incense, and even the curtain wall and the tabernacle tent and veil, all are necessary to create the conditions under which God can dwell in the Holy of Holies among His people. God begins with Himself, in the beginning God!!! "Let them make ME a sanctuary" and beginning with Himself in the Holy Place He works outward detailing the conditions that must obtain before He can take up residence in the midst of His people. How the lessons gush out of the tabernacle.

God in the midst, His rightful place, everything centred around Him, and so it must ever be with this God who never changes, always in the midst. When the incarnate Son was here He was always in the midst of the people. When they would cast Him over the brow of the hill He went through the midst of them, (Luke 4 vv 29 & 30), and even on Calvary's cross they crucified two malefactors with Him and Jesus in the midst. Today, where two or three are gathered together in His name there is He in the midst of them (Matt. 18 v 20) and throughout eternity the picture is, "in the midst of the throne a lamb as it had been slain." We might almost call this one of the prime lessons of the tabernacle and apply it to ourselves, for it is no use seeing lessons or even listening to them unless we apply them. Is the Lord in the midst of our lives? Does He occupy the central position? Does everything gyrate round Him? The scriptures reveal that without Him was not anything made that was made. Can we say in our lives that without Him is not anything done that is done?

Prior to the building of the tabernacle God did not dwell among men. He was for them and in this sense with them but He did not dwell among them. Consider the sacrifice offered by Abel, the first recorded sacrifice in the word of God, and we read that Abel "brought of the firstlings of his flock and of the fat thereof" (Gen. 4 v 4) but there is no mention of the blood. How astonishing! Surely the blood was the most important part of the sacrifice for without it there could be no remission. Search through the rest of Genesis and in all of the sacrifices there is no reference to the blood for cleansing. Why?

God could not come down to dwell among men until provisions had been made for an atonement (a covering) for sin and, says the apostle Paul in Romans 7 v 7, "I had not known sin, but by the law" and again in Romans 3 v 20 " for by the law is the knowledge of sin." In other words man could not know sin in its fulness until the mind of God was revealed by the giving of the law and with the giving of the law God also made provision for the sin offering.

Prior to the law Christ was presented before Jehovah as the burnt offering, that which God could find pleasure in but was not the aspect that would enable God to deal with man's sin and come to dwell in his midst.

Look at God's dealing with man in the early chapters of Genesis and we find such expressions as, "Go to, let us go down

. . ." (Gen. 11 v 7), "and God went up from Abraham" (Gen. 17 v 22), "I will go down now . . ." (Gen. 18 v 21), "And the Lord went His way, as soon as He had left communing with Abraham" (Gen. 18 v 33), "The angel of the Lord called unto him out of heaven" (Gen. 22 v 11), "The angel of the Lord called unto Abraham out of heaven the second time" (Gen. 22 v 15). God was for men and with certain men but He did not dwell among them. Not until the sin question was dealt with could Jehovah take up His position in the midst of His people and the sin question could not be dealt with until there was the knowledge of sin given by the law. That in itself was not sufficient, there had to be an atonement, a covering for sin furnished by the aspects of the sin and trespass offerings. When the children of Israel said, "All that the Lord hath said will we do, and be obedient." (Exod. 24 v 7) then the scene was set for God to give Moses divine instructions for the conditions that must obtain in order that God could dwell among His people. This is the progression of God's dealings with men. Prior to the giving of the law God was FOR and WITH certain men. After the giving of the law God could dwell AMONG men. After Pentecost God could dwell IN men.

It therefore follows that if we are to understand anything of this wonderful phenomenon of a sanctuary being built wherein God could dwell, it must be complete before we can begin to learn its lessons. We cannot begin to understand the mysteries of the Holy Place, still less the sanctity of the Holy of Holies, until we have the laver for the cleansing of the priests and the altar with all its sacrificial significance allowing some sort of approach for sinful man to a thrice holy God.

How right it is that God should begin with Himself in the Holy of Holies and work outward towards erring Israel, thus establishing His holiness and showing from the very first that there is only one gate, one way of approach and that must be by way of sacrifice if any access to His presence is to be obtained. There is, most emphatically, no other way. It would be of little use for a democratic Israelite to come to Moses and say that an old, yet wonderful Levite, who was full of good works even as Dorcas was, desired to enter the tabernacle compound but, as he lived on the west side he could not make even the short journey round to the east where the wide gate was. Would it not be possible, indeed would it not be humane and right to allow one of the western curtains to be pulled aside a little? It would not need a great effort. Just this one exception for a truly good man, could it not be? The answer is obvious. Whether the Levite be young or old, whether he be good or bad, there is only one God-appointed way and that is by the gate. What a wonderful lesson so soon in this tabernacle study. God, beginning with Himself, finishes a mighty and wonderful work through His servant. If we are to understand anything of that work we must approach it as a finished work. This is the way that God ever deals with sinful man. He sets before him a finished work accomplished by His Obedient Servant. When He came down and trod this bare earth as a man and dying upon that fearful cross He cried, "It is finished." The work began with God Himself. "God is love" (1 Jno. 4 v 8). That is His very essence. Anticipating the cross, for the Lord knew all that was to befall Him (Jno. 18 v 4 & Luke. 9 v 22), the Lord said to Nicodemus, "For God so loved (beginning with Himself) the world, that He gave His only begotten Son, that whosoever believeth in Him should not perish, but have everlasting life"(Jno. 3 v 16). A finished work by Jehovah's obedient Servant. We must approach the tabernacle as a finished work. Somewhere inside those perimeter curtains dwells a God of love whose heart is set on revealing Himself to men, and it is only through a finished work that this can be accomplished. The fact of the tabernacle being a picture of God coming down to dwell on earth is stamped firm and hard on its types and teaching. There is to be no floor in the tabernacle, not even in the Holy of Holies with its gilded boards and cunningly wrought curtains, the floor is to be bare earth. When God was manifest in the flesh in Bethlehem no one laid out the red carpet for Him, even although His advent was foretold in great detail as we see in hindsight. There was no human reception committee. He walked about on the bare earth and even although foxes had holes and the birds of the air had nests there was no comfort for the Son of God to lay His head but He went, as He was wont, to the mount of Olives at night. (Luke 22 v 39). Here

He met Nicodemus, here was a Garden called Gethsemane where He fell to the ground sweating as it were great drops of blood. God come down to earth. Selah! Pause and ponder a moment, think of that one who though He was rich, and how very rich, yet for our sakes He became poor, and how very poor, that we through His poverty might become rich, and how very, very rich (2 Cor. 8 v 9). (Someone, somewhere, we forget who, has told us that "Selah" means, "Pause and think of that". It is in this sense that we use it in this book.)

There are three sanctuaries that are described with any structural details in scripture, the tabernacle, Solomon's temple and Ezekiel's temple. True there were other temples such as Zerubbabel's and Herod's but no structural details are given of these and we suggest that they were built in order to maintain a temple continuity so as to teach us other sets of lessons. For example, it was necessary that there should be a temple when the Lord was upon earth in order that much of His teaching could be related to a temple but we know nothing of the construction of Herod's temple beyond perhaps the fact that it took forty-three years to build. So that we have three basic edifices, the tabernacle, Solomon's temple, and Ezekiel's temple. To try to combine Solomon's temple with that of Ezekiel must be wrong, they are two separate structures. The tabernacle is the only one with no floor. What then is the overall lesson? May we suggest for your meditation and consideration that the tabernacle teaches us the lesson very clearly that this is a picture of God dwelling among men. Sufficient detail is not given of Solomon's temple for any man to make a reasonably accurate model and this had led some to make the error of trying to fill the gaps from Ezekiel's temple. Surely we must ask ourselves why God stops short in His description of so glorious an edifice as Solomon's temple. And how about Ezekiel's? Read the description in Ezekiel chapters 40-43 and the greatest architect in conjunction with the greatest builder could not even begin to understand the structure.What then is God teaching by these three sanctuaries? God tells us clearly about the tabernacle. Everything is detailed, or almost everything. We are not told what the pillars that support the outer curtains are made of, neither are we told the size and shape of the laver. We should therefore be very careful of models of the tabernacle, but the picture is clear, this is God coming down to man. How about Solomon's temple? Have a look at Solomon's prayer of dedication in 1 Kings 8 vv 22-53. He commences by reminding God of His promises then in verse 27 he raises the query, "Will God indeed dwell on the earth?" and eight times over in his prayer he uses words like "hear Thou in heaven" (vv 30, 32, 34, 36, 39, 43, 45, 49). So that the picture is that God is no longer on earth, thus the temple has a floor, as it were separating God from it. God is in heaven, what has happened? Has God become more distant?

The children of Israel have finished their desert wanderings, they are now in the land possessing their possessions. There is many a fight and many a battle in front of them before the Prince of Peace shall reign in their midst, and Solomon directs the gaze upwards to where God is in heaven. Perhaps the New Testament would put it rather like this, "If ye then be risen with Christ, seek those things which are above, where Christ sitteth on the right hand of God. Set your affections on things above, not on things on the earth". (Col. 3 vv 1 & 2). It is rather like saying that although we are still down here we should not be so much occupied with the wilderness journey, for if we are we shall be a moaning and complaining people even as Israel was, but God is asking us to enter the land, fight the battles and as long as we are obedient we will triumph. Come into His temple, not the eternal state, for the battle is not yet over. Now read the first two chapters of the Ephesian epistle and you will be gently lead along a pathway showing how we were chosen in Him, how we have obtained an inheritance in Him, our portion in the promised land, not the full inheritance but the earnest of it by God's Spirit, and He tells us that even now He has made us sit together in heavenly places in Christ Jesus. Thus the overall lesson of Solomon's temple is that God is in heaven, we are still on earth and God is saying in effect, I came to earth once – the tabernacle – now although you are still on earth I am in heaven, enjoy the things of heaven now. You cannot see it clearly, the detail is somewhat obscure, parts of the design seem to be missing. How like Solomon's temple, enough description for us to see that it is a glorious building, possibly the finest that was ever built, but we can never understand it completely. Where is the saint who, even although he has known the present power of his Lord, can turn round and say that he also knows all about heaven? He can see that it is wonderful in itself but even more wonderful because the Lord is there. Although he sees and experiences these things he also knows full well that when faith gives place to sight he will joyfully acknowledge that the half had not been shown or told him.

How about Ezekiel's temple? If we find it difficult to understand Solomon's edifice we are completely adrift with Ezekiel. What do we do, abandon him as being impossible? No, take a general look at the thing that characterises this third sanctuary. This temple is full of little chambers, side chambers, holy chambers, chambers, chambers, chambers. In chapter forty and verse five the description of the temple commences and from there until the end of chapter forty-two where the prophet leaves the temple building we have the word "chamber" mentioned about thirty-five times. Why? Try and construct Ezekiel's temple. Try even to visualise it. Chambers and arches, palm trees and cherubim. Let's combine it with Solomon's temple. No, we must not do that, this is a separate picture. Well, it is obviously prophetic, obviously future, it will sort itself out in eternity. Eureka! you've got it. It is future, chambers, chambers, many chambers! "In my Father's house are many abiding places: if it were not so, I would have told you. I go to prepare a place for you." (Jno. 14 v 2). Of course you cannot understand Ezekiel's temple for "eye hath not seen, nor ear heard, neither have entered into the heart of man, the things which God hath prepared for them that love him." (1 Cor. 2 v 9). What a relief. So we need not study Ezekiel's temple because we shall not understand it anyway. Just a moment, read on in 1 Cor. 2 vv 10-12, "But God hath revealed them unto us by His Spirit . . . the things of God knoweth no man, but the Spirit of God . . . that we might know the things that are freely given to us of God." Back to your study of Ezekiel's temple if you would know the deep things of God.

To summarise the thoughts expressed on the three edifices,

we have the tabernacle teaching us about God coming down to dwell among His people, Solomon's temple in which God calls us to dwell with Him in heavenly places, even although we are still on earth, Ezekiel's temple – God calling us home to glory to dwell with Him, in many abiding places for all eternity.

Now let us consider the tabernacle in more detail. Four is the number that is connected with the earth. The fourth day saw the completion of the terrestrial scene as described in the first chapter of Genesis. Days five and six were concerned with the animals and birds that inhabited the earth. There are four seasons, spring, summer, autumn and winter. There are four cardinal points of the compass, north, south, east and west. In the biblical prophecies concerning the dominion of the earth only four powers are recognised, Babylon, Persia, Greece and Rome. There are many more less obvious uses of the number four being connected with the earth but the foregoing are adequate to demonstrate the significance of the number.

If we are correct in our understanding and interpretation of the tabernacle, that the overall picture is God dwelling on earth in the midst of His people, we should expect the number four to be prominent in the design. Let's have a look. Nothing that is described in the tabernacle is circular, speaking of that which is eternal, and nothing that is described is any other shape than four-sided (beware of models). Four structural materials are used, wood, brass, silver and gold. Four decorative agents are employed, blue, purple, scarlet and fine twined linen. There are four coverings of the tent, goats' hair, rams' skins, badgers' skins and fine linen. There are four curtains at the gate of the tabernacle (this will be amplified when we deal with the perimeter curtains). Finally the Holy of Holies, God's dwelling place upon earth is not circular, speaking of that which is eternal, but four square, of the earth and transient.

As God, in sovereign grace even in the Old Testament, deigns to come and dwell among sinful men, there must of necessity be strict conditions for man to come near to the deity. Indeed, in the ultimate figure only one man can be presented before Him and that in the capacity of High Priest, his view screened from beholding the holy dwelling place between the cherubim by the smoke of the holy incense and not daring to approach without the blood of atonement in his hands. Ever remember that God has not, nor ever will, abandon His first declared purpose, "Let us make man in our image." (Gen. 1 v 26). This seemingly impossible task God is committed to accomplish and in the process no inherent glory will be evidenced in man, all will be bestowed upon him by divine love and grace to the glory of His only begotten Son.

Let us then approach the tabernacle, the construction of which is described twice over in the book of Exodus, with humble and, if possible, open minds and seek to learn some of the lessons as we see the Word made flesh and tabernacling among us, for if we succeed we shall behold His glory, the glory as of the only begotten of the Father , full of grace and truth. (see Jno. 1 v 14). We must emphasise again that the understanding of the types and pictures of the Old Testament can only be appreciated as the Holy Spirit reveals them to us. So, taking the guide book, the New Testament, in our hands, let us pause and lift up a silent prayer perhaps couched in the words of the hymn writer, as mentioned in our preface,

> *Open my eyes that I may see,*
> *Glimpses of truth Thou hast for me,*
> *Place in my hands that wonderful key,*
> *That shall unclasp and set me free.*

# CHAPTER FOUR

# The Approach, The Overall Lesson

The tabernacle has been built. The people have given bountifully of their substance, so bountifully that their giving had to be restrained. Everything has been done exactly as Jehovah has ordered, so exactly that in the last chapter of Exodus the Holy Spirit records "according to all that the Lord commanded him, so did he" (v 16). When we turn to our guide book how worthy a tribute is paid to this great leader by the apostle in Hebrews 3 v 5, "Moses verily was faithful in all His (i.e. God's, according to Newberry) house, as a servant, for a testimony of those things which were to be spoken after." And here we are, some three thousand five hundred years later speaking of those things that Moses did under the command of God for our instruction and edification in God's dealings with mankind. The apostle then goes on to say that if we hold fast, that is, obey the divine instructions as meticulously as Moses did, then we are His house, thus giving us a further indication that we are to consider the tabernacle, not only as a picture of the Godhead; Father, Son and Holy Spirit, but also as a picture of ourselves as being part of His house, "if we hold fast the confidence and the rejoicing of the hope firm unto the end." (Heb. 3 v 6).

The people gave abundantly. Moses served meticulously. Yet when the tabernacle was finished and God gave instruction to the tribes concerning their camping order He said, "far off about the tabernacle of the congregation shall they pitch" (Num. 2 v 2). Although the children of Israel had given their all in substance, time and skill, these things did not entitle any man to approach or go near to God. Even when it came to the crossing of Jordan, no one (other than the Levites who carried the ark) could approach closer than half a mile to that symbol of Jehovah's presence, and Aaron himself was told, under penalty of death, that he must not approach Jehovah "at all times" (Lev. 16 v 2). What a lesson. No man can gain favour with God by giving, by working or by religious observance. How then can sinful man approach a thrice holy God? The omissions of scripture are often as important as the inclusions. Consider the materials used for the tabernacle and they include no iron. Yet an immense amount of iron was used in Solomon's temple. It is often assumed that iron was unknown at this time. In the light of Gen. 4 v 22, Num. 31 v 22, Num. 35 v 16 etc. this cannot be true. Why then was no iron in the tabernacle? Commentators often draw attention to the brass or native copper as being the fire-resistant metal but it was not, for iron has a higher melting point than brass. Then why not at least make the grate of the altar of iron so that it could withstand more heat? Why not indeed. We will consider this aspect when we come to the brazen altar, let it suffice here to observe that God did not want any iron in the tabernacle, and the reason? Oh, how wonderful and glorious. Iron speaks of judgement, punishment and iron rule. The Lord is going to rule the nations with a rod of iron, yet God is saying most clearly in the materials of the tabernacle that although man cannot approach God by anything that he can do, yet there is a way that this God who is longsuffering, merciful and gracious, has provided for man to come close to Him, not on the grounds of man's worthiness for that must be punished by death (the iron), but on the grounds of sovereign grace for although the sacrifice on the altar could not be seen outside the court, yet the ascending smoke and the smell of the sacrifice being consumed speak of great mysteries even before any approach to the actual structure of the tabernacle is made.

Consider this tabernacle as it stands amidst the tents of the children of Israel. Immediately surrounding the court are the tents of the Levites. The family of Gershon pitched behind the tabernacle westward. The tribe of Kohath pitched on the side of the tabernacle southward, and the family of Merari pitched on the side northward, while the eastern side was taken up by

Moses and Aaron and his sons. The total number of the males from one month old and upwards counted from the tribe of Levi was twenty-two thousand. Include the women and the children under two and we possibly have a company of some forty-five to fifty thousand souls so that there was never any shortage of labour when it came to the duties of the tabernacle. We can also understand that with this vast company of Levites camping close to the tabernacle, the instruction was given to the other twelve tribes (Ephraim and Manasseh being each counted as a tribe) to camp far off, became an absolute necessity. Now consider this strange thing. Here is a camp that must have stretched some two or three miles in each direction, an immense number of people, yet in the midst, as the shrine of Jehovah their God, is a comparatively insignificant little structure, no bigger than a modern tennis court (allowing for the side clearances and the run back at either end). Nothing glamorous about it, just a courtyard surrounded by white curtains. Rising somewhere inside there is a tent covered with badgers' skins. The only colour visible to the outsider was the ornamentation of the gate and perhaps the top part of the door to the tent. What a contrast to the temples of Egypt. How the children of Israel must have looked in wonder at this comparatively puny effort. It was not as though the children of Israel could not have done better, after all they had to be restrained in their giving. Gladly would they have provided the materials to ornament all of the curtains. Willingly would they have furnished a covering of glory for the tent. They would even perhaps have given Moses sufficient to make the tabernacle twice the size, but this was not in the hands of the children of Israel. Right from the start God was teaching them that His ways were not their ways. (Isa. 55 v 8). Jehovah was intent on having a structure that although it may not have appealed to man, yet it was to be full of lessons both for Jacob's offspring and also for those of us who, living many centuries later have come to know this same God in a fuller and deeper way.

Surely when we consider the simplicity and unadorned exterior of the tabernacle we are reminded that when God was manifest in the flesh and came to dwell among men, there was no external beauty that we should desire Him (Isa. 53 v 2). He did not come clothed in the glory of this world but as a man of sorrows and acquainted with grief. The Israelite had to look beyond the external, past the white curtains and see first of all the ascending smoke of the burnt offering and then the pillar of cloud resting on the Holy of Holies and there he could see and know that the God of his father Jacob was indeed dwelling in the midst of His people. The apostle John looked beyond what the natural man saw, even beyond the perfect, unsullied whiteness of the Lord as He walked down here and he says, "We beheld His glory, the glory as of the only begotten of the Father, full of grace and truth." (Jno. 1 v 14).

Look again at the tabernacle structure. Here was a courtyard one hundred cubits long and fifty cubits wide. What a strange arrangement. Here we have twelve tribes that are to surround the tabernacle, three on each side, the sensible and obvious thing would be to make the tabernacle square, perhaps a little more imposing, say one hundred cubits in all directions. That is not what God ordered, the tabernacle must be one hundred by fifty. Why? Surely God is telling us that He is not coming down into a perfect world, not like the Holy of Holies where He will dwell, and therefore God tells Moses to make the tabernacle oblong, the unequal square, for He is coming down to dwell in an unequal world, a world that lacks symmetry, a world that has been marred by sin. Then why not make the tabernacle one hundred cubits wide and fifty cubits deep? Because the attributes of God are always deeper than they are wide. Take the love of God, "For God so loved the world", here is the width, I can understand that. Every man, woman and child comes within the scope of that love. "That He gave His only begotten Son", that I cannot understand. Why God, in His love towards men, should allow the Son of His love to come here to earth and suffer on Calvary's cross, that is beyond my comprehension. The depth is greater than the width. Let us approach closer to the tabernacle and see some of the lessons taught by the curtains and the gate surrounding the court.

CHAPTER FIVE

# Of Curtains

In seeking to understand the perimeter curtains we should take note of two particular verses. The first is found in Exodus chapter twenty-seven and verse eighteen. "The length of the court shall be an hundred cubits, and the breadth fifty everywhere"., from which we may conclude that it was the divine intention that at no point should the tabernacle courtyard exceed these parameters. Any understanding of the tabernacle that places a separate set of curtains in front of the tabernacle to act as a gate must be a violation of this instruction and therefore completely wrong. The tabernacle must present an unbroken wall of curtain about 7'6" high. This would mean that no man could enter or even see inside the tabernacle unless he gained admittance by the gate. The second important text is that found in Exodus chapter thirty-eight and verse eighteen, "and twenty cubits was the length, and the height in the breadth was five cubits, answerable to the hangings of the court." (A.V.). J.N.D. makes this passage a little clearer by translating it as, " and the length was twenty cubits and the height like the breadth, five cubits, just as the hangings of the court." From this description of the gate we can arrive at the following conclusions. All of the curtains, whether for the walls or for the gate must be of the same size, every curtain must measure five cubits by five cubits and seeing that the gate was twenty cubits wide there must be four curtains in the gate and not three as some would have us believe.

Now the difficulty with the gate, and indeed with all of the perimeter curtains concerns the number of pillars that it takes to hold up the specified number of curtains. A little exercise in logistics will demonstrate the problem. To hold up one curtain we need two pillars, to hold up two we need three pillars, to hold three up we need four pillars and to hold up four curtains we need five pillars. Now the word of God states specifically that the gate must have four pillars (Exod. 38 v 19), so that if our assumption is correct that there must be four curtains then we are one pillar short for we need five pillars to hold up four curtains. Neither is this problem confined to the gate for we find that the hangings on the south and north sides of the tabernacle were to be supported by twenty pillars each (Exod. 38 vv 10 & 11). Now if the length was to be one hundred cubits and each curtain was to be five cubits wide then we shall have twenty curtains. But twenty curtains need twenty-one pillars, so that if we only use twenty pillars then the last curtain will have no support and will flap around like a flag:. The same condition obtains with the curtains on the west side where we have ten curtains and only ten pillars.

Before proceeding further we should note that the word translated 'fillets' in our A.V. should really be 'connecting rods' even as Mr. Darby translates it. Now if we consider each unit as consisting of a pillar, a curtain and a connecting rod, we can begin to make sense of the instructions that are given. This concept of each unit consisting of the three components is further borne out by the constant use of the little word 'their' in Exodus chapter thirty-eight verses 10-19. Now with these verses before us let us place ourselves in the position of Bezaleel and his helpers and try and construct the perimeter curtain wall.

Exodus 38 vv 9 & 10 says, "And he made the court: on the south side southwards the hangings of the court were of fine twined linen, an hundred cubits: their pillars were twenty, and their brazen sockets twenty; the hooks of the pillars and their fillets (connecting rods) were of silver." Refer to illustration number one and mentally erect this wall with twenty pillars (number from right to left) and twenty curtains, every curtain joined to the next pillar by its connecting rod of silver, except for the last curtain for although it has a connecting rod of silver it has no pillar upon which it can be hooked. All right, we have done the best we can with the south wall. Let us continue the wall round to the west side. Visualise what we have done as a plan. We have constructed the bottom wall, the south, and working from east to west (right to left) we have finished up with a curtain on the extreme left, that is the west end, with no supporting pillar. Now proceed with the wall for the west side and put our first pillar into position at the bottom left of the south wall, in doing so we have furnished a pillar that not only supports the first curtain of the west side but also we have provided a pillar on to which the last curtain of the south side can be hooked. The position now is that we have the south wall complete with twenty curtains and twenty pillars and the twentieth curtain instead of being left with no support is hooked on to the first pillar of the western side. Proceed with the western side and we will finish at the top, the north, with an unsupported curtain. Don't worry, construct the north wall and we will find that this odd curtain on the west side can be hooked on to the first pillar of the north side. Proceed with the north wall and once again we have an unsupported pillar, this time at the eastern end. Now the eastern end contains the gate about which there are specific instructions. Set those instructions aside for a moment, not permanently whatever we do, but continue our construction of the wall on the principles outlined above. Very well, proceed with the east wall and for the time being use white linen curtains all round. We start at the top right hand corner, the north east, and proceed with our ten curtains, their pillars ten, and their sockets of brass ten, and we find that at the bottom end, the south, we have a curtain with a connecting rod but no pillar. Wait a moment, we have a pillar, for the first pillar of the south side is already waiting for us just to hook our loose curtain on. Rather neat isn't it? The two long sides have each twenty curtains and twenty pillars and the two short sides have each ten curtains with a corresponding ten pillars, yet by hooking the last curtain of each side on to the first pillar of the adjacent side the wall is complete as one whole. So far, so good. Now what about those specific instructions with regard to the gate? Have a look at the eastern end. We are faced with our wall of ten curtains. Now the instructions with regard to the gate are that there must be a fifteen cubit wall of white curtain on each side of the gate. All right, leave the first three white curtains, commencing from the left, in position. That gives us our fifteen cubits of white curtain. Now unhook the next four curtains and replace them with the four curtains that are of needlework, of blue and purple and scarlet and fine twined linen. This will give us the twenty cubits needed for the gate. Now how are we going? Reading from the top we have three curtains, fifteen cubits, of white. Then we have four curtains, twenty cubits, of embroidered curtains, the gate, giving us a further twenty cubits of colour. Now if we add the three cubits of white to the four cubits of colour we have a total of thirty-five cubits. Thirty-five from fifty (the total width of the eastern side) leaves us with fifteen cubits of white curtain. This matches up rather nicely with verses fourteen and fifteen of Exodus chapter thirty-eight, "The hangings of one side of the gate were fifteen cubits; their pillars three and their sockets three. And for the other side of the court gate, on this hand and that hand, were hangings of fifteen cubits; their pillars three and their sockets three."

Before we come to the spiritual application of the perimeter curtains let us summarise the scene before us. Here is an oblong courtyard measuring one hundred cubits by fifty, as we have already said, about the size of a modern tennis court. Walking at about four miles an hour it would take us just three minutes to circumnavigate. The courtyard is surrounded by a wall of curtains some seven feet six inches high. All of the curtains are white except four at the centre of the eastern end which are coloured. Each curtain is supported by a pillar and a silver connecting rod, and the pillars are set in sockets of brass.

Now in seeking to understand this type bear in mind the purpose of the tabernacle. This is specified in Exodus chapter 25 and verse eight, "And let them make me a sanctuary; that I may dwell among them." Its purpose was to create conditions such that God could dwell among men, and presumably, so that man could approach as near as he dared to Jehovah.

The prospect does not look very promising. Somewhere, behind this curtain wall God has taken up His residence. Man can neither approach Him, nor even see anything beyond the curtain wall. What does it mean? Turn to the guide book, the

New Testament. There we will see in the nineteenth chapter of the book of the Revelation and verse eight these words "for the fine linen is the righteousness of saints". God does not change His types but gives us constant indications as to how we are to understand the pictures set before us. Very well, the fine linen is our righteousness, yours and mine, if we have availed ourselves of the provisions of salvation with which God has provided us. The apostle Paul in the first letter to the Corinthian believers and chapter three, verse seventeen says, "for the temple of God is holy, which temple ye are." Peter takes up a similar strain in his first epistle and chapter two, verse five where he states, "Ye also, as living stones, are built up a spiritual house." (Newberry). The apostle Paul again takes up the theme in the second chapter of his letter to the Ephesians for in verse twenty-two he writes, "In whom ye also are builded together for an habitation of God through the Spirit." Now where is this going to lead us? Here we have this wall of white curtain through which no man can pass and this represents the believers' righteousness. But in myself I have no righteousness, for as we often quote from Isaiah 64 v 6 "all our righteousnesses are as filthy rags;". Turn to the guide book again. The fourth chapter of the Roman epistle which describes how righteousness was imputed to Abraham concludes with these words, "Now it was not written for his sake alone, that it was imputed to him; but for us also, to whom it shall be imputed, if we believe on him that raised up Jesus our Lord from the dead; who was delivered for our offences, and was raised again for our justification." (Rom. 4 vv 23-25). So we see that the person who believes on Him that raised up Jesus our Lord from the dead has a righteousness imputed to him, not of works but of faith. What then does the unconverted man see as he tries to approach God? A wall of imputed righteousness. Not the inherent righteousness of the saint himself but the righteousness that the Lord imputes to him by faith. The natural man cannot understand this righteousness. That men, whom he once knew to be sinners like himself, should have the audacity to imply that their sins are forgiven, that heaven is their home, not a maybe, but a certainty. How can a man surmount this wall? How can he get round it? How can he be righteous before God?

And the trusting saint has to turn to him and point out that there is no way through him. His righteousness has a twofold effect, it shows the sinner that there is no entrance to God's presence by any saint or even the virgin Mary; and also that there is only one way in and that is by the gate. A gate that is unmistakeable. A gate that is wide. A gate that has four curtains, details of which we will consider later.

Let us return to our white linen curtains for we are nowhere near exhausting the lessons that they teach us. Firstly have a look at the shape, perfectly square, five cubits by five cubits. The number five, expressive of human weakness and divine grace. Human weakness? Yes, take away the pillar and the connecting rod and the curtain will fall to the ground, a huddled heap, spattered with the dust and dirt of the desert, with no strength to raise itself up, helpless and hopeless. How like us, but glory be to God "when we were yet without strength, in due time Christ died for the ungodly." and we have been lifted up, the perfect square, God saying to us as He did to the apostle Paul, "My strength is made perfect in weakness." (2 Cor. 12 v 9). We must not think from this that we have arrived at a state of sinless perfection, but rather that in God's sight the imputed righteousness of Christ renders us perfect and it is as though God turns to the whole world, indeed to the whole universe and issues the challenge, "Who shall lay anything to the charge of God's elect?" God has justified them. Christ has died for them, they stand perfect before God, angel, man and demon,so that God holds His own up for display as perfect but only if that righteousness is that imputed to them by the Lord. This is typified to us by the pillars. Every curtain has its own pillar, and strange though it may seem, every saint has his own Christ. Don't raise your hands in shocked amazement, we all accept this when we come to singing hymns but when we see it written in black and white it pulls us up short and we begin to shy at the suggestion. Do we never sing, "Jesus my Saviour, dying on Calvary, purchased my pardon, setting me free," or "Mine, mine, mine, I know Thou are mine, Saviour, blest Saviour, I know Thou art mine." What? a personal Saviour, yes, wonderful isn't it? The Lord is so great, so marvellous and wonderful that none of us can encompass His worth or glory. To one believer He is the embodiment of love, another is occupied with His moral perfections, another with His glory. We cannot comprehend who He is in Himself and so we view Him from all sorts of angles and from each viewpoint we say, "He is altogether lovely." What is your particular Christ like? Perhaps slightly different from mine for your experiences of Him have been slightly different. This is why we are not told the material from which the pillars are made, your personal Christ may be as a golden pillar, you are occupied with His glory, or it may be a silver pillar, you become engaged with the glory of redemption, or maybe brass, the eternal character of God's purposes revealed in Him, or perhaps your pillar is of wood, God manifest in the flesh, to think that the Son of God should come to earth to show forth God to man, here is glory indeed. Whatever your appreciation of your Lord you will never encompass the wonder of His person. This is one of the things that makes the Lord's Supper so precious, where brethren can gather and hear him say, "Come near to me I pray you . . . and ye shall tell my Father of all my glory in Egypt." (Gen. 45 vv 4 & 13). Not one of us can do it on our own but collectively how the worship rises, how the Lord is exalted.

Now although we are not told specifically what material was used for the pillars of the court, by a process of deduction we can conclude that they were of wood for there would not have been sufficient of the other materials. Then why did not God tell us that they were of wood? In order that we might appreciate the lessons detailed above and then realise that all of these glories emanate from the fact that the pillars must have been of wood. Now wood in scripture speaks to us of humanity. The righteous are likened to palm trees, the blind man saw men as trees walking and we shall find that in our consideration of the tabernacle the thought of wood speaking of humanity and gold speaking of the glory of the Godhead furnishes us with some wonderful and glorious lessons, and this perhaps is the first, no matter whether our experience of the Lord has been as gold, silver, brass or wood, all are only fundamentally possible in that the Lord became flesh (the wood) and tabernacled among us.

Two metals are connected with the curtains and pillars.

Consider the pillars first, they are set in sockets of brass. Now brass was the most enduring metal used in the tabernacle, not from the point of view of it being incorruptible for gold excels it in this, but from the point of view that it was of solid and practical value and thus speaks to us of the eternal purposes of God. That firm foundation settled before the world was, wherein the Son in obedience to the will of the Father came to earth as man and died on Calvary's cross. Purposes that were eternal and that could not be shaken, purposes that, wonder of wonders, included our being chosen in Him before the foundation of the world. So the pillars are presented to us standing in sockets of brass, immovable, certain, unshakeable. Such are the purposes of God in Christ Jesus and those purposes did not finish at Calvary's cross, this was the basis, but those purposes bringing many sons to glory, "that in the ages to come he might show the exceeding riches of his grace in his kindness toward us through Christ Jesus." (Eph. 2 v 7). Does not that thrill you? Do you not find that exciting? It is as certain that I shall be with Him in glory for all eternity, enjoying the riches of His grace, as certain as the fact that one day He came to earth and suffered upon Calvary's cross. Sockets of brass, sure and certain.

The other metal in the curtain complex is silver. Now we know that silver speaks of atonement and redemption. A half shekel of silver had to be given for every one that was twenty years old or above, and that silver had to be given for the service of the tabernacle of the congregation. (Exod. 30 vv 13-16). The crowning glory of the pillar was the chapiter and that was of silver. The crowning glory of the Lord was not the creation of the universe, great though that was, but the marvel of redemption through sovereign grace. Whatever our conception of the Lord, whether our pillar is of gold, silver, brass or wood, the crowning glory is still of silver. Every saint looks upward to his Lord and sees the crown of thorns turned into a crown of glory, singing in his heart, "The head that once was crowned with thorns is crowned with glory now.", and rejoicing in this fact he looks and sees that he (the curtain) is joined eternally to that pillar with hooks of silver and again his heart overflows and he changes his tune and sings, "My Redeemer, my redeemer, Oh, what joy to call Him MINE." How we could linger here but there are more lessons to be learned from the silver. Contrary to popular understanding, that atonement money paid in Exodus chapter thirty was a one-off event. It must have been, for the silver that was collected was carefully appointed for the construction of the tabernacle. Exodus 38 v 25 reads, "And the silver of them that were numbered of the congregation was an hundred talents, and a thousand seven hundred and threescore and fifteen shekels, after the shekel of the sanctuary: a bekah for every man, that is, half a shekel, after the shekel of sanctuary, for every one that went to be numbered, from twenty years old and upwards, for six hundred thousand and three thousand and five hundred and fifty men. And of the hundred talents of silver were cast the sockets of the sanctuary, and the sockets of the vail; an hundred sockets of the hundred talents, a talent for a socket. And of the thousand seven hundred seventy and five shekels he made hooks for the pillars, and overlaid their chapiters, and filleted them." Now this passage is very precise, repeatedly determining the exact shekel, that it must be the shekel of the sanctuary, and accounting for every last bekah. None was left over for the upkeep of the tabernacle. The whole lot had to be used as a permanent memorial "unto the children of Israel before the Lord, to make an atonement for your souls" (Exod. 30 v 16). How like us to be occupied with ourselves, to look upon the silver and rejoice in our salvation, but how much greater it is to know that God looks upon the redemptive work, the silver memorial before the Lord.

If He were not satisfied with that work, if the sacrifice of Calvary had not been acceptable in His sight, of what avail would it have been to us? The resurrection and the ascension puts the seal upon that, God has highly exalted Him and we find almost as much satisfaction in that as we did in looking at the silver chapiters and knowing that we are the redeemed of the Lord. Surely it is not irreverent to lift up our hearts, especially as we remember Him in the Lord's Supper, and pray that He will continue to look upon that blood even as He did in Egypt, "When I see the blood, I will pass over you". (Exod. 12 v 13). Brethren, this and all that it represents, is all that stands between you and me and an eternity in hell. As we have written, the payment of the atonement money was a one-off event. It is widely taught that the punishment that overtook David as a result of his numbering the people was the result of his not having collected the half shekel atonement money from the children of Israel. First of all look at the date of the first atonement levy. The exact month or day does not appear to be given but it must have been before the tabernacle was completed for the silver was used in order to complete that edifice. Now we know the date of the completion of the tabernacle for it was erected "in the first month in the second year, on the first day of the month." (Exod. 40 v 17). Let us now refer to the first chapter of Numbers and verse one which reads, "And the Lord spake unto Moses in the wilderness of Sinai, IN THE TABERNACLE OF THE CON-GREGATION, on the first day of the second month, in the second year after they were come out of the land of Egypt, saying, 'Take ye the sum of all the congregation of the children of Israel,'". Now this was a month after the completion of the tabernacle, the atonement money had been taken and used, yet here is the Lord telling Moses to number again the children of Israel but there is no mention of atonement money. True, the result of this census was the same as that taken earlier but this could possibly be accounted for by the fact that the Levites were excluded in the latter census but it is probable that they were included in the census in Exodus thirty for the Levites needed an atonement in Leviticus sixteen just as much as any of the children of Israel.

If the census in the first chapter of Numbers does not suffice, try the census in the twenty-sixth chapter where Moses and Eleazar were told to count the people in the plains of Moab by Jordan near Jericho. Verse two reads,"Take the sum of all the congregation of the children of Israel, from twenty years old and upward." No mention of the half shekel of silver, and we sit back and ask ourselves why, why, why? Many teach that the tribute money paid by the Lord in Matt. 17 v 24 was the half shekel demanded on the principle of Exod. 30 vv 11-16. This may well be, but if we look at the Lord's reply it would almost appear that He is saying that this tax should never have been imposed in the first place. Learn a most important lesson.

When the children of Israel were brought out of the land of Egypt, God instituted a solemn feast of remembrance, the Passover. A lamb was killed and its blood sprinkled on the lintel and two side posts of the doors of the houses of the children of Israel. They were told to keep the feast by an ordinance for ever, but, and this is the important point, they were never told to sprinkle the blood again. They were a redeemed people. Having sheltered beneath the blood there was never any chance that God would visit them with death. The blood was shed once. Apply this to ourselves. We go to that cross of Calvary and see the Lamb of God slain for us. We shelter beneath that blood, taking God at His word "When I see the blood I will pass over you." It is a full and complete salvation, my sins, past, present and future have all been dealt with so that the apostle John could state, "I write unto you little children, because your sins are forgiven you for His name's sake." Lay hold of this great truth and the sixth chapter of Hebrews begins to make sense. In verse four the apostle writes, "For it is impossible for those who were once enlightened, and have tasted of the heavenly gift and were made partakers of the Holy Ghost, and have tasted the good word of God, and the powers of the world to come, if they shall fall away, to renew them again unto repentance; seeing they crucify to themselves the Son of God afresh, and put him to an open shame." To try and convince ourselves that the believer described here is a professing Christian, does violence to our intelligence. What more can be added to describe this man as a true believer? He's been enlightened, he's tasted of the heavenly gift, he's made a partaker of the Holy Ghost, he's tasted of the good word of God and also of the powers of the world to come. What can you add to that description to identify a true believer? Surely the apostle is emphasising the truth that is demonstrated by the redemption money only being paid once. If you are saved, you are saved. No matter what happens you cannot go back to the cross of Calvary and be saved a second time otherwise you are virtually crucifying the Son of God afresh.

This lesson is taught more than once in the Word of God. In Exodus chapter 17 we read that the children of Israel pitched in

Rephidim and there was no water for people to drink. God told Moses to take the rod with which he smote the waters and to go and strike the rock. Moses did so and the water flowed. Now have a look at Numbers chapter 20. Here the cildren of Israel have come to Kadesh and a similar problem has arisen, no water. The remedy is similar. Take the rod but this time do not smite the rock, simply speak to it. Moses disobeyed and in his anger he struck the rock and because of his disobedience God barred him from entering the land. What a harsh punishment. Moses had suffered at the hands of the people and occasionally at the hand of God for many long years in the wilderness. His faithfulness and obedience had been exemplary. Now, for one act of disobedience caused by an anger that was amply justified, God punished Moses most severely. Why? Moses, you have spoiled God's type. The same lesson was being taught (not necessarily to the children of Israel but certainly to us) that the rock must only be smitten once, afterwards it is only necessary to speak to the rock. We can have no doubt as to the interpretation of this type for the apostle Paul tells us distinctly in the Corinthian epistle, "That rock was Christ." (1 Cor. 10 v 4). The lesson is apparent and very important. The Lord dies for our sins once. We drink of the smitten rock once and once only, after this it is only necessary for us to speak to the Lord. If it is a question of sin then the request is that He might restore unto us the joy of our salvation, but whatever happens that rock must not be smitten twice in your soul's history or mine.

We may well complain that this is an Old Testament type, where is the evidence of it in the New? Apart from the epistle to the Hebrews already quoted, refer to the first chapter of John's gospel. John the Baptist looks upon Jesus as He walks and says, "Behold the Lamb of God which taketh away the sin of the world." (Jno. 1 v 29). Read on a little and in verse thirty-six we read that John looks upon the Lord the second time and says, "Behold the Lamb of God" and he stops short, he does not add, "that taketh away the sin of the world." Why not? That was dealt with in verse 29. He takes away sin once, one sacrifice for sins for ever. It is not arrogance on your part or mine to say emphatically that our sins are forgiven us, heaven is our home, nothing can alter that for none can pluck us out of His hands or out of the Father's hands. (Jno. 10 vv 27-29). The final emphasis of this lesson comes from the Lord himself. In John chapter 13 the Lord washes His disciples' feet and in response to the remonstrations of Peter the Lord says, "He that is washed needeth not save to wash his feet but is clean every whit." (Jno. 13 v 10).

Doubtless there are many more lessons to be learned from the curtains but we must pass on to the connecting rods.

CHAPTER SIX

# Of Connecting Rods

Before leaving the perimeter wall of curtains we must not forget the "fillets of silver". We have already pointed out that JND, and others, translate these as "connecting rods". These connecting rods were entirely of silver and were joined to the silver crowned pillars by silver hooks. All was of silver. part of that redemption money that was to be a "memorial unto the children of Israel before the Lord." (Exod. 30 v 16).

What are we to learn from this? The Lord does not tell Moses to look for a certain hall-mark, or a distinctive engraving on each connecting rod. Its only qualification for being a connecting rod is that it is made of the redemption silver. The chief lesson that we must learn from this is that every believer is joined to his fellow believers, no matter what the man-made denomination or cult may be. The redeemed of the Lord are one. The prayer of the Lord in John seventeen is being answered, "that they all may be one". (Jno. 17 vv 21-22).

Every blood-bought saint who is trusting in the Lord and His finished work is joined, by redemption, to every other believer. After all, we have to share eternity together. This is not ecumenism. To try and unite all of the different denominations and creeds is impossible and a complete waste of time. There are so many unbelievers, good living men and women, yet unconverted and unredeemed in all religious systems, the "mixed multitude" that follow with God's people (Exod. 12 v 38 & Num. 11 v 4), that it is futile to try and make one homogeneous whole of Christendom. The wheat will not form one loaf with the tares.

You will note that it is the top of the pillars that are joined and the only junction is by the hooks and connecting rods of silver.

On the grounds of redemption we are "All one in Christ Jesus." (Gal. 3 vv 27 & 28). It is the tops of the pillars that are joined, not the foundations. We must each hold firmly to those principles that we see in the scriptures, our individual foundation and appreciation of the Lord yet, at the same time, we must recognise that in the Lord's sight (the top of the pillars), His assembly is one.

We feel that we must explain this further, even although it means quite a digression from the tabernacle. This digression is justified if it helps us to understand some of the basic lessons and principles of our faith.

We have already stated that in the Lord's sight His assembly is one. We use the word "assembly" rather than "church" because man has taken the latter word and corrupted it to mean a building with stained glass windows, a spire, and crucifix ornamentation etc. Such mundane things are in no wise connected with the Church or Assembly referred to in the New Testament. The Church is composed of called-out chosen believers. It is a living body. In spite of Rome claiming to be "mother Church", and the Church of England or Scotland claiming to be the great protestant churches, or the Exclusive Brethren, (and indeed some Open Brethren) claiming that they are the Church on Earth. In spite of these claims the truth of the matter is that there is no Church on Earth. What! Take it easy. Let us state that a bit clearer and seek to explain more fully. There is no Universal Assembly on earth, this is a heavenly body, What we do have on earth is local assemblies, each one representing that great Universal Church.

The great Universal Assembly, composed of every believer who has trusted the Lord since Pentecost is entirely in the Lord's hands. Praise the Lord for that. What a mess we would have made of it had it been left to us. Just look at the state of some of our local churches. Let us trace the story from the beginning.

We write these words with a great deal of trepidation lest some should feel that we are criticising those great men who were the founders of the "Brethren Movement". Never lose sight of the fact that these early brethren deserve the accolade of being "David's mighty men". These were men of outstanding moral and spiritual fibre, leaving organised religion because they could see the evil therein, some giving up their livelihoods as ordained priests and all seeking to follow those things that they saw in the scriptures. They left us a precious heritage. Unfortunately they were human. Although many of them had great learning, especially in ancient Hebrew and Greek, nonetheless, in hindsight we can see that they, in common with us, made their mistakes, and the greatness of the mistakes is directly proportional to the greatness of the men.

Surely one of the legacies of these great men is that we should profit from their mistakes, and the following is written with the conviction that if these early brethren had appreciated the truths that follow, many of the sad divisions that so mar those who are called "Brethren" (whether exclusive, open, or any brand in between) would have been avoided.

For the sake of clarity we will refer to that great company who were, and are being, called out of the world since the giving of the Holy Spirit at Pentecost, as the "Universal Assembly". Gatherings of disciples in localised districts we will refer to as "Local Assemblies".

Consider the Universal Assembly. That this does not include Old Testament saints is evidenced by the Lord's statement to Peter in the sixteenth chapter of Matthew's gospel. After the Father's revelation to Peter concerning the person of the Christ, the Lord turns to him and says, "Upon this rock I will build my church (or assembly, the word is the same). (Matt. 16 v 18).

We cannot enter into the controversy as to whether the Lord was referring to Peter or to the foundation truth that the Lord was, "The Christ, the Son of the living God." (Matt. 16 v 16) when He referred to the "rock", rather would we draw your attention to two other indisputable truths. First of all the words concern something that was going to be formed in the future, "I WILL found my church". Old Testament saints are therefore excluded. Secondly, whatever our contention concerning Peter, one thing is certain, it is the Lord who will found His church. These two points are important. The assembly was to be formed after the death of the Lord, and it was the Lord Himself who was going to do it.

In Acts chapter two we have the commencement of this Universal Assembly, the "called out ones", for Peter says that the promise is to "as many as the Lord our God shall call" (Acts 2 v 39). The expansion of this called out company was rapid indeed, for the last verse of Acts chapter two says, "there were added to the church (assembly) daily such as should be saved.". WRONG! WRONG! WRONG! The last verse reads, "And THE LORD added to the church daily such as should be saved."

In order to keep things clear in our minds let us summarise the points so far. We saw in Matthew sixteen that the formation of the assembly was future and from the Acts we learn that the actual date was the Day of Pentecost. The second point from Matthew sixteen was that this was to be the Lord's doing, "I will build MY church". Note this well. The Lord was the founder of the assembly.

What points did we learn from Acts chapter two? In verse thirtynine we read "as many as the Lord our God shall call." So once again the Lord is in control of this assembly. He does the calling. Who does the adding to the church in verse fortyseven? Peter or John? No. Paul is not yet on the scene so it could not have been him. Who then? THE LORD. So we learn that in the Universal Church the Lord is the Founder, He is the Builder, He is the Caller, He is the One who adds to that company. All is of the Lord.

Having founded this wonderful Universal Assembly, having added to it at Pentecost, the process continues right through the New Testament and on until today. Such as are being saved are being added to that body every moment of the day and perhaps of the night also. A great and mighty company in which the Instigator, the One who builds, the One who calls, the One who adds, is exclusively THE LORD HIMSELF.

Who are in this great and mighty company? Have we got to be Jewish, for Peter was addressing Jews from every quarter in Acts chapter two? No, for the gentiles were added to this company as we see when we read the Acts of the Apostles. Must we belong to "Mother Church" as Rome describes herself? No. What then, some other religious denomination? No. How then can we join? On our own we cannot. "THE LORD added to the assembly daily those that were to be saved." (Acts 2 v 47 – JND). If we have been called by the Lord and have trusted in Him and His finished work, then we are saved and belong to the "Universal Church". We may remonstrate that we have done nothing to join. We have signed no membership card, our name has not been written by a priest or pastor on to a church register. What steps must we take to join? Absolutely none. If you are saved then the Lord will do the rest. Having responded to His call, the Lord will add you to this great company of "called out ones". Where can we meet with this great company? We cannot. Possibly the greatest portion of the Universal Church is already absent from the body and awaiting that great summons when the Lord shall call them to be for ever with Him. So that is the end of the Universal Church saga? No, far from it, for we read in Ephesians chapter five and verses twentyfive to twentyseven, "Christ also loved the church, and gave Himself for it; that He might sanctify and cleanse it with the washing of water by the word, that He might present it to Himself a glorious church, not having spot, or wrinkle, or any such thing; but that it should be holy and without blemish.". Quite a number of points here. Let us add them to those that we have already established. The assembly was founded by the Lord at Pentecost. The Lord called men and women to Himself. The Lord added such as were being saved to this great company. The Lord is still calling men and women and adding to His Assembly. Now the additional points. The Lord loves this great assembly sufficiently to give His life for it. May we pause a moment and ask a very pertinent question. Are you among this great company that the Lord so loves? Maybe the Lord is calling you at this very moment; listen, to the words of the poet, "I heard the call, 'Come follow,' that was all. Earth's joys grew dim, my soul went after Him . . . Will you not follow when you hear His call?"

Not only does the Lord love His assembly enough to give Himself for it but He is also going to sanctify and cleanse it then present it to Himself a glorious assembly without any blemishes, spots or wrinkles, but a completely holy assembly. What? us as a part of that, holy and without blemish? We cannot walk one day and say at the end that we have been completely holy. We cannot make the grade. Now here's a wonderful thing, we do not have to, He is going to do it. What a Saviour!

We think that we have emphasised these points sufficiently to show that everything connected with the Universal Assembly is entirely the Lord's doing. Much as it may hurt our ego, we have no rule, authority, or jurisdiction in the Universal Assembly. All is entirely of the Lord. The Universal Church is a heavenly company. There is no one church on earth at the present time. This is the mistake that was made by some of the early brethren causing them to excommunicate whole local assemblies. Some still make this claim today as does Rome and many of the systems. The Universal Church is a heavenly people, (Israel was Jehovah's earthly people) the Lord alone having complete and sole authority in it.

In the world now, what we do have is a number of local assemblies, each one entirely autonomous and answerable directly to the Lord. Yet these assemblies do not operate in isolation but are bound together in one great fellowship even although no one assembly can exercise any direct control over any other. Sounds complicated and therefore we will seek to explain in broad outline the formation and function of the local assembly. Much could be written about the local assembly but we must confine ourselves to that aspect that has a bearing on the connecting rods of the tabernacle.

When the Holy Spirit was first given to indwell the disciples at Pentecost there was only one assembly and that was at Jerusalem. As the Word went forth and the strangers in Jerusalem returned to their own localities with the wonderful news of a risen Saviour, local gatherings of Christians were established in various centres.

That this was the work and design of the Holy Spirit there can be no doubt for much of the instruction in the New Testament is given to, and through, these local churches.

The local assemblies were established, not so much for the proclamation of the gospel, that was to be done outside the assembly among the populace at large, but the object was to instruct the saints in the things of Christ and primarily to form a place of gathering where the Lord could be remembered as He requested on the night of His betrayal.

In the gospels you will find that at the last Passover Supper, the Lord asked His disciples to take a loaf and a cup of wine and by partaking of it together they were to call Him to mind. This remembrance of bread and wine is given to us in the four gospel accounts. WRONG! But . . . we repeat again that this statement is WRONG!

Have a look at the gospel accounts. Matthew recounts the Last Supper and mentions the bread and wine but there is NO MENTION OF REMEMBRANCE. (Matt. 26 vv 26-30). Mark also tells us about the Last Supper and the bread and wine but again NO MENTION OF REMEMBRANCE. (Mark 14 vv 22-26). Luke gives an account of the Last Supper and he does mention remembrance but only with regard to the bread. (Luke 22 vv 19 & 20). John does not mention the bread and wine at all.

Therefore the statement that all of the gospels mention the remembrance of the Lord is completely incorrect. Only one gospel, Luke, gives a reference to remembrance, and that is only for the bread. Now note this, Luke himself was not even present at the last supper, only Matthew and John were there and neither of these mention remembrance. What do we learn from this?

First of all we learn that there was a Last Supper. Secondly that the Lord did take bread and wine with His disciples. Thirdly that He did ask that this should be done for a remembrance of Him although the fact is kept very low key and barely mentioned. From which we can assume, as so many do today, that the remembrance of the Lord is of little importance. Let us just tack it on to the end of some other meeting, perhaps once a month, it does not really matter a lot. WRONG AGAIN. Then why not emphasise it in the gospels?

One of the local assemblies that was formed after Pentecost was at Corinth and through Paul's letters to that church the Holy Spirit tells us much about their constitution and function. If we turn to the eleventh chapter of Paul's first letter to Corinth we find that repeatedly the apostle uses words like, "when ye be gathered together into one place" (vv 17, 20, 33, 34). We must understand that what follows is not to be celebrated by individuals but by the local church gathering together in one place. This is why the thought of remembrance is suppressed in the gospels. This remembrance could not, indeed should not, be performed by individuals. There is no benefit that accrues to the individual by partaking of this remembrance, it is entirely for the Lord, therefore the remembrance had to wait until after Pentecost, until after the local assemblies were formed. As soon as this was done the Lord gave Paul a special revelation as to how this remembrance should take place. The apostle tells us that he did not receive his information and instruction from the other apostles or disciples but direct from the Lord Himself. Read the first chapter of the letter that Paul wrote to the churches of Galatia. Verse twelve summarises the way in which he received the good news, "For I neither received it of man, neither was I taught it, but by revelation of Jesus Christ." No wonder that Paul knew so much of the mind of the Lord. Perhaps we should be more careful when we listen to learned professors telling us that we can disregard some of Paul's teaching. Maybe we should place Paul among that select company of holy men who wrote as directed by the Holy Spirit.

Let us return to 1 Cor. 11 and verse twenty-three. "For I received from the Lord that which I also delivered unto you . . ." (Newberry translation) and he goes on to detail what the Lord did at the Last Supper and how the remembrance is to be celebrated. Like Mark and Luke, Paul was not present at that Supper but he speaks positively and with complete authority because he had received all the details direct from the Lord.

This is the only full account that we have in the New Testament of the way in which the local assembly is to gather together in one place and collectively remember the Lord. It was possibly the first instruction that Paul gave to the church at Corinth for in the scripture quoted he says that he had already delivered this instruction to the saints at Corinth but they had got it wrong and he now begins to give the fullest details as to its celebration.

We do well to note that this was not to be a feast (although some of our hymns suggest that it is). One Hymn writer pens the words, "What food luxurious loads the board, when at His table sits the Lord." Is the bread and wine intended as food? Is it luxurious? "Here the feast of love is spread." Is it? If you wish to feed turn to John chapter six where you will find no mention of remembrance. This is why John does not mention the bread and wine lest we should confuse it with the Bread from Heaven which is for our sustenance. This bread and wine that we take to celebrate the Lord's Supper is not intended for our nourishment, (although it is true that we will never come away from such a gathering without us saying in our hearts that it was good for us to have been there) this is for the Lord, "this do for a remembrance of ME". Surely this was where the Corinthians had got it wrong. This was not to be a feast, this was the Remembrance of the Lord, the LORD'S SUPPER. Paul challenges them directly and says, "What? have ye not houses to eat and drink in?" If you want an agape or love feast (although this might be a doubtful practice for it had its origin in pagan rites), then your home is the place for it, not the assembly.

We learn from the scriptures that it was the custom for the saints to gather together on the first day of the week (Luke 24 v 1, Jno. 20 v 19, Acts 20 v 7). True this was probably the most convenient day for the slaves to be free to gather, but all the saints were not slaves, indeed the majority of the saints referred to in the New Testament seem to be free men and women. Could it not rather be that the Holy Spirit was guiding and leading these early saints in order to set an example for us who were to follow. Remember that the Lord rose on the first day of the week. The risen Lord appeared to His disciples twice on successive "first days of the week". Poor Thomas had to wait seven days before his faith could be confirmed. Why did not the Lord appear to him on the second or third day of the week and thus establish his faith sooner? Surely the important lesson being taught is that the first day is the resurrection day, and the Lord is establishing this as His day. This was the day on which He would appear to His disciples. This was the day on which the disciples were to gather together into one place. This was the day on which the local assembly was to carry out its most important function and assemble to remember Him. (See also Acts 20 v 7, "And upon the first day of the week, when the disciples came together to break bread", some manuscripts read "the bread").

Does your local church get its priorities right? Do you assemble on the first day of every week (some of us feel that it should be the very first thing on the first day of the week, for the Lord rose and appeared to Mary and the other sisters very early in the morning) to remember Him. This is the only occasion on which we gather specifically to give to Him rather than receive from Him. It is His Supper. Remember His words to His disciples on the night of His betrayal, "With desire I HAVE DESIRED to eat this passover with you before I suffer" (Luke 22 v 15). And the disciples had to do all of the preparation for that supper. Much could be written but we are drifting too far from the tabernacle lessons.

The local assembly was to be the centre for the remembrance of the Lord, and, as we find in other church epistles, the place of instruction for the saints. Here they were to learn of Him. Here they were to learn the principles of church government. Here they were to learn about the pathway that they must tread. Here they must learn how to conduct themselves in the House of God. Much could be added but the lesson that we are endeavouring to teach is that the local assembly is not primarily the place for evangelism, this should be done in the world outside. The local assembly is the place for the remembrance of the Lord, putting Him first and in the midst of His people. The place where the Lord comes before the sinner and his needs. It is the place where the saints should be instructed in the things of the Lord. No Bible Schools, Colleges or Seminaries, but instruction in the things and person of the Lord in the local assembly.

It has been pointed out that no saint, however gifted, has any jurisdiction in the Universal Assembly. This is the Lord's domain. He will perfect it and present it to Himself. The local assembly is different. Although the Lord is also the Head of the Local assembly, He has delegated certain responsibilities to elders, bishops, or overseers. The meaning of the word is the same. Not one bishop of a diocese and over a group of churches, but, if needs be, several bishops in one local church. A great responsibility rests on these elders and one of their requirements is that they should be apt to teach. (1 Pet. 5 v 2, Tit. 1 v 9). We cannot off-load this responsibility to others outside the assembly. You so-called elders, get down to studying your Bibles so that you can function according to your calling.

Each of the local assemblies now has a leadership composed of several elders, (nowhere in the New Testament is this word used in the singular when applied to church government) not just one, and collectively they are answerable to the risen Lord. Look briefly at the way in which the local assemblies are to perform. In the second and third chapters of the Revelation we have seven letters written to seven distinct local churches. They were not the only churches in existence at that time but were taken as representative. The churches have been formed. The apostolic presence has been removed. These churches are now standing on their own responsibility and each one is answerable directly to the Lord.

In these seven churches we have all sorts of evils described. False doctrine, false prophets, idolatry, fornication. You name it and you will find it in one or other of these letters. Now note this very, very important point. Nowhere is any one church told to interfere in the affairs of another. Even when there is wrong doctrine and all manner of evil, each individual church is told to rectify that evil itself. Ephesus could not interfere with Thyatira, or Pergamos with Sardis. Each was a separate assembly before the Lord and He, the Lord, will judge His people. He is the one who is in the midst of the assemblies, watching, correcting and judging, that in due course He might present them to Himself as one body, one Universal Church, which He will perfect in that future day. In the meantime we are separate local assemblies seeking to do the will of the One who is in the midst.

These churches are described as lampstands surrounding the Lord. If the Lord is in the midst then the largest portion of the light generated in the assemblies must fall on Him – what a lesson.

The ultimate punishment for a rebellious church who will not listen to the Lord's word, is the removal of that lampstand (Rev. 2 v 5). Come along, brethren, let us start a holy crusade. Which assemblies are holding wrong doctrine? Which are behaving unseemly? Let us have a purge and cleanse the assemblies. What proud egocentric brethren we are. Our job is to look to our own assembly. If there is any excommunicating of assemblies to be done, you and I have no authority to do it. The Lord Himself, and He alone, has the authority to remove a lampstand. So we see that we are completely isolated as local churches. WRONG AGAIN. The apostle John is told to write all of these letters in a book (Rev. 1 v 11), and circulate it to all of the churches. Why? Certainly not for the purpose of any church interfering with the affairs of any other, but in order that we might learn the lessons of each church and apply them to our own. In this way we can learn the mind of the Lord and pray for our brethren and have fellowship with them, although this fellowship may be limited according to the state of each church. We should never hate any believer no matter what his man-made denomination. It is the systems that the Lord hates, not the saints. (Rev. 2 v 6 & 15). In this way we may profit from each other's examples and lessons without seeking to impress our own will or understanding upon any other assembly.

This is a wonderful theme but we must leave it otherwise we shall find that the Levites have packed up the tabernacle and removed it out of our sight. How does all this talk of a Universal Assembly and Local Assemblies affect our understanding of the connecting rods? God's view is to look down from heaven upon man. This principle is developed more fully in chapter twenty six when we consider the garments of the High Priest. What did God see when he looked down upon the perimeter of the tabernacle? Illustration one should help us to visualise this. As Jehovah looks down He sees an unbroken ring of silver composed of the silver chapiters on each pillar, the silver hooks for attaching the connecting rods, and the silver connecting rods themselves. (Exod. 38 vv 17-19).

"Let them make me a sanctuary that I may dwell among them" (Exod. 25 v 8). Such was the objective and purpose of the taber-nacle, and here, right at the outset, before any other component is detailed, Jehovah tells the Israelites that He can only dwell in the midst of a redeemed people. None other must be allowed in and every pillar must be included, in order that the circumference is unbroken. There is no room for a man to obtain acceptance by God through a jihad or sacred war, even although Joshua and David and a host of others fought battles for the Lord, their acceptance had to be on the grounds of redemption. No matter what great works of charity or how good and moral a man may be, God cannot dwell in him unless he be redeemed.

There is a popular notion that provided a man is sincere and worships God with fervour, then all will come right in the end. Not so! The first requirement of God is that a man must be redeemed and sheltering beneath the blood. Mohammedans, Buddhists, and even professing Christians will not have God dwelling among them even although they pray five times a day. They must be redeemed.

Now we can see why the silver perimeter extends over the gate. Every saint is linked to the Way by the silver connecting rods of redemption.

A great deal of thought was necessary before deciding whether to refer to the entrance as "I am the door", or "I am the way". Finally we decided that "Way" was to be preferred for this suggests an on-going route rather than a door which, once entered, can be closed and left behind.

We still have not connected this silver perimeter with the Church. What did Jehovah see as He looked down upon the tabernacle? An unbroken ring of redemption silver. So, when the Lord looks down upon His assembly, He sees an unbroken, undivided company composed of every believer, past, present and future, who has been redeemed since Pentecost. One great company which belongs to Him; which He has purchased; which He has called; which has been added to by Himself; which He has kept; which He is purifying; which He has loved unto death; which He will present to Himself without spot or wrinkle or any such thing; upon which He will lavish the fulness of His grace throughout eternity. (Eph. 2 v 7). The Lord does not deal in half measures. Every redeemed soul, no matter what their creed or denomination, will be in that company, caught up to meet the Lord in the air, "so shall we ever be with the Lord." (1 Thess. 4 v 17). What a God! What a Saviour! Such is the Lord's view of His Assembly, the Universal Church.

Now for man's view. Oh dear! All separate curtains, (reckon this is why Moses was not told to make one big curtain to go right round) each with its own Pillar and individual foundation. No large complete unity but separated into isolated curtains. Not quite as bad as that, for although separate, these curtains are still joined together at the top by the silver of redemption. The curtains still function as a wall inside which God can dwell. It therefore follows that it does not matter what we believe as long as we are redeemed. WRONG AGAIN. Every curtain was supported by a pillar which stood upright and firm in a foundation of brass. Your pillar and the pillar of your local assembly is the appreciation of the Lord. Maybe it is a wooden, brass, silver, or golden pillar, but this will determine the character of your assembly. All will not be the same. We are finite, we cannot fully comprehend the infinite person of the Christ. It is a very interesting exercise when visiting other assemblies, to try and assess their appreciation of the Lord. What is their pillar made of? Do not do this from a critical or condemnatory point of view but rather to learn lessons, even as John's book was circulated among the assemblies in the Revelation. Have we never visited an assembly and felt that perhaps they had something that was lacking in our own assembly, something from which we ought to profit and perhaps emulate? Do visitors come to our assembly and see that which is of Christ and seek to emulate us? Selah!

So much for the pillars but what about the sockets of brass? The eternal purposes and principles of God. We are responsible to see that our assembly is founded and stands firm in its brazen socket. The elders of an assembly should know the fundamental truths on which the assembly stands, why sometimes it has to be aloof, complete in its own right and answerable to no man, or man-made organisation, but answerable to the Lord and Him alone. This must be done through the elders of the assembly. You younger saints are very important in the assembly but you must not take the bit between your teeth and rebel. Of course the elders in your assembly are old fuddy-duddies. Of course they are old stick-in-the-muds who do not move with the times, and I am sure you could think of a lot of other scurrilous descriptions of those that the Lord has put over your assembly.

GOD'S SANCTUARY

True, maybe! but one of the lessons that youth must learn is obedience. Perhaps the hardest lesson ever. Israel did not learn it. Perhaps we shall never learn it but we must try. There is no test of obedience if we always get our own way or always agree entirely with what is being done. Do not think that this gives the elders the right to dominate in the assembly. Peter puts it rather nicely in his first letter, chapter five and verses one to six. Firstly he delineates some of the responsibilities of an elder, finishing with these words, ". . . neither as being lords over God's heritage, but being ensamples to the flock.". He then goes on in verse five, "likewise, ye younger, submit yourselves unto the elder. Yea, all of you be subject one to another, and be clothed with humility." How the Holy Spirit changed stormy, tempestuous Peter. God is just the same today and can work in us as He did in Peter.

Forgive a personal testimony. In the assembly of which I was part as a young man, we sometimes rebelled against our elders, doubtless causing them many hours of anxiety. We were wrong. We should have asked our elders to reason with us and perhaps teach us the way of truth more perfectly. Looking back after half a century of walking the Christian pathway and being called upon to be an elder myself, how the assessment changes. Those elders of old, yes, they had their faults, they made their mistakes, but overall they did a wonderful job in their assembly. Pray God that some rebel young saint may, in a later day, pass such a verdict on me. (Ours is such a perfect assembly that we have no such rebels!!! President Bush once invited his audience to "watch my lips". I say here, "watch my tongue, it's firmly in my cheek!").

In this respect we can even learn a lesson from a purely secular writer. Because he is such I cannot quote chapter and verse, but I believe it was Mark Twain who wrote to the effect that, when he was a lad of fourteen his father appeared to be the most foolish and unwise of men. It surprised him that his father improved so much during the next seven years. No comment!

To summarise. The Lord looks down and sees His Assembly as one glorious whole, fulfilling His prayer in John 17 v 21, "That they all may be one; as Thou, Father, art in me, and I in Thee, that they also may be one in us: that the world may believe that thou has sent me." A wondrous and great Universal Assembly.

74

On the other hand, we function here as separate assemblies, joined in fellowship with every other redeemed soul, but being responsible to the Lord, and Him only, for the way in which our company is conducted as the local assembly.

CHAPTER SEVEN

# Of Pins and Cords

As soon as we read of "pins and cords" we immediately think of tent pegs and guy ropes for the simple reason that this is the way we have always seen them illustrated in pictures of the tabernacle. Take a fresh look. Recall that verse in Exodus twenty-seven, eighteen, "The length of the court shall be an hundred cubits, and the breadth fifty everywhere." If we put guy ropes on the outside of the tabernacle we are obviously increasing the width at certain points for the guy ropes were certainly part of the tabernacle. To have guy ropes on the inside of the pillars only would be worse than useless for they would be applying tension to one side without a corresponding force on the other. This would tend to make the pillars less stable rather than more firm. Furthermore, these pillars are set in sockets of brass, a firm foundation, and being only five cubits high they would not need any other stabilising factor. If our understanding of the type is correct and the pillars teach us of the Lord upholding each individual believer can we possibly conceive of the pillars being inadequate in themselves to support the curtains?

What then shall we do with the pins and cords for they are mentioned more than once. Consider the perimeter curtain wall. Every curtain is supported by pillars and a connecting rod holds the top of each curtain. A slight wind blows across the wilderness. What happens? The curtains are held at the top but what of the sides and bottoms? With every little breeze our curtains will cease to function as a wall but will rather look like a line of washing. If, however, brass pins were driven into the ground at the bottom of each curtain and cords were threaded through the pins to fasten the bottoms of the curtains securely, then the winds could blow but the curtains would remain unmoved, fulfilling the function for which they were designed.

Are there any lessons for us in the pins and cords? First of all look at Ephesians 4 v 14, "That we henceforth be no more children, tossed to and fro, and carried about with every wind of doctrine." This, we learn from verse twelve, is the work of the teachers, edifying the body of Christ. We can only be stable in our Christian path if we are anchored to those fundamental truths that have stood the test of time (the enduring brass) and the work of the Holy Spirit is to take the things of Christ and reveal them unto us that we may, as it were, be bound by strong cords to these firm pins of truths. The apostle Jude speaks of those who are blown about like clouds in the wind, those who speak evil of those things which they know not, and Jude gives us the remedy, almost as though he is saying, batten yourself down securely, tighten the cords against those firm brazen pins, "building up yourselves on your most holy faith, praying in the Holy Ghost, keep yourselves in the love of God, looking for the mercy of our Lord Jesus Christ unto eternal life," (vv 20 & 21). The pins and the cords are such little things but how important they are. Without them the curtains are completely ineffective when the slightest wind will cause them to flap and when the gales come they are useless and fail in the purposes for which they are intended. "Therefore we ought to give the more earnest heed to the things which we have heard, lest at any time we should let them slip." (Heb. 2 v 1)

# CHAPTER EIGHT

# The Gate . . . "I Am The Way"
(Jno. 14 v 6)

It would appear that the major items of the tabernacle correspond to the seven "I AM's" in John's gospel and this is the first, "I am the way." There can be no doubt as to where the gate is in the tabernacle. Every white curtain is a fixture, every one is saying, "I cannot let you in", every one is saying, "There is the gate, there is no other way", and such is the message that the believer has for men and women today. The scripture clearly states the truth that "None can by any means redeem his brother, nor give to God a ransom for him: for the redemption of their soul is precious." (Psa. 49 v 7). In the fourteenth chapter of John' gospel and verse six the Lord says, "No man cometh unto the Father but by me." That is surely clear and precise. No evangelist, however great and renowned he may be can save a soul. There is only one way. "Neither is there salvation in any other: for there is none other name under heaven given among men, whereby we must be saved," (Acts 4 v 12). Seeing then that the gate is the only approach to God let us examine it more closely and try and unfold its lessons.

We have already seen that the gate has four curtains and it also has four pillars. By arranging the curtains of the tabernacle, including the gate, so that each curtain has its own pillar, what wonderful lessons God is teaching us.

We have considered the white curtains, each with its own pillar, socket and connecting rod. Now we come to the gate we have a completely new set of types. This is THE WAY. There can be no doubt that this must speak of the Lord, presumably as men would see Him, that they might know how they can approach a thrice holy God. In himself man has no hope whatsoever. Man is a born loser, born in sin and shapen in iniquity. "Behold, I was shapen in iniquity; and in sin did my mother conceive me." (Psa. 51 v 5). If such be the case, how can a just God condemn me for being a sinner? Trace the story from the beginning.

In the first chapter of Genesis God gave effect to an important decision, something that He had decided in a past eternity, if we can use such an expression, for it is impossible to try and evaluate eternity in the terms of time. Before the worlds were created God planned to make man. This must have been so because we were chosen in Him before the foundation of the world. (Eph. 1 v 4). God gave substance to this decision in Genesis 1 v 26 by saying, "Let us make man in our image." God put this into effect and the Holy Spirit records, "And the Lord God formed man of the dust of the ground, and breathed into his nostrils the breath of life; and man became a living soul." (Gen. 2 v 7). This made man unique. God did not breathe the breadth of life into any of the animals, only into man, "and man became a living soul", eternal even as God is. Had Adam not sinned he would never have died, Adam, the eternal perfect man, but God put a condition upon man's eternity of life on earth, saying that if man broke that condition then his life on earth would cease. Concerning the fruit of the tree of the knowledge of good and evil God said, "For in the day that thou eatest thereof thou shalt surely die." (Gen. 2 v 17), but Adam lived on for several hundred years and begat sons and daughters. How could this be? Had God gone back on His word? Much has been made of the fact that the words "Thou shalt surely die" could be translated, "Dying, thou shalt surely die", it being argued that this proves that it was an extended process and when God said "in the day" He meant that on that day the process would begin to take effect. Maybe this is correct. On the other hand may we suggest a more satisfying solution. What is death? Death is separation. Physical death is separation of the soul from the body, but what about spiritual death? Refer to one of God's other pictures, this time a parable in the New Testament. Luke chapter fifteen gives us a threefold parable, the last section of which is the wonderful story of the prodigal son. When this wandering son returns to his father part of the paternal greeting was, "For this my son was dead, and is alive again;" (v 24). The prodigal son had never died physically. He might have wished he had, but here he is back safe and sound in his father's house. What did the father mean? Whatever our interpretation of this parable we must concede that the father is a picture of God and as his son was in a far country, away from the parental home, then the father regarded him as dead, giving us this principle that as physical death is separation of the soul from the body, so spiritual death is separation of man from God. This is further borne out by Romans chapters six, seven and eight, crystallised in these words, "For to be carnally minded is death." (Rom. 8 v 6). Now this is written to Christians, those who are born again, who have been baptised (chapter six) but the apostle says, if you are carnally minded you will be separated from the Lord who bought you, not permanently, but rather like the prodigal son, while he was away he was counted as dead, so if we obey the flesh we are distanced from the Lord and reckoned dead. May we suggest that this is what happened to Adam. The day that he sinned he was separated from God, God's first question being "Where art thou?", separated for all eternity for there was no way back, and as man had been given an eternal soul, God having "breathed into his nostrils the breath of life", then man was lost for all eternity, dead towards God. Either God had to banish man from his presence, send him to hell, or a way back must be found.

God knew the end from the beginning. With God there are no problems, only solutions. The answer to man's rebellion was already there, formulated in the plans of God, "In the beginning", formulated so that the Son of His love could be exalted and given a name that is above every name, that at the name of Jesus every knee should bow, of things in heaven, and things on earth and things under the earth. (Phil. 2 vv 9 & 10). God had made the decision that he was going to make man in His own image. This is what Satan was out to prevent. If God failed to make man thus then Satan wins and God is no longer God. How glorious that scripture becomes, "But we know that, when He shall appear, we shall be like Him; for we shall see Him as He is", (1 Jno. 3 v 2), God's purpose finally accomplished, man made in God's image, so that God is faced with this problem (speaking after the manner of a man, for as we have said, with God problems do not exist); either Adam must be consigned to hell or else God must allow him to continue to dwell on the earth as a sinner, with God providing the ultimate answer; but if man is allowed to continue to live on the earth then he must be allowed to fulfil God's other command to him, "Be fruitful, and multiply, and replenish the earth, and subdue it." (Gen. 1 v 28). Now here is a state of things. Man has sinned, yet man must multiply on the earth and the result must be a world full of sinners, bringing in its train all the misery of sickness, deformity, famines and wars. Perhaps this helps us to understand the mystery of God allowing such awful things to happen in His wonderful world. Surely the only solution is to send Adam to hell and have done with it. It's what he deserves anyway. How little we understand of the ways and the love of God. His Son has already made His delights among the sons of men. God has decreed that He is going to bring not only Adam, but many sons to glory, thereby the captain of their salvation making them perfect through suffering. The prime purpose of salvation is the glorification of His Son; so you and I are born in sin, shapen in iniquity. We had no option. We did not ask to come into this world and being here we cannot escape. We are faced with this supreme problem that by nature "all have sinned, and come short of the glory of God." (Rom. 3 v 23). This is not so much an accusation but rather an inescapable fact. When we are born into this world we are certain of one thing only, that we are going to die. This is surely the built-in evidence that we are sinners for the Word of God declares that "the soul that sinneth, it shall die." (Ezek. 18 v 4). Man does not realise the enormity of his sin. It is so much his constant companion that he ceases to measure himself against God's law, so much so that in Proverbs chapter 21 v 4 we read, "the plowing of the wicked is sin". What an astonishing statement. What is God saying? Surely this, that the man who does not recognise that even the very strength that he has wherewith to earn his daily bread in plowing the field, that failure to recognise Him is in itself a sin. How do we stand? How can any man stand against such a standard? Whether we like it or no the facts are staring us in the face, we are indeed "dead in trespasses and sins" (Eph. 2 v 1), so that when Adam sinned a gulf was opened that only divine love could bridge. How wonderful that in glorifying His son we are brought into the greatest possible blessing, sins forgiven, a home in heaven and, wonder of wonders, made like Him for all eternity. God puts the picture bold and clear in the gate of the tabernacle. He is not willing that any should perish, the gate is wide and plain for all to see. Look at that gate, for therein is depicted the only way to eternal life. Four pillars, four curtains, each curtain foursquare. The message must be to the inhabitants of earth. That is only a perfunctory lesson of the gate. There are only four authoritative accounts of the Lord's life here on earth. Four gospel accounts showing the way, four curtains. There were four different writers of those four gospels, each presenting the Lord in a slightly different light, in the same way that we each have a slightly different understanding and experience of the Lord – four pillars, Matthew, Mark, Luke and John, – one gate, four curtains – one gospel, four accounts. Each pillar is holding out its curtain for all to see, the invitation is clear and plain, so with the gospel. Each pillar has the same foundation, a socket of brass, the eternal purposes of God. Each pillar has the same chapiter of silver, each gospel has the same crowning glory of redemption. Each pillar is joined to the next by a connecting rod of silver, one common theme of salvation runs through all the evangels. Let us draw closer and examine these curtains in more detail.

In all of these types and pictures we must never forget the third person of the trinity. The Holy Spirit is always active, functioning as the Lord promised He would, "He will guide you into all truth: for He shall not speak of Himself . . . He shall glorify me: for He shall receive of mine, and show it unto you." (Jno. 16 vv 13 & 14), so that when we come to the curtains of the gate and see that they are foursquare we must not think of the evangelists as perfect in themselves, but rather that the Holy Spirit was able to use weak and sinful men to present a gospel message that is perfect in every detail. We have clear indication both in fact and type that the Father and the Son were present at Calvary. On that dread occasion the Lord spoke directly to His Father but we find little indication of the presence of the Holy Spirit. In type we have that wonderful picture in Genesis 22, where God tested Abraham. Twice over in this chapter we read "And they went, both of them together " (vv 6 & 8), the Father and the Son but no mention of the third person. Just a moment, look for it, remember, God does not change His types. The Holy Spirit descended at Pentecost in cloven tongues "like as of fire" (Acts 2 v 3). Return to Genesis 22 and we read that one of the things that Abraham took with him to the place of sacrifice was "the fire in his hand" (Gen. 22 v 6). Are there any indications that the Holy Spirit was present during the suffering of the Lord? Luke records these words in his twenty-second chapter, "And there appeared an angel unto Him from Heaven, strengthening Him." (v 43). Wonderful sermons have been preached concerning the condescension of the Lord in allowing Himself to be comforted by an angel. We must surely ask ourselves, could any angel, or even the archangel, enter into the sufferings of the Lord in such a way as to be able to strengthen Him? Was not the Lord strong enough, as part of the Godhead, to be sufficient to bear the agony and suffering that were to follow? The angelic hosts must have looked on in awe and wonder to see the Lord of Life laying down His mortal life on the cross, and for what? – for rebels, for sinners. Indeed Peter tells us that the angels knew little of what was happening concerning these wonderful events for he writes that the prophets of old enquired and searched diligently concerning the grace that should come to us which is contained in the gospel that has been preached "with the Holy Ghost sent down from heaven; which things the angels desire to look into." (1 Pet. 1 vv 10-12). That little word "angel" is the same word in the Greek as "messenger". There came a messenger from heaven and He strengthened the Lord in his dire need and distress. Who else could have accomplished this mission? Call to mind the way in which the Lord introduced the Holy Spirit to His disciples in John fourteen and fifteen. He referred to him over and over again as "the Comforter". Perhaps the Lord already knew that comfort on His pathway down here, on those occasions when He spent the night in prayer. May we suggest that the Lord as man knew from practical experience that one of the chief functions of the Holy Spirit was to act as the Comforter, therefore would it not be within the understanding of scripture to think that the messenger from heaven, sent to strengthen the Lord in that dark garden of Gethsemane was none other than the third person of the trinity, the Holy Spirit? – seldom prominent, yet always in the background.

A contentious soul may argue that this was in the garden. Have we any evidence to show that the Holy Spirit was at Calvary? John records that the soldiers broke the legs of the two thieves that were crucified with the Lord, "But when they came to Jesus, and saw that He was dead already, they brake not his legs." (Jno. 19 v 33). Who stopped the soldiers from breaking the Lord's legs? After all it was done so that the scriptures might be fulfilled. "A bone of Him shall not be broken." Ah! so it was not just His legs, none of His bones may be broken. Scholars tell us that the Lord was crucified by having the nails driven through his wrists. Perhaps the words of scriptures give us the true picture, "They pierced my hands and my feet." (Psa. 22 v 16). Have a look at the palm of your hand. Any bones there – hardly room to get a penknife between them, yet the soldiers drove great chisels through the palms of the Lord's hands without breaking a bone, they must have done if the scriptures were to be fulfilled. Who guided those chisels with such accuracy? If we look for it we can see the work of the Holy Spirit even at Calvary, but always in the background. Perhaps we should examine very carefully those cults or sects that seek to make much of the Holy Spirit and place Him to the fore. Remember that, as quoted above from John 16 vv 13 & 14, the work of the Holy Spirit is not to speak of Himself but to glorify the Lord.

As we have seen, the pillars were four, the curtains were four, and the curtains were each foursquare. In addition four decorative materials were used in their construction; blue, purple, scarlet and fine twined linen and these seem to correspond to the characters of the four gospels. Many have noted that Matthew presents the Lord as the earthly king, rejected, it is true, but nevertheless, the king. The scarlet mentioned in Exodus is the "worm scarlet" and is suggestive of kingship which is of the earth. The Lord was the Messiah but he came unto His own and His own received Him not. The kingly line is indicated in scripture by the scarlet thread. In Genesis 38 vv 28-30 the midwife sought to establish the first-born of the royal line by tying a scarlet thread on the hand of Phares. The second chapter of Joshua and verse eighteen tells us that the house of Rahab was to be distinguished by a scarlet thread and Rahab is among the women mentioned in Matthew's first chapter as being of the royal line. A king must have a genealogy and Matthew traces that genealogy back to David the king, the son of Abraham. Matthew's is the only gospel that refers to 'the kingdom of heaven' for this king's realm and rule is a heavenly one, not belonging to the kingdoms of this world. At the Lord's trial, according to Matthew, the Lord was dressed in a scarlet robe and mocked as the king of the Jews. Matthew's is the kingly gospel, the scarlet gospel, showing forth the scarlet in the gate.

Mark's is the purple gospel. Purple is made of two colours, red and blue. Red is the colour of man, this is the literal meaning of Adam, while blue is the heavenly colour. Here in Mark's gospel we have the combination of the Son of God and the Son of man presented as the servant of Jehovah, "Behold my servant, whom I uphold; mine elect, in whom my soul delighteth;" (Isa. 42 v 1).

A servant has no genealogy therefore Mark gives none. A faithful servant takes the shortest route for his mission, Mark's is the shortest gospel. There is an urgency found in Mark that is not present in the other gospels, such expressions as "immediately" in chapter 1 v 12, "and immediately the spirit driveth Him into the wilderness". An analysis shows that Matthew uses the word six times, Luke three, John four, while Mark uses it no less than fifteen times. Similarly with the word "straight-way", Matthew uses it seven times, Luke three, John does not use it at all while Mark employs it nineteen times. This is the language of the perfect servant, urgently and diligently doing the will of Jehovah. Mark's is the only gospel that records the Son's limitation in knowledge concerning the Father's purposes, "But of that day and that hour knoweth no man, no, not the angels

D

which are in heaven, neither the Son, but the Father." (Mark 13 v 32). "For the servant knoweth not what his lord doeth" (Jno. 15 v 15). Mark presents the Lord as the servant and is the purple gospel with the emphasis on the red as the Son of man here among men doing Jehovah's perfect will. The suffering servant of Jehovah is set before us in Isaiah 52 v 13 to 53 v 12, "Behold my servant . . . He is despised and rejected of men; a man of sorrows, and acquainted with grief; . . . He was wounded for our transgressions, He was bruised for our iniquities: the chastisement of our peace was upon Him; and with his stripes we are healed . . . He was oppressed, and He was afflicted, yet He opened not His mouth . . . He was taken from prison and from judgement . . . He was cut off out of the land of the living: for the transgression of my people was He stricken . . . Yet it pleased the Lord to bruise Him . . . He hath poured out His soul unto death: and He was numbered with the transgressors; and He bare the sin of many, and made intercession for the transgressors.", the holy judgement of God against sin being borne by the willing servant.

Red is also the colour of judgement. The lust of Esau after the red pottage earned him the name of Edom or red (Gen. 25 v 30) and brought him under the judgement of God, "Concerning Edom, thus saith the Lord of hosts . . . I have made Esau bare, I have uncovered his secret places, and he shall not be able to hide himself: his seed is spoiled, and his brethren, and his neighbours, and he is not." (Jer. 49 vv 7-10). The one who came up from Edom in Isaiah 63 has his glorious apparel dyed red for He had trodden the winepress of judgement alone, treading down the people in His anger, yet remembering the remnant of Israel and saying, "Surely they are my people . . . so He was their Saviour." (Isa. 63 v 8).

Consider other instances of red in scripture, the red heifer of Numbers 19, the judgement of sin in the believer; the red waters of 2 Kings 3, the judgement of Moab; the red dragon of Revelation 12, the judgement of Satan. Mark shows Jehovah's willing servant bearing the judgement for sin, but we must never forget that although the Lord was Jehovah's willing servant, yet He was also the Son, and so Mark commences his gospel, "The beginning of the gospel of Jesus Christ, the Son of God.", the Lord from heaven, and as blue is the heavenly colour it is as though the Holy Spirit throws a dash of blue into the red of Mark's gospel and therefore in the judgement hall the Lord is clothed in a purple robe, a mixture of red and blue, with the emphasis in Mark's gospel on the red. Purple is also the colour of royal robes. Now turn to our guide book and look at Philippians chapter two. Here we have the Lord taking upon Himself the form of a servant, "and being found in fashion as a man, he humbled himself, and became obedient unto death, even the death of the cross. Wherefore God hath highly exalted Him, and given Him a name which is above every name: that at the name of Jesus every knee should bow, of things in heaven, and things in earth, and things under the earth; and that every tongue should confess that Jesus Christ is Lord, to the glory of God the Father" (Phil. 2 vv 8-11). Jehovah's obedient servant, exalted and crowned above all and invested in the royal purple.

John's gospel shows the Lord as the Son of God. He summarises his gospel thus, "these are written, that ye might believe that Jesus is the Christ, the Son of God; and that believing ye might have life through His name." (Jno. 20 v 31). John begins his gospel with a genealogy, but as this genealogy is that of the Son of God it must of necessity be very short, for the Son, like Melchisedec, has neither beginning nor end of days. He has no ancestors for He was "In the beginning". He was the Word; He was with God, and He was God (Jno. 1 v 1). It is this presentation that makes John's gospel so different as he emphasises again and again the deity of Christ. In the very first chapter note verse 14, "we beheld His glory, the glory as of the only begotten of the Father", and verse 18, "No man hath seen God at any time; the only begotten Son, which is in the bosom of the Father, He hath declared him.", also, verse 34, John the baptist, "saw and bare record that this is the Son of God.", and finally Nathaniel's testimony in verse 49, "Thou art the Son of God."

No other gospel contains such a revelation of the Father and the Son's relationship to Him as is found in the fifteenth, sixteenth and seventeenth chapters of John's gospel, and when we come to the nineteenth chapter we read these words, "Then the soldiers, when they had crucified Jesus, took His garments, and made four parts, to every soldier a part; and also his coat: now the coat was without seam, woven from the top throughout." (v 23). What has that got to do with the Lord being the Son of God? Why record it at all? Is it just a superfluous remark or is the Holy Spirit drawing our attention to the fact that the Lord was clothed in a garment, without seam, woven from the top throughout? Consider the Lord as He appeared when He walked upon earth. Here was the One foretold right from the initial chapters of God's book, the seed that should bruise the serpent's head. Trace Him back even before that as John does in the opening verses of his gospel, telling us that He was in the beginning;. Recall the prophecies concerning Him, as though God was weaving this garment from the top to the bottom. Thread upon thread, the coat grows throughout the centuries, a perfect coat woven without seam, no joins, no blemishes, and the Lord Jesus wears this coat and John tells us to look on this coat, look at the wearer, and even as the sacrificial lamb was without blemish so the Lord wore this coat, perfect, without seam, and John points to Him telling us that this is indeed the Son of God. If, therefore, John's is the gospel of the Son of God we should expect the Lord to be robed in the heavenly colour, blue. True, but even John will not let us lose sight of the fact that the Son of God is also the Son of man, recording that "Jesus answered them, saying, 'The hour is come, that the Son of man should be glorified'." (Jno. 12 v 23). As in Mark's gospel we must not think of the Lord only as a servant and therefore the splash of blue is mixed with the red to give us the purple robe, so in John's gospel, although the unique Son of God is presented, we must not forget that He is also the Son of man, hence a splash of red must be added to the blue once again to give us a purple robe, "and the soldiers platted a crown of thorns, and put it on His head, and they put on Him a purple robe." (Jno. 19 v 2).

Luke presents the Lord as the Son of man. As a man He must have a genealogy and in chapter three the genealogy is traced along the human line, Joseph the man right back to Adam the first man, for these are the generations of the Son of man. The

Lord is heralded by the angels as bringing "on earth peace, goodwill toward men." (Luke 2 v 14). Luke gives us the fullest account of the Lord's birth and childhood and goes on to present Him as the perfect man, summarising his gospel in chapter 19 v 10, "For the Son of man is come to seek and to save that which was lost.". The Lord walks as the perfect man among sinful men, showing God's love and righteousness, as in the stories of the good Samaritan, the lost sheep, the prodigal son, the Pharisee and the publican, Zacchaeus and the cry of the penitent thief, "This man hath done nothing amiss." (Luke 23 v 41), all of which incidents are exclusive to Luke. Is it to be wondered at that Luke records the robe in which Herod's soldiers dressed the Lord as being "a gorgeous robe". No colour is given, for Luke represents the fine twined linen.

We must digress a little here in order to understand more lessons about the gate, repeating some of the lessons detailed in chapter two on "The Priesthood" but seeing them as a practical application. In Exodus 19 vv 5 & 6 we read, "Now therefore, if ye will obey my voice indeed and keep my covenant, then ye shall be a peculiar treasure unto me above all people: for all the earth is mine: and ye shall be unto me a kingdom of priests, and an holy nation." It is true that Israel did not entirely obey the Lord's voice yet they were, and still are, a peculiar people unto Him. God still has great blessing in store for His people, neither did God rescind His word that they should be a kingdom of priests. Addressing Jacob and the children of Israel in Isaiah 43 v 21 God says, "This people have I formed for myself; they shall shew forth my praise." Consider then the priesthood as set up in Moses' day. Here was the whole nation regarded as a priesthood. In the eyes of the nations round about these were the people who belonged to Jehovah, they served Him, they worshipped Him, they kept His feasts and offered His sacrifices, so that among the heathen Israel shone out as a kingdom of priests serving the only one true God. Within the nation there was another order of priests, in its broadest sense all of the children of Levi, for we find that the Levites are called priests in Joshua 3 v 3, "When ye see the ark of the covenant of the Lord your God, and the priests the Levites bearing it, . . .", but within the tribe of Levi there was another division and that segregated the sons of Aaron, for Exodus 28 v 1 says, "And take thou unto thee Aaron thy brother, and his sons with him, from among the children of Israel, that he may minister to me in the priest's office, even Aaron, Nadab and Abihu, Eleazar and Ithamar, Aaron's sons.", so we see that we have really a three tier priesthood. In the eyes of the nations round about, all Israel were priests of Jehovah, He was the one they served, and He was the one they worshipped. In the eyes of Israel the Levites functioned as the priests, while in the eyes of the Levites the sons of Aaron were the priests. We have become so scared of the evils of priesthood, so concerned that there must be nothing like a priestly class, that we have taken the words of Peter's epistle, which are actually quoted from Exodus, and opened wide the doors and said that all believers are priests – perfectly true. In the eyes of the world these are they who serve and worship the Lord, but inside the assembly the function of the priest takes on a special character. A priest had to undergo intensive training and even in the assembly a deacon must not be a novice. It is wrong for a young convert to minister straight away in the things of the Lord. He is a priest, yes, in the broadest sense, but he is not a Levite or a son of Aaron, that comes with experience. All men, even of the tribe of Levi were not allowed to function as priests. The lame, the hunchback, those who had any blemish, they still came under the broad heading as part of the nation of priests, but when it came to serving as the representatives of the people before the Lord they were barred. We have gone deeper into this subject in chapter two, suffice it to say that although every believer is a priest, as being one that serves the Lord, not every believer can represent the saints in worship for if his walk is wrong or his back bent his priesthood is forfeit. Now to return to the gate. This was the entrance to the tabernacle courtyard, a small enclosure, a large portion of which was taken up by the actual tabernacle tent, the brazen altar and the laver. Perhaps we have always imagined that all of the children of Israel could gather within the tabernacle courtyard. It would have been impossible. If there were more than perhaps thirty people within its confines it would have been impractical for them to perform any type of worship whatsoever. It rather looks as though the children of Israel were not allowed past the gate, only the Levites having access to the courtyard, and it looks as though only the sons of Aaron had access to the Holy place for in Hebrews 9 v 6 we read, ". . . the priests went always into the first tabernacle, accomplishing the service of God. But into the second went the high priest alone once every year." This is further borne out by the instructions issued when the tabernacle is to set forward on its travels for we read in Numbers 4 v 15, "And when Aaron and his sons have made an end of covering the sanctuary, and all the vessels of the sanctuary, as the camp is to set forward; after that, the sons of Kohath shall come to bear it: but they shall not touch any holy thing lest they die.", and thus, even the Levites were not allowed to look upon or handle the holy things of the sanctuary. That the children of Israel were not allowed into the courtyard seems to be shown on the occasion of the dedication of the priests, for Moses was told by God to gather "all the congregation together unto the door of the tabernacle of the congregation" (Lev. 8 v 3). A further confirmation is given after the sin of Korah in Numbers 16. As a sequel the rod of Aaron budded to show that he was the anointed priest of the Lord and the reaction of the people can be read in Numbers 17 v 12, "And the children of Israel spake unto Moses, saying, 'Behold we die, we perish, we all perish. Whosoever cometh anything near unto the tabernacle of the Lord shall die:'". This point is again emphasised in the eighteenth chapter of Numbers. The whole chapter should be read but a summarising extract of the point that we are making is found in verse three. Speaking of the sons of Levi, the Lord told Aaron, ". . . only they shall not come nigh the vessels of the sanctuary and the altar, that neither they, nor ye also, die".

From the foregoing it would appear that all that the mass of the children of Israel saw concerning the tabernacle was a wall of white with the gate clearly identified. Maybe they got a glimpse of the smoke from the altar or perhaps a small portion of the actual tent was visible, just sufficient for them to know that there was something beyond the gate. Was that all that they saw? Have a look at Leviticus chapter one and verse three,

". . . he shall offer it . . . at the door of the tabernacle . . . before the Lord" . . . v 5 " . . . and he shall kill the bullock before the Lord." See also chapter three verse two, ". . . and kill it at the door of the tabernacle of the congregation." See also verses eight and thirteen and on into chapter four, so that it looks as though the majority of the offerings were slain before the gate of the tabernacle, for the word "door" really bears the connotation of "entrance".

Let us review the scene again in order that we may have clearly in our minds that which the ordinary Israelite would see. Remember the Israelite was a redeemed person, he had crossed the Red Sea, Egypt was a thing of the past, (except perhaps in lustful memory). Here is the gate of the tabernacle, clearly visible with all its colours and the glory of the fine twined linen. Ah! but what takes place there? The sacrifice is slain, the blood is shed, the horror of death, the suffering, the life being given. What a marvellous picture. We have already seen that the gate speaks to us of the gospel story as depicted by the four evangelists. Here we see the wonders of the Christ, the king, who though now rejected, will one day reign over all, the servant, accomplishing the will of Jehovah, going even into death but finally being exalted above all that is in heaven or on earth or even under the earth. Here we view the perfect man, God's man, and we obey Pilate's command, "Behold the man", crucified and slain but raised in power and seated on the right hand of the Majesty on high until that day in which His enemies will be made His footstool, and in awe and wonder we behold Him as the Son of God, God manifest in the flesh, unfathomable mystery. All of this and more is shown forth in the curtains of the gate, but wait, one thing is essential, something that the natural man would fain do without. He is prepared to grant that the Lord was a great man, a wonderful teacher, a perfect example, but look again, this is the place of sacrifice, here is where the blood is shed, here is where the life is laid down. Here, oh Israel, is the basis of your redemption, the picture that you must ever look upon, the way, but only made possible by the blood

What is the lesson for us? We have perhaps formulated our own thoughts as to what the gospel is and unconsciously we tailor the scriptures to fit in with our ideas. Always remember this, it does not matter what you think, it does not matter what I think, neither does it matter what this or that professor or teacher says, neither is the import of statements of archbishops or popes of much importance, what does matter and what must be paramount in our spiritual lives is what the Word of God says. Now exactly what does the Word of God say with regard to salvation? Call to mind the conversion of the Philippian jailor in Acts chapter sixteen. In his extremity he calls to Paul and Silas, "Sirs, what must I do to be saved?" The answer is simple and straightforward, "Believe on the Lord Jesus Christ, and thou shalt be saved." (vv 30 & 31) In other words, just look at the gate man, look and live. How about that most popular of all gospel texts, John 3 v 16, what is the condition laid down there? "Whosoever believeth in Him shall not perish but have everlasting life." Consider the simple statement in Acts 2 v 21, "Whosoever shall call on the name of the Lord shall be saved." What wonderful simplicity, nothing for man to do except realise his need. How this is shown forth in the thief upon the cross. There was no time to teach him the doctrine of salvation, his need was too pressing, he was face to face with death, on the brink of eternity and his cry: "Lord, remember me!" He looked, he saw the gate, the way, he saw the sacrifice, perhaps as none other has ever done. How much he understood who can say, except that he called upon the name of the Lord and received the promise, "Today shalt thou be with me in paradise." (Luke 23 v 43). What then is necessary for our basic salvation? An understanding of the truths of baptism? An appreciation of the principles of church doctrine? All of these are important, terribly important, but the basics of salvation are to look and believe. Perhaps some are already holding up holy hands and crying for the excommunication of this rebellious priest, pointing out that when the apostles were preaching in the Acts of the Apostles they urged the people to repent and believe. Have a look at the meaning of that word "repent" and we find that its import is "to have another mind". Now in Acts chapter two the apostle Peter is accusing his audience of taking the Lord and with wicked hands crucifying and slaying Him. Now he turns to them and tells them that they must change their minds about Him, they must repent and as an evidence of that repentance, that change of mind concerning Him, they should make their altered opinion public to all, in the same way that their hatred against Him had been public to all, and be baptised in His name. A similar state of affairs obtains in Acts chapter three and also in chapter eight. The apostles are urging men and women to change their minds concerning this one, look and see that this is the Christ the Son of God. Then baptism, the Lord's Supper and all of these other things do not matter at all? Patience, patience, we are only just on the outside of God's tabernacle. We have not yet entered into the company of the Levites, let alone the sons of Aaron. Before we proceed past the gate, pause to look at Christendom at large, that vast company who in some measure or another call themselves after the name of Christ. Obviously to many the appellation "Christian" is nothing more than a name, but in every denomination and sect there are those who have looked and seen salvation in the Lord. Maybe their knowledge is not very profound, they only see the gate with some sort of a sacrifice that in some peculiar way God has initiated for the forgiveness of sins. They are saved. Even as the children of Israel came from various tribes, even although their knowledge was limited, even although they oftentimes did those things that displeased Jehovah, yet nonetheless they were a redeemed people; so today, men and women out of every tribe and nation, out of every man-made denomination, if they turn in faith to the Lord, experience the truth of the fact that "Salvation is of the Lord."

CHAPTER NINE

# Concerning The Levites

To try to place the Levites as distinct from Aaron and his sons is not easy. That the tribe of Levi had put themselves into a very special position with regard to Jehovah is shown by their action after the episode of the golden calf, and when Moses blessed the tribe just before his death it is recorded in Deut. 33 vv 8-11, "Let thy Thummim and thy Urim be with thy holy one, whom thou didst prove at Massah, and with whom thou didst strive at the waters of Meribah; Who said unto his father and to his mother, 'I have not seen him;' Neither did he acknowledge his brethren, nor knew his own children: For they have observed thy word, and kept they covenant. They shall teach Jacob thy judgements, and Israel thy law; They shall put incense before thee, and whole burnt sacrifice upon thine altar."

The problem is compounded even more when we find that in some respect their tribal aspect was lost, for Moses was told to take "the Levites from among the children of Israel instead of all the firstborn." (Num. 3 v 11). Moses had to be very meticulous in this for when the firstborn of the children was more than the number of Levites, the balance had to be made good by the payment of five shekels apiece. (Num. 3 v 47). This money is spoken of as the Redemption Money (Num. 3 v 49), but the redemption money had already been paid for all of the children of Israel in Exodus chapter thirty verses eleven to sixteen. Now the scripture clearly shows that we cannot be saved more than once, but it also shows that there are at least two parts to our salvation, maybe three. Someone has expressed it thus; I am saved, that is once and for all my sins were forgiven at Calvary's cross; I am being saved, that is a day to day process, drawing me closer to the Lord and fitting me more fully for the glory that is to follow; finally I shall be saved, that is when this body of corruption shall put on incorruption, when that root of sin that is within me shall be finally dealt with, when seeing Him I shall be like Him.

Let us look again at one or two of God's pictures, or types if you will, especially with regard to the children of Israel and remember that these things happened to them as examples to us (1 Cor. 10 v 6). The children of Israel were brought out of Egypt with a high hand. God did it all. You and I have been saved with a high hand. God did it all. Israel was saved from the Egyptians, we are safe for all eternity, but the children of Israel were not yet in the land, they were not possessing their possessions, they had to cross Jordan. To enter into all the teaching of these two wonderful events would be too much of a digression from the tabernacle, sufficient to say that on the latter occasion, the crossing of Jordan, the children of Israel did have to do something, they had to take twelve stones, every man had to be identified through their representatives with a stone. These stones were placed in the midst of Jordan and twelve other stones were taken up out of the river and erected on the bank, giving us a picture of baptism. The old stones were put into the river and were covered and the new stones came up out of the river. A similar lesson is being taught by the waters of Massah (Exod. 17 v 7) and Meribah (Num. 20 v 13). The children of Israel needed the waters from the smitten rock as a picture to us of the cleansing that comes from the work of redemption but they also needed the waters from the rock that should have been spoken to, not smitten, in order to refresh and cleanse themselves on the journey and also for the service of the tabernacle. This will be dealt with more fully when we come to look at the laver.

In the aspect of the Levites which we are considering, the children of Israel have already been redeemed by the half shekel payment in Exodus thirty. Have we now another redemption by silver? No, that cannot be, it must be another aspect of that redemption. Could it be that as the children of Israel had each been identified with a stone that was placed in the bottom of Jordan, so in this instance the children of Israel were being identified with the Levites? Every man had to be identified with a Levite through the firstborn. In type the firstborn ceased to exist and his place was taken by a Levite. To what purpose? That they might act in the service of Jehovah. Every Israelite was a purchased possession by the redemption money but only a few went forward as Levites. Was it not the same with the crossing of the Red Sea? All of the children of Israel crossed in safety, but what of Jordan? Only Joshua and Caleb of those who left Egypt entered the land. Why? – because they obeyed the Lord, because the purposes of God were dear to them, because they believed that God would accomplish that which He had promised to do. The picture is similar with regard to the Levites. The Levite was in a special position because he honoured God even before his brethren and relatives. (Exod. 32 v 25-end & Deut. 33 vv 8-11). How this reminds us of the Lord's words in Matthew 10 v 37, "He that loveth father or mother more than me is not worthy of me". The firstborn, comparatively few in number, were identified as Levites. Those who were to serve Jehovah were to come from all sorts and types of men but were typified by the Levites. If this be so what is the function of the Levites? Before we attempt to answer this question let us re-cap on the three pictures; picture one, the crossing of Jordan; picture two, the exchange of the firstborn for the Levites; picture three, baptism. We are told explicitly in Romans chapter six exactly what baptism represents. The natural man, the old man, goes down under the water where no man can live and figuratively he is left there even as the stones which represented the children of Israel, God's redeemed people, were left in the bottom of Jordan. Romans tells us in effect that a new man comes up out of the water, one who will walk in newness of life, a living testimony. How we wish we could enter more fully into the teaching of baptism but our subject is the tabernacle and we must only keep digressing in order to make certain points clearer; so that in broad outline the baptismal picture is that of a new man taking the place of the old. Is not this what happened in type with the Levites? Every man of Israel was identified with a Levite through the firstborn. The Levite took the place of the firstborn and became the exclusive servant of Aaron and

Jehovah. A picture of baptism? You must decide for yourself, but one thing is certain, the Levite must now walk apart from other men. His tribe is no longer counted among the twelve that surround the tabernacle at a distance. (The two half tribes of Manasseh and Ephraim have filled the gap.) Henceforth the Levites are to camp in close proximity to the tabernacle with Moses and Aaron and his sons occupying the position before the gate.

Here then we have three aspects of the work of redemption, and there may be many more. Each aspect is in two parts. THE CROSSING OF THE RED SEA AND JORDAN – the waters of death. The Red Sea. Christ dying for us, we had nothing to do except pass over, the Lord did it all. Crossing Jordan we had to die, the stones had to remain at the bottom of Jordan, the lesson, "I am crucified with Christ: nevertheless I live; yet not I, but Christ liveth in me." (Gal. 2 v 20). The second aspect is THE WATER OF CLEANSING AND REFRESHMENT, again in two parts; the smitten Rock, "If any man thirst, let him come unto me, and drink." (Jno. 7 v 37), very little for the thirsty man to do, just drink. When we come to John 13 however, we are told, "He that is washed needeth not save to wash his feet." (v. 10), something that we have to do repeatedly. The third aspect, THE REDEMPTION BY SILVER. In Exodus 30 vv 12-16 every man had to give a piece of silver as a ransom for his soul. Man buying his own redemption? No, the price was insignificant, just half a shekel. Even the poorest in the land could afford it and the richest was forbidden to give more. When we put our faith and trust in the Lord Jesus there is just that little bit that is required of us, just belief – whosoever believeth in Him – insignificant in itself and no man can give more, but when we come to the other part of the lesson of redemption by silver the price is higher. When the firstborn was exchanged for the Levite God could quite easily have made the number of the Levites exactly the same as that of the firstborn, but He did not. A redemption price had to be paid, not an insignificant amount like a half shekel but ten times as much, five shekels. It costs us practically nothing to trust the Lord and receive everlasting life, it costs everything to live for Him.

That the Levites were not allowed to handle the most holy things, including the brazen altar, is evident from Numbers 4 v 15. What then would they do? Bear in mind that to start off with there were only two priests apart from Aaron. Nadab and Abihu had died offering strange fire before the Lord, leaving only Eleazar and Ithamar. These had to handle certain duties connected with the daily sacrifices and with all of the offerings of the children of Israel, and seeing that the camp must now include some two or three million the work load could have been quite heavy. We can understand that the Levites were given, not only to Jehovah, but also to Aaron and his sons in the service of the tabernacle. The Levites could not touch the brazen altar, how then could they help in the sacrifices? – mainly outside the gate. An Israelite brings a "burnt sacrifice of the herd" (Lev. 1 v 3). Follow the procedure as recounted there. The offering has to be a male without blemish. Someone has to examine this animal to assess its acceptability, a job for the Levites? Someone has to hold the animal while the offerer kills "the bullock before the Lord", the blood must be caught ready for Aaron's sons to sprinkle the blood round about upon the altar, more work for the Levites? – yes, but what are the lessons? The Levite, the man set apart for the service of Jehovah must lead the Israelite to the door of the tent, to that which is a picture of the Lord as "The Way" and show him that the sacrifice is a very personal one. The priest must not slay the animal, the Levite must not slay the animal, the man himself, the one who comes with the sacrifice, must, himself, do the killing. How do we react to that? Do we shrink from it? Do we say in our hearts that we could not bring ourselves to slay an animal in such a way that the Levite could catch its blood. What a terrible picture. Come to "The Way" as depicted in the guide book, the New Testament. There you will see the Lord in all His glory represented by the cunning work of the curtains, there you will also see the blood of the sacrifice. The Lord has died, but come closer still, part of that sacrifice was for each one of us. I had my part in nailing the Lord to that tree. Terrible? Horrible? Ghastly? – yes but sadly true. Remember how the apostle Peter threw this at the crowd assembled at the feast of Pentecost in Acts chapter two. This event happened seven weeks after the crucifixion but Peter says, "Him . . . ye have taken, and by wicked hands have crucified and slain". (Acts 2 v 23), and Peter was taking no excuses for as a remedy he says, "Repent and be baptised, every one of you." It was your sins and my sins that nailed the Saviour to that cross almost as surely as though we had taken that hammer and driven in those chisels. Now in type this is the lesson that the offerer has to learn, there is no priest that can come between the sinner and the sacrifice. The scripture says emphatically. "For there is one God, and one mediator between God and men, the man Christ Jesus." (1 Tim. 2 v 5). Even the law of God cannot take us past that gate. There is only one way, only one gate, and the Lord says, "I am the way". We must not disparage or under-estimate the law, for Paul says, "the law was our schoolmaster to bring us unto Christ." (Gal. 3 v 24). Now that word "schoolmaster" carries the sense of a "pedagogue", one who leads us step by step towards a certain goal. Another picture; consider Abraham's servant when he went to seek a wife for Isaac in Genesis 24. In verse ten we read, "and the servant took ten camels of the camels of his master, and departed." Here goes the servant to bring back a bride for his son. With him he takes ten camels, plodding beasts, going step by step, never deviating. They have a purpose in view, to bring back the bride. How like the law, the pedagogue, the ten commandments, step by step, on a mission to bring us to Christ, but what happens? The servant comes to the city of Nahor where there was a well of water, but the camels are helpless to draw that water, they are on their knees. There is the water, they have gone thus far but now they are impotent, just like the law. Paul tells us that "the law is holy, and the commandment holy, and just, and good." (Rom. 7 v 12), but great and good although the law is it cannot give life, in the same way that the Levite could not push the Israelite through the gate. The way had not yet been made.

In seeking to understand some of the lessons of the tabernacle never forget its purpose. It was not made so that man could approach to God, the purpose was "that He may dwell among them." (Exod. 25 v 8). This was to create the conditions under which Jehovah could dwell among His people. It failed and failed miserably. Think of all the indignities to which the holy ark was subjected in Israel's history. The fire on the altar was extinguished. The holy vessels presented before strange gods. Jehovah is farther away from His people at the end of the Old Testament than He was at the beginning. The first book of the Bible begins with a man into whom the Lord God had breathed the breath of life, the book ends with a dead man in a coffin in Egypt. (Gen. 50 v 26). The Old Testament begins with Jehovah blessing Adam telling him to be fruitful and multiply and replenish the earth; it ends with God threatening to smite the earth with a curse. (Mal. 4 v 6), the tragedy of it all. Man cannot even create the conditions for God to dwell in his midst, so the curtain comes down at the end of the Old Testament and four hundred years of silence ensues. The priests, the Pharisees, the Sadducees, and goodness knows who else sought to create the conditions for Jehovah to dwell among His people; even that wicked man Herod built a temple, an empty temple, a temple with no God therein, no shekinah glory, so that when God was manifest in the flesh, when He was shown among men, the conditions were such that they cried, "Away with Him, away with Him, crucify Him." (Jno. 19 v 15). As we look at the tabernacle we can see how far man is removed from God. Speaking very reverently, but trying to make a point, it looks as though the tabernacle was rather like an obstacle course; the gate, all could come to the gate but few could go through; the altar and the laver, the Levites could see but only the priests could touch; the holy place, only the priests could enter; the Holy of Holies, only one man could go in, Aaron, the High Priest, and that only once a year with the atoning blood. If there is to be any approach to God of all these difficulties must he overcome, thus we can understand that if each one of these types correspond to the seven "I ams" in John's gospel, then the only approach to God, not only for salvation but also as priests and Levites must be through Him. So much then for the gate. It is there, all can see it, but the way is not yet open even although the type is there of the wonders and glories of the Lord and ever and foremost the sacrifice being slain and the blood shed. Do you wish to go beyond the gate? Are you a priest or a Levite? The tragedy of Christendom is still the same today. Christians can see the gate, they can see the sacrifice, they can realise it is for them and there they stop. This is only the beginning. To label a church as "Evangelical" is like saying, "We are immature, we only know that Christ died for us," (this is a wonderful truth and do not in any wise belittle it), but this is only the commencement of the Christian pathway. Now we can understand why the great apostle Paul writes in Hebrews 6 vv 1-3, "Therefore leaving the principles of the doctrine of Christ, let us go on unto perfection; not laying again the foundation of repentance from dead works, and of faith toward God, of the doctrine of baptisms, and of laying on of hands, and of resurrection of the dead, and of eternal judgement. And this will we do, if God permit." Paul, Paul, what are you saying? – that we have got to scrap all of those basic things that are so dear to us, those things whereon our very salvation rests? No, Paul is not saying that. What Paul is saying is that we must move on, there is a progression based on these fundamentals. Remember that Peter tells us that as newborn babes we should desire the sincere milk of the word (1 Pet. 2 v 2) and the purpose is "that ye may grow thereby". Now when we come to 1 Cor. 3 v 2, the apostle Paul has assumed that the saints have grown thereby, that they have fed on the milk of the Word, and they are now mature enough to take of more solid food, but he is disappointed, telling them that he has had to feed them with milk when he should be feeding them meat. He is not belittling the milk, it is good and wholesome milk, but there is more, there is meat. That is what the apostle is saying in Hebrews chapter six, and this is the lesson that we have got to learn if we are to progress in the things of the Lord. We are saved, good. Our sins are forgiven, excellent. We can see the truth of baptism, we believe in the resurrection, wonderful, but there is more, much much more, so that the apostle whose knowledge seems to us so wonderful, so complete, yet in the Philippian epistle chapter 3 vv 10-12 expresses the desire, "that I may know Him, and the power of His resurrection, and the fellowship of His sufferings, being made conformable unto His death: if by any means I might attain unto the resurrection of the dead. Not as though I had already attained, either were already perfect: but I will follow after, if that I may apprehend that for which also I am apprehended of Christ Jesus." – strong meat indeed. Who can hope to show all of the deep mysteries of Christ, when even the great apostle seems to say that he is still learning. Such a task is indeed impossible, but as we consider the furnishings and construction of the tent and courtyard, may we get a glimpse of the deeper things, those that are reserved in particular for the priests, that we may fulfil in fuller measure our calling as a kingdom of priests and a people peculiar to Himself.

# THE BRAZEN ALTAR

**"HOLLOW WITH BOARDS SHALT THOU MAKE IT"**
(Exod. 27.8)

The boards on one side have been removed and laid against the carrying staves, thus showing the ease with which the priest could attend to the sacrifices and the perpetual fire. Note also the "pan to receive his ashes" and the "firepan". (Exod. 27.3).

# CHAPTER TEN

# The Brazen Altar

"I am the GOOD SHEPHERD: the good shepherd
giveth His life for the sheep." (Jno. 10 v 11)

In connecting the brazen altar with the Good Shepherd it
should be noted that in John chapter 10 the Holy Spirit does not
speak of the Lord so much as the one who feeds the sheep, but
of the Shepherd laying down His life for the sheep. He had the
power to lay it down, even as He also had the power to take
it again (Jno. 10 v 17) and this was a commandment that He
had received from His Father. This was not only the Good
Shepherd laying down His life for the sheep, it was also Jehovah's
Shepherd obeying the command of His Father, so that the
prophet Zechariah could write, "Awake, O sword, against MY
shepherd." (Zech. 13 v 7), and as we shall see, everything
connected with this altar belongs to Jehovah. It is His altar.
When the Lord had detailed to Moses the sacrifices that were
to be offered on this altar he again emphasised the purpose of
the tabernacle and of the altar, "And I will dwell among the
children of Israel, and will be their God." (Exod. 29 v 45). It is
interesting to note that when the Lord refers to Himself as "The
Good Shepherd" He introduces the thought of the Father's
appreciation, almost as though the fragrance of the burnt offering
is ascending into heaven as He says, "Therefore doth my Father
love me, because I lay down my life." (Jno. 10 v 17).

Let us approach this brazen altar, and let us do so with due
reverence for Jehovah lays great store on the fact that it is holy
and that no stranger should approach thereto. If, therefore, you
have not learned the lessons of the gate you may not see the
glories of the altar. Many would look at this, the largest of the
furnishings of the tabernacle, and tell themselves that this was

only a structure of wood and copper (or brass if you wish, it matters little), and how right they would be.

The thing that made these base materials holy was the use to which they were put. Many of us today appear to have lost the sense of the holiness of the Lord and the things pertaining to Him. We are so conscious of the wonderful way that has been opened up for us, by the truth that we may go in and out and find pasture, that we forget that the Lord is still a thrice holy God. The word holy is the only word that is repeated three times in both the Old and New Testaments. It is important. Because the Lord is gracious enough to call us His brethren raising us to a level that is beyond belief, we are not entitled to drag Him down to our level and refer to Him as "our elder brother". He is the Lord. Learn a lesson from the apostle John. John rested his head on the Lord's breast at that last supper. John delighted to refer to himself as the disciple whom Jesus loved, but when John saw the Lord in all his risen glory in the vision of Revelation chapter one he writes, "And when I saw Him, I fell at His feet as dead." The Lord's condescension and love towards us does not entitle us to familiarity. Another word of warning, view with suspicion any company of people who constantly refer to the Lord simply as Jesus. At best they are immature, at worst they border on blasphemy. The altar was holy, not because of the material of which it was made but rather for the use to which those materials were put. How do we treat the bread and the wine when we remember the Lord? Oh, it's true as the hymn writer has put it that it is "only bread and only wine". How true and how wonderful, but remember to what use that bread and wine are being put, representing His body and his blood. Surely they become sanctified, not for what they are but for what they represent. Surely loving hands, redeemed hands, should take those emblems and with love and reverence place them upon the table. We are not suggesting that a fetish be made of the emblems, we see enough of that in the High Church and the Church of Rome, but we should certainly distinguish the holy from the profane. Similarly, after the remembrance it should be counted as a priestly service (not as part of some priestly caste or office) that those things that have been used to represent such divine and wonderful things, should be handled as still being holy. How do we dispose of the bread that is left over? We know of one brother who takes it home and feeds it to his pigs. That must be wrong. What then do we do? If we have any indication at all in scripture it must surely be the passover lamb. The instruction there was, "and ye shall let nothing of it remain until the morning; and that which remaineth of it until the morning ye shall burn with fire." (Exod. 12 v 10). How well might the Israelite have argued that this was good food, even if not fit for human consumption, well at least give it to the animals. God says, "Ye shall burn it with fire." Whatever we do we must not get caught up in a "Nehushtan" situation as the children of Israel did in 2 Kings 18 v 4 and worship the emblem rather than the Lord, neither must we become involved in a system of priestcraft, for the word of God does not envisage a two tier system for believers, with the amateurs and the professionals, the paid and the unpaid, or even the fulltime worker and the casual labourer. What it does envisage is a company of blood bought saints called upon to serve their Lord in various ways according to their Lord's calling and in this way they should exercise their priestly function in His love and in His fear. There is a world of difference between worshipping an object and showing respect and reverence for those things that have been sanctified for the Lord's use.

The brazen altar presents us with a hollow box made of wood overlaid with copper. The altar is to be five cubits by five cubits, it is to be foursquare and from this we must conclude that there were no parts that protruded beyond this measurement except for the minor items specified, namely the four rings for carrying and perhaps the four horns on the top corners. No mention is made of steps leading up to the altar, this was strictly forbidden, (Exod. 20 v 26) neither do we read that Moses had instructions to build a ramp so that the priests could attend to the sacrifice. Obviously we are going to be faced with problems. It would seem that oftentimes God does not explain all the details of His plans and He leaves us wondering. May it not be that this is God's intention, that we should ponder and think about these things and in so doing learn some of the wonderful lessons that the scriptures hold for us? There are those who claim that the Spirit has taught them all things and therefore they know it all, how regrettable. The most erudite saint only knows a fraction of the truth contained in the Word. The older we get the more we realise how much there is still to be unfolded. Teaching is an on-going process, daily learning more and more.

Perhaps we should be well advised in considering the brazen altar to state in full the instructions given to Moses, "And thou shalt make an altar of shittim wood five cubits long, and five cubits broad; the altar shall be foursquare: and the height thereof shall be three cubits. And thou shalt make the horns of it upon the four corners thereof: his horns shall be of the same: and thou shalt overlay it with brass. And thou shalt make his pans to receive his ashes, and his shovels, and his basons, and his fleshhooks, and his firepans: all the vessels thereof thou shalt make of brass. And thou shalt make for it a grate of network of brass; and upon the net shalt thou make four brazen rings in the four corners thereof. And thou shalt put it under the compass of the altar beneath, that the net may be even to the midst of the altar. And thou shalt make staves for the altar, staves of shittim wood, and overlay them with brass. And the staves shall be put into the rings, and the staves shall be upon the two sides of the altar, to bear it. Hollow with boards shalt thou make it: as it was showed thee in the mount, so shall they make it." (Exod. 27 vv 1-8).

In seeking to understand the lessons of the tabernacle we do well to remember that a cubit is roughly 18" or 46cm long. It is as well to envisage the various items in cubits for, if the numbers in scripture have any significance, it is the number of cubits that should be taken into account. This renders some modern translations unsuitable for the serious study of the Word of God, for they metricate all of the measurements. Another thing that should be borne in mind is that some translations refer to the brass as copper. Brass is a mixture of zinc and copper, and as the native copper which was evidently used contained certain impurities it could easily be classified as brass. It was not the most durable metal known but it was certainly the most durable metal used in the tabernacle. It had this important characteristic that it was one of the greatest conductors of heat, a most important factor as we shall see when we consider the altar in detail.

From the description given to Moses we can see that this altar was a hollow structure made of boards of shittim wood that had been overlaid with brass. Try to visualise this hollow structure measuring 7'6" square and being some 4'6" high. Illustration two will help. At the top of each of the four corners there is a horn, it may have been a straightish one like a cow's or it may have been a curled one like a ram's, we are not told, just that there should be horn on each corner, and Moses is told that, "His horns shall be of the same", suggesting that the horns should be made an integral part of the altar. Halfway down in the altar there was a grate or grill, and where this grate met the four corners of the altar a ring was constructed. This gave four rings through which two brass covered wooden poles could be placed in order that the altar might be carried on the shoulders of the Levites.

Forget for a moment the horns and the rings. We are confronted with a hollow square box made of brass covered boards. In the middle and halfway down inside the box is a grating made of brass. Certain brazen implements were to be provided for the altar. Three of these implements are easy enough to understand, the shovels for dealing with the fire, the basons for dealing with the blood, and the fleshhooks for manipulating the sacrifice. What about the other two, the firepans and the ashpans? (Exod. 27 v 3). If their names mean anything it must mean that there was a pan to contain the fire, and another pan to collect the ashes. Add these two items to the altar that we have already constructed in our minds, a hollow square box made of brass covered boards with an internal grating halfway down. Now we have got to add a firepan and an ashpan. The ashpan will obviously be the lowest so that we can place that on the floor. If we are going to have a firepan it must mean that the fire must go in this and presumably the sacrifice must have been burnt on the grating of the altar, and the fire, in the firepan, would come between the grating and the ashpan. This would make an ideal arrangement for there would be no danger of the fire being extinguished when a whole, wet, freshly slain lamb was placed on the altar. The fleshhooks could place the sacrifice exactly where it was wanted and it could even be moved into position during the burning. The fire, being in the firepan, could easily be tended. If necessary the whole fire could be withdrawn and replaced. What could be better than to have an ashpan underneath to catch the ashes as they fell through. When one ashpan was full it could be removed and an empty one inserted. Any small amounts of ash that fell over the sides could be catered for with the shovels; quite a well organised altar.

How did the priests attend to the sacrifice? The problem is that the altar is three cubits high (4'6"), almost shoulder height for the average man. The sacrifice was half way down in the altar on the brazen grate, or some 1½ cubits (27") below the top of the altar. The priest could not approach too close for the altar would be very hot and wood smoke and the acrid smoke of burning flesh would act as an effective barrier to the priest trying to put his head over the edge of the altar. We said there would be problems. Think a little. God had told Moses to make the altar "hollow with boards". Why did God give such an instruction? Might it not have been simpler to make the altar in one piece? No, God says it has got to be hollow with boards. Which way did the boards run, horizontal or vertical? If vertical they could serve no useful purpose, but if horizontal the priest could remove the boards from the top half of one side of the altar and he would be faced with a platform or table formed by the grate, just at comfortable working height, 1½ cubits (27") from the ground. How easy it would be for two priests to lift the sacrifice on to this grate, push it into position with the fleshhooks and replace the boards. If further attention need be given to the sacrifice the appropriate boards could be removed, the adjustments made and the boards replaced. What a well thought out altar, no wonder God said that it was to be made with boards; but there is a further use for these boards. Consider the lower half of the altar, the area where the fire burned and the ashes were collected. Remember that the altar was made of brass. Now brass has a melting point of about 1,000 degrees centigrade. A great deal of care and skill would be required to keep the fire at such a level that it was sufficient to consume the sacrifice but not melt the grate or the firepan. By removing boards from the bottom of the altar the priest could control the access of air to the fire in much the same way as we use a damper in a modern boiler. Indeed, if he took the bottom board away all round the altar he would virtually create a miniature blast furnace. When it came to refuelling the fire, access was easy by the removal of the appropriate boards. When it came to clearing out the ashes, the boards on one side could be removed, the ashpan dragged out and a new one inserted; complete control, complete access; rather an excellent design, but really that is what you would expect, and these were some of the things in which each generation of priests had to be instructed.

Another strange thing about this altar is that it is made of wood with a brass overlay. At first sight we would consider it an unfortunate choice of materials. On the first lighting of the altar fire, all that would remain of the boards would be a charred core with a brass case. Wrong! May we repeat that, WRONG! We have already pointed out two important factors concerning brass. Firstly it has a higher coefficient of heat transfer than most metals. This is why we have copper kettles and copper-bottomed saucepans. Secondly it has a melting point of just under 1,000 degrees centigrade. It therefore follows that the firepan and the grate must never be subjected to greater heat than 1,000 degrees. The centre of the fire might possible exceed this temperature because the heat would rise and the firepan would tend to dissipate the heat very quickly. Similarly the heat on the grate might occasionally exceed the optimum because the wet carcase and the heat dissipation of the grate would help. If the centre of the fire had to be kept to this limit then the outer portion of the grate must be well below this, and as brass is such a good conductor of heat it would mean that the walls of the altar would be cooler still. In fact the altar would act as one gigantic heat sink, dissipating the heat as fast as it was generated; and the wood in the boards? – absolutely untouched. Experiments have been conducted on this and a blowlamp temperature well in excess of 1,000 degrees applied as close as 6" to the corner of the altar leaves the internal wood absolutely unmarked, with no charring at all. Of necessity the altar description has been lengthy for the lessons are most wonderful. Let us examine them in detail.

Consider the two materials that were used in the construction of the altar, brass and wood. Brass was the durable metal of the tabernacle, not as durable as iron, but earlier on we have given the reason why iron was not employed in the tabernacle. Another reason why iron is not used in the altar is its unsuitability; – but iron is more durable, iron will resist a higher temperature without melting. That is true, but iron will not dissipate heat nearly as quickly as brass, and it is essential in the picture that God is giving us that the heat should be dispersed so that the wood remained uncharred. How important this is in the type we can see if we turn to our guide book, the New Testament. It was necessary that the Lord's humanity should remain intact even through the trials and sufferings of Calvary. Not only does the Holy Spirit record that no bone of His should be broken but when He appeared to His disciples after His resurrection He turned to them and said, "Behold my hands and my feet, that it is I myself: handle me and see; for a spirit hath not flesh and bones, as ye see me have." (Luke 24 v 39). How wonderful are these truths. There is a man in the glory, not a spirit, not a shadow of His former self, but a man who has endured the cross, despising the shame, and is set down on the right hand of the throne of God. (Heb. 12 v 2). How could it be otherwise? This was God's perfect man. Was man going to be allowed to destroy Him? Surely this was why His legs were not broken. The thieves on either side were villains of the deepest dye. Their walk had been anything but perfect, but when we come to the Lord, He never took one step that was out of place, doing always those things that pleased the Father, (Jno. 8 v 29), perfect in all His ways. His legs must not be broken not only because the scriptures must be fulfilled but also because He has fulfilled the scriptures.

This leads us to the wood. The wood was the shittim wood or the acacia, the wood of the wilderness and God wants this used in the structure of the altar. Earlier on we pointed out that wood is a picture of man and humanity. See a lovely use of this type in Genesis chapter twenty-two. Abraham and Isaac are setting out on their journey to the place of sacrifice. There we read, "And Abraham took the wood of the burnt offering, and laid it upon Isaac His son;" (Gen. 22 v 6). Ponder that a moment. Think of the wonder and the glory of it. The father laid the burden of the wood upon Isaac his son. The Father laid on the Lord the burden of humanity, how marvellous; and what a burden that was. Here was the one who neither slumbers nor sleeps (Psa. 121 v 4) feeling weary and sitting by a well in Samaria (Jno. 4 v 6). Here is that One by that same well asking for a drink when He could give fountains of living water. The Son of God when He walked here, looked upon Jerusalem and wept. He attended the grave of Lazarus and wept there. What a burden the wood was. How heavy a weight, when the Father laid upon Him the limitations of humanity. It was not only on the cross that the Lord suffered, it was all along. "That path uncheered by earthly smiles led only to the cross". We are so self centred that everything we read in the scriptures must be concerning us. Not so, it should be concerning Him, so that when upon the cross the Lord cried, "It is finished." (Jno. 19 v 30) we rush in and acclaim the work of redemption as complete; but was it? The burial, the resurrection and the ascension, even the gift of the Holy Spirit were all needed before redemption's work was fully finished. What then of the Lord's cry upon the cross, what did He mean by, "It is finished."? May we with respect suggest that this was a cry from the Lord's heart. He had come down to dwell among men. He wrote the story of sins forgiven in the dust of humanity. (Jno. 8 v 6). Now the earthly pathway was finished, He had reached the bottom of the valley, henceforth the pathway was an upward one, the resurrection, the ascension, the Father's right hand, the waiting to receive His bride. The burden of humanity had been taken from His shoulders. Oh, the glory of that redemption.

The wood was covered with the brass, and as the brass speaks to us of the durability of God's counsels, so we can see this One, who was God manifest in flesh (1 Tim. 3 v 16) fulfilling every prediction concerning the Saviour of the world. Those predictions were unshakable, as durable as the Godhead itself, and the Lord walked here in such a way that not one jot or tittle was left unfulfilled. Surely the wood was overlaid with the brass.

Working from the top of the altar, we are first confronted with the horns on the four corners. The only instructions that Moses and Aaron received with regard to these was that they must be an integral part of the altar, and on certain occasions these horns were to be anointed with blood, notably at the consecration of the priesthood, (Lev. 8 v 15) and on the day of atonement. (Lev.16). In both instances Aaron had to take of the blood with his finger and either put it (Lev. 9 v 9) or sprinkle it (Lev. 16 vv 18 & 19) upon the altar, another indication that the altar could not have been red hot at the perimeter. There was no instruction that any animal should be tied to them. It is worthy of note that the altar of incense in the Holy Place had horns on the four corners, and no animal was ever to be offered thereon – pretty pointless to try to tie down incense. Wonder what those horns were for? We will come to them later.

It would have been impossible to tie any animal, especially a young bullock, to a hot altar, for remember the fire of the altar must never go out. At one time there were only two priests, for of the four of Aaron's sons two, Nadab and Abihu, were dead, leaving only Eleazar and Ithamar. Furthermore the sacrifices were killed at the door of the tabernacle of the congregation and would therefore be dead when placed upon the altar. It is not until we come to the prophetic Psalm 118 that we read, "Bind the sacrifice with cords, even unto the horns of the altar." (Psa. 118 v 27). Surely the flames of the fire would burn through the cords in no time and pandemonium would be let loose. Perhaps the hymn writer had an inkling of the truth when he wrote, "Was it the nails, O Saviour that bound Thee to the tree? Nay, 'twas Thine everlasting love, Thy love to me, to me." This was only one of the cords that bound Him there. Christ loved me and gave Himself for me. (Gal. 2 v 20). Another cord surely was His obedience to His Father's will. How often we repeat those words of Matthew 26 v 39, "O my Father, if it be possible, let this cup pass from me: nevertheless not as I will, but as Thou wilt." A third cord was that the scriptures might be fulfilled, brought home to us by words like, "Thus it was written," or "That the scriptures might be fulfilled.", surely a threefold cord, not quickly broken. (Eccl. 4 v 12), not easily seen either. Perhaps this is why the horns had to be made of brass and an essential part of the altar, the durable and eternal purposes of God. Here is a picture of the Lord when, "He steadfastly set His face to go to Jerusalem." (Luke 9 v 51), when He went to the place of sacrifice, and as the Lamb of God bore away the sin of the world, yet in spite of the fierceness of the wrath and the holy judgement of God against sin, His humanity remained intact.

Halfway down the altar we come to the grating or hearth of brass. It was here that the sacrifice was placed for burning. No one could see the burning for the altar was three cubits (4'6") high and the grating was halfway down in the midst of the altar. None could see it except Jehovah. This was Jehovah's altar. See what was offered on this altar in Exodus 29 vv 38-42, "Now this is that which thou shalt offer upon the altar; two lambs of the first year day by day continually. The one lamb thou shalt offer in the morning; and the other lamb shalt thou offer at even." Besides this and one or two other small items such as the fat from certain offerings, little else seems to have been burnt on this particular altar. Keep in mind the purpose for which the tabernacle was built, "That I might dwell among them." This was Jehovah's altar and none might look therein. Maybe there is a slight modification to that. When the priests removed a board or two in order to attend to the sacrifice or the fire, then perhaps a Levite would catch a glimpse of either the fire or the sacrifice. Pause a moment and consider the type. The altar is God's appreciation of His Son as the perfect sacrifice. He alone could fully see all that happened on that altar. The fragrance ascended to Him. This is that aspect of Calvary that only the Father can appreciate, that ascending fragrance that no saint can fully enter into, yet perhaps occasionally the wind would blow that fragrance to the nostrils of the priests, especially on the fast days. How good that smell must have been. So with us, we cannot enter fully into that fragrance that arises to the Father but just occasionally the Holy Spirit, (likened to the wind in John three) causes us to appreciate something, only a very little, of the Father's satisfaction in that sacrifice. Perhaps this is one of the things that is made more acute by prayer and fasting. Linger a moment more. Perhaps as we remember the Lord at the Lord's Supper some brother exercises his priestly function and removes a board from the top part of the altar, and we catch a glimpse, fleeting perhaps, but how glorious, of what that sacrifice meant to the Father. Maybe another brother will remove a board from the base of the altar, and we see the fierceness of the fire, the intense suffering, not only physical, but moral and spiritual; fleeting glimpses perhaps, but how precious, and the odour and fragrance rises more strongly. If for one moment in all eternity God does not smell the sweet savour of the sacrifice of Calvary then the ransomed will fall from glory into a lost eternity; but even as it is impossible for us to refer to "a moment in eternity", it is equally impossible for God to cease from saying, "This is my beloved Son, in whom I am well pleased." How terribly important this is. If the sacrifice had proved unacceptable to God, what use would it have been to you and me? God has placed His seal upon Calvary by raising the Lord from among the dead and seating Him at His own right hand. Selah!

There were four rings, one at each corner of the grate. These were so arranged that poles could be inserted in them so that the altar could be carried, a constant reminder that the children of Israel were still wanderers in a hostile wilderness.

Before leaving the altar consider the way in which it was divided by the grating. One half of the altar pointed upwards, and one half downwards. One half was heavenward, one half earthward, one half Godward, one half manward. Now consider the seven sayings of the Lord on the cross. Three were Godward: "My God, my God, why has Thou forsaken me?" (Matt. 27 v 46), "Father forgive them; for they know not what they do." (Luke 23 v 34) and "Father, into Thy hands I commend my spirit." (Luke 23 v 46). Three of the sayings were manward: to the thief, "Verily I say unto thee, Today shalt thou be with me in paradise." (Luke 23 v 43), to Mary and John, "Woman, behold thy son . . . Behold thy mother." (Jno. 19 vv 26 & 27), as a man the Lord said, "I thirst." (Jno. 19 v 28); three sayings Godward and three sayings manward. This leaves one to go in the middle, as it were on the grating, the missing saying, "It is finished." (Jno. 19 v 30). Which way does this face, Godward or manward? Note it well, it comes in the middle, both Godward and manward. God was satisfied with the work, it was complete as far as He was concerned, all the prophecies had been fulfilled, "IT IS FINISHED", – Manward, yes, reconciliation, finished. After all of those long years of man's separation from God, God was now coming down to dwell among men.

Much has been made of the fact that the hearth of the altar was on the same level as the top of the ark or the mercy seat. Wonder what the real lesson is? God dwelt between the cherubim on the mercy seat, at the same level as the sacrifice. The floor of the Holy of Holies was bare earth, speaking of God coming down to dwell among men, but the time had not yet come when God could actually walk upon earth. He could only descend as far as the sacrifice. It was not until God became incarnate, until the place of sacrifice was rooted on earth, that is, when the grating was lowered to the ground, "And the Word was made flesh, and tabernacled among us." (Jno. 1 v 14), that the Baptist could cry, looking upon Jesus as He walked (note that – as He walked), "Behold the Lamb of God!". (Jno. 1 v 36). God (and we write this very reverently) now had His feet on the bare earth. "How wonderful, that Thou the Son hast come, and here for us as Son of Man hast died.".

At first we may wonder how such a small altar coped with all of the sacrifices that the children of Israel offered. Here were two or three million people who had professed their dedication to Jehovah. The fact that they meant it is shown by the willingness with which they parted with their substance in order to build the tabernacle. Surely as soon as the altar was commissioned there would be hundreds of sacrifices waiting to be burnt. The altar could never have coped. It would have burnt out. Let us cast our minds back to the murmurings of the Israelites. One of their chief complaints was their lack of food and in particular the lack of meat. God satisfied them with manna, and, although it angered the Lord, with quails, the eating of which caused a

E

great many deaths at Kibroth-Hattaavah. (Num. 11). Moses was loth to kill the flocks and the herds to suffice them (v 22) for obviously these were essential to the camp for provision of milk and for transportation, so that the availability of sheep, goats and bullocks was very limited indeed. Jehovah had already placed a strain upon resources by asking for a lamb night and morning, but such a state of affairs was not going to continue always and provision was made for other altars to be built, although it seems essential for the type that we should regard it as only one altar. In the same way there were many thousands of sacrifices offered but they must only be regarded as a picture of that one sacrifice for sins for ever. (Heb. 10 v 12). That provision was made for other altars is shown in Exodus twenty. Moses was in the mount receiving the commandments of Jehovah and also the details and pattern of the tabernacle. In the twenty-fourth verse the Holy Spirit records, "An altar of earth thou shalt make unto me, and shalt sacrifice thereon thy burnt offerings and thy peace offerings, thy sheep, and thine oxen: in all places where I record my name I will come unto thee, and I will bless thee", so it would appear that God intended that there should be altars other than the brazen one of the tabernacle. This is why it appears as though this is essentially Jehovah's altar. All that Moses was directly told to offer thereon was for Jehovah. There may even have been other altars at the same time as the tabernacle was standing, for remember that the tabernacle was in existence right up until the time of Solomon. An inkling of this may be contained in Leviticus 1 v 7 where we read, "And the sons of Aaron the priest shall put fire upon the altar, and lay the wood in order upon the fire:". Now the fire on the brazen altar must never go out. How then could "the sons of Aaron the priest put fire upon the altar" when it was already there, and how could they lay the wood in order if the whole lot was already burning? A further indication is given in Leviticus chapter 17 vv 1-9. Here we are told that if an Israelite or a stranger living with him killed any beast, whether in the camp or in the open field, then he must present it before the door of the congregation as an offering. It would appear that all that was necessary was for the slayer to bring the hard fat of the animal together with its blood. The blood would be poured out and the fat burnt. If the number of animals killed was ever very great, then the altar would not be able to cope with the vast amount of fat that had to be burned. The fact that the blood was sprinkled on the altar identified each sacrifice with the brazen altar wherever it may have been burned afterwards. Although Hebrews 13 v 11 may be restricted to the sin offering, maybe it has a wider significance. In any event we have records of other altars being built. Balaam built several in Numbers 23 and although perhaps we should not use Balaam as an example, yet Goes does not condemn his building the altars. Moses gave instruction to the people, that when they had passed over Jordan, "there shalt thou build an altar unto the Lord thy God, an altar of stones: thou shalt not lift up any iron tool upon them. Thou shalt build the altar of the Lord thy God of whole stones: and thou shalt offer burnt offerings thereon unto the Lord thy God." (Deut. 27 vv 5 & 6), an altar that complied with the instruction given in Exodus twenty and remember that the tabernacle was still in existence. Deuteronomy sixteen verse twenty-one forbids the planting of any trees near "unto the altar of the Lord thy God.", hardly an instruction that could be given with regard to the brazen altar. Surely no one would attempt to turn the tabernacle courtyard into a garden, even although some seem keen on doing so with the assemblies, overdoing the floral decoration. Joshua carried out Moses' instruction and built the altar on the other side of Jordan. (Josh.8v30). Solomon offered a thousand burnt offerings upon the altar that Bezaleel had made. (2 Chron. 1 v 6). At first sight we look and think what a marvellous thing for Solomon to have done. Now refer to the account in 1 Kings 3 vv 3 & 4, "And Solomon loved the Lord, walking in the statutes of David his father: ONLY HE SACRIFICED AND BURNT INCENSE IN HIGH PLACES. And the king went to Gibeon to sacrifice there; FOR THAT WAS THE GREAT HIGH PLACE: a thousand burnt offerings did Solomon offer upon that altar." How gracious was the Lord not to smite him as He did Uzziah (2 Chron. 26). A thousand burnt offerings? If this took place within twelve hours it would mean that more than one animal would have to be burnt every minute. Possibly he may have destroyed that altar, melted it in his enthusiasm and the glory of the greatness of his sacrifice, unless of course the sacrifices took place over a longer period. In any event we read nothing more of Bezaleel's altar for Solomon built one that was far bigger being sixteen times the area and over three times as high, but even this was not sufficient to accommodate all of Solomon's sacrifices, some had to be burned in the middle of the court. (2 Chron. 7 v 7). Perhaps Solomon had learned the lesson that you cannot overload a brazen altar, who knows.

CHAPTER ELEVEN

# The Laver

"I am the resurrection, and the life." (Jno. 11 v 25)

In some respects we know less about the laver than any other article of furniture in the tabernacle. We do not know its shape, neither do we know its size. All that we know in this direction is that it had the facilities whereby Aaron and his sons might wash their hands and their feet. In another respect we know more about the laver than about any other article for Exodus 38 v 8 tells us, "he made the laver of brass, and the foot of it of brass, of the lookingglasses of the women assembling, which assembled at the door of the tabernacle of the congregation.", or, as J.N.D. translates it, "of the mirrors of the crowds of women who crowded before the entrance of the tent of meeting." Now here is a strange thing. The laver was made from the mirrors of these women who gathered at the door of the tabernacle, yet the laver was made before the tabernacle was built, what a glaring anachronism. How could Moses collect mirrors from those assembled at the entrance when the entrance was not yet in existence? Does the Word of God throw any light on this elsewhere? Some three hundred years after the appointment of the first High Priest, another occupied that position. His name was Eli and he had two dissolute sons, Hophni and Phineas. It is recorded of the two reprobates that among their many sins "they lay with the women that assembled at the door of the tabernacle of the congregation." (1 Sam. 2 v 22). Could it be that "the women who assembled at the door of the tabernacle of the congregation" might be a euphemism in Israel for women of easy virtue, in the same way that we might call them "women of the streets"? It is certain that this was their character at the time of Eli. It seems strange that the Holy Spirit should use this expression only twice in scripture, and He tells us what it means on the second occasion.

Working on this assumption we can understand that a mirror would be an essential part of their stock in trade. Perhaps it would be good to note that it was the harlots of olden time who used lipstick and eye shadow. Now note, there was nothing wrong with the mirrors, it was the image that they portrayed that was at fault. Where is all this getting us, what does the laver represent? Consider the laver again, shapeless, sizeless, obscure yet very important for the priests could not function without it. Call to mind the Lord's conversation with Nicodemus in John's third chapter, how He explained the elusive character of the Holy Spirit, likening Him to the wind, shapeless, boundless, imperceptible, but powerful and mighty. Consider the words of 1 Cor. 6 v 11, "ye are sanctified, but ye are justified in the name of the Lord Jesus, and by the Spirit of our God" and also Titus 3 v 5, "according to His mercy He saved us, by the washing of regeneration, and renewing of the Holy Ghost". The guide book seems to suggest that the Holy Spirit plays an important part in the washing and cleansing of the saints. If then the laver is a picture to us of the Holy Spirit, how come that it was made from the mirrors of these immoral women? As we have already stated there was no fault in the mirrors. We should remember that these mirrors were not made of silvered glass as in our modern production but were made of polished brass or copper. The fault lay not in the mirror but in the image. How like the Spirit operating through the Word of God, each one of us had no moral standing in the sight of God, even our righteousnesses were as filthy rags. We look into the Word of God and the Spirit shows us what we are, painted images, looking good on the outside but rotten and corrupt within, how like the painted harlot, but God used that same Word, part of His eternal purposes, to minister the cleansing power of His Holy Spirit, in the same way that Moses took the mirrors that had reflected the vanity of these sinful women and from them constructed the laver for the washing of the priests.

The laver was accessible only to Aaron and his sons, those who were priests. Ever the way of approach is getting narrower and narrower. The stranger could not approach the tabernacle on penalty of death. The multitude of Israel could gather at the door of the tabernacle as at the consecration of the priests in Leviticus 8 v 1-4, but they could not enter the court. The Levites could enter the court but must not touch the holy things. The priests, Aaron's sons, could minister at the altar and enter the Holy Place, and only one man could go into the Holy of Holies and that only once a year on the day of atonement and even then his vision has to be screened by the smoke of the incense. Perhaps we tend to lose sight of the holiness of God. The word 'holy' is the only word used three times over in both the Old and New Testaments. Perhaps when we read such glorious scriptures as Hebrews 10 vv 19 & 20 "Having therefore, brethren, boldness to enter into the holiest by the blood of Jesus, by a new and living way, which He hath consecrated for us, through the veil, that is to say His flesh:" we tend to forget the holiness of God and think that we can dash in and out of the Holy of Holies like children coming in and going out to play. Such is not the case. We must never take a scripture out of its context. The apostle continues, "let us draw near with a true heart in full assurance of faith, having our hearts sprinkled from an evil conscience, and our bodies washed with pure water." Here it is, the laver, the washing that is necessary before we dare go into the Holy Presence. Let us not lose sight of this. No matter what meeting we are attending, no matter in what way we seek to handle eternal things, whether it be ministering the Word, listening to the Word, or even washing the cups or sweeping the floor after a conference, this is the service of our God, of a thrice holy God and remember we must always approach Him with clean hands. Listen to the turbulent and aggressive James, "Cleanse your hands, ye sinners; and purify your hearts, ye double minded . . . Humble yourselves in the sight of the Lord, and He shall lift you up." (Jas. 4 vv 8-10). Ponder this lesson. All of Israel was called to be a kingdom of priests for they were a redeemed people. Only the Levites, representing the firstborn from every tribe, could approach beyond the gate. Only the priests, Aaron's sons, could go into the Holy Place, and Aaron alone could go into the Holy of Holies. The Holy Place is not a free for all. It is a place for those who have gone on in the things of the Lord, who constantly wash their hands and their feet and approach God in reverential fear, conscious of His love and mercy and knowing that they are accepted in the beloved. Maybe we cannot see these things, neither could the mass of the children of Israel. Even when they gathered outside the gate, when perhaps the curtains were drawn wide, all that the Israelite could see clearly was the brazen altar, the place of sacrifice accepted by Jehovah. He could see that there was something beyond. Maybe he could not see the laver (what a lesson) but he could see the entrance to the tabernacle proper, but the mysteries contained therein remained covered. They were for the priests. There is progression in our Christian growth. We do not know it all at once. Daily we learn its lessons; let us seek to function as the Levites and go on to a full priesthood.

To equate the Holy Spirit with the aspect of the Godhead presented by "I AM the resurrection and the life." may at first seem strange, but hark back to the Lord's conversation with Nicodemus in the third chapter of John. Here the Lord is telling this teacher of the Jews that there must be a new birth, a new life; not a patched up old entity but something born of the Spirit of God. Romans chapter six puts it graphically as our old man, our old nature, being buried in the waters of baptism, and a new man rising up from those waters. That the resurrection is not just something that will happen some time after we are dead was the mistake that Martha made in John chapter 11 verse 24, "Martha saith unto Him, 'I know that he shall rise again in the resurrection at the last day.'" The Lord replied, ... "Whosoever liveth and believeth in me shall never die.", telling her that eternal life is something that we have here and now. This is supported by the thirty-sixth verse of John 3; "He that believeth on the Son hath everlasting life." It is a present possession, and this is brought about by the new birth so that the apostle Paul writes in Galatians 2 v 20, "I am crucified with Christ: nevertheless I live; yet not I, but Christ liveth in me: and the life which I now live in the flesh I live by the faith of the Son of God, who loved me, and gave Himself for me." This is accomplished because "God has sent forth the Spirit of His Son into your hearts." (Gal. 4 v 6).

Never make the mistake of trying to isolate the persons of the Godhead. They are three and yet they are one. In the previous quotation from Galatians four we can see that the Father and the Son and the Holy Spirit are all active in causing the Holy Spirit to dwell in our hearts thus enabling us to call God, Abba, Father. Perhaps the easiest way for us to understand something of this is to remember that when God made Adam he planned to make him in the image of God, and this He did, "So God created man in His own image, in the image of God created He him." (Gen. 1 v 27). Now we know that God is tripartite, the Father, the Son, and the Holy Spirit. Man too is tripartite. He has a body, that part of him that all can see. May we reverently liken this to the Son who was God manifest in the flesh. This is what man could see of the Godhead. Man also has a soul, that part of him that is largely exercised with his will. Broadly this corresponds to the Father. "The Father sent the Son to be the Saviour of the world." Finally man has a spirit, that ability to reach out Godward. No animal has this. No tribe of man has ever been discovered that had not some form of deity, fetish or idol that it worshipped. No species of animal has ever been discovered that had this God-conscious desire. This spirit, this indefinable something was given to man when God breathed into him the breath of life. Adam sinned, and in the day that he sinned he died. The divine spirit that was in him died and a new spirit was born within him. This was the old nature, referred to in 1 Cor. 2 v 11, "For what man knoweth the things of a man, save the spirit of man which is in him? even so the things of God knoweth no man, but the Spirit of God.", so that man still retained his tripartite structure of body, soul and spirit, but the spirit portion was now dominated by the will of man rather than by the will of God. In order to put this right the old nature, the spirit of man must die, and be replaced by the spirit of His Son. A death and a rebirth must take place, a death and a resurrection. How then does a born again man differ from the original Adam that God created? As we have seen, Adam was body, soul and spirit, but that spirit was of such a character that when put to the test it could sin, and it did. Man was dead in trespasses and sins, walking "according to the course of his world, according to the prince of power of the air, the spirit that now worketh in the children of disobedience." (Eph. 2 vv 1 & 2), but, and herein is a marvellous thing, with the resurrection of a new birth we are indwelt, not with the original spirit that was in Adam, a spirit that although God-given was capable of disobeying God and sinning, but a new spirit, the spirit of His Son, and that cannot sin. How we could dwell on this theme but we needs must turn to the tabernacle. However, before leaving the laver it must be imperative to point out the wonder of this indwelling of the Holy Spirit. At the time of the crucifixion the disciples were weak, helpless and useless. Peter denied his Lord and none of the others were any better for they all forsook Him and fled, yet after Pentecost these selfsame men stood firmly and boldly, and every one of them, as far as we know, died a martyr's death. What had happened? The explanation is in John's gospel chapter fourteen. Referring to the Holy Spirit the Lord says, "But ye know Him; for he dwelleth with you, and shall be in you." (v 17). What the Lord is telling them is that they have the Holy Spirit with them, even as the prophets of old. The presence of the Holy Spirit was enough for them to see and dimly understand those things that the Lord taught them, so that, when in Matthew 16 the Lord asked them who they said He was, Peter replied, "Thou art the Christ, the Son of the living God." (v 16). The Lord then turned to Peter and said, "Blessed art thou, Simon Bar-jona: for flesh and blood hath not revealed it unto thee, but my Father which is in heaven." (v 17). The revelation was not a natural one, it came from the Father who was in heaven. The spirit was with Peter but not yet in him. It is this indwelling of the Holy Spirit that drives us on in our Christian pathway. After all, surely if we are saved, and saved eternally, what more do we want? The Spirit of God takes of the things of Christ and shows them to us. We see wonderful things in the Word of God, and what do the scriptures say concerning the dealings of the Holy Spirit with the Lord when He was upon earth? "And immediately the Spirit driveth him into the wilderness" (Mark, the servant gospel, 1 v 12). The Holy Spirit is just the same today with the Lord's people, He drives them on, showing them the emptiness of this world and the glory that shall follow. Again we must not linger for the rest of the tabernacle proper is calling us.

One last question, however, where did the water for the laver come from? Here we must do a little arithmetic. Horeb and Sinai, according to some authorities, were identical. Others say that Horeb was a mountain range and Sinai was one particular peak. It matters little, sufficient to say that they were close enough to warrant little distinction between them. For convenience we will use the Jewish year of 360 days, giving each month 30 days. Now the children of Israel came to Sinai three months (90 days) after leaving Egypt (Exod. 19 v 1). For forty days Moses was in the mount (Exod. 24 v 18) receiving the pattern of the tabernacle and the law. He returned to the people and broke the tables of stone then went back up the mount for another forty days (Exod. 34 v 28). Now note the time factor. The children of Israel came to Sinai three months after leaving Egypt, say 90 days. Moses spend two periods of 40 days in the mount, bringing the total time after leaving Egypt to 170 days. Add the few days that must have elapsed between Moses' two visits to the mount and we have a period of about six months (180 days), the position now being that, six months after leaving Egypt, the Israelites were at the foot of Mount Sinai with the completed God-given plans for the tabernacle in their possession. They were feeding on the manna and the quails and drinking the water from the smitten rock at Horeb.

The seventeenth verse of the last chapter of Exodus records this important date, "And it came to pass in the first month in the second year, on the first day of the month, that the tabernacle was reared up." This would mean that less than one year after leaving Egypt, for they left Egypt on the fifteenth day of the first month, the tabernacle was finished, but six months had elapsed before Moses delivered the full plans of the tabernacle to the children of Israel. It therefore follows that the tabernacle with all its curtains, its woodwork and metalcraft, its embroidery and the graven stones for the High Priest were all completed in the short space of less than six months, an outstanding achievement when we consider that the Israelites could not go to the department store and buy so many yards of double width material. All had to be woven specially for the job, neither could they go to a timber merchant and buy planks of wood already planed. Everything had to be done from scratch by men and women who often had to learn fresh trades and skills, and all in six months. There was no time for journeyings. The tabernacle must have been built at the foot of Mount Sinai. What, you may ask, is the import of that? Such intense activity carried on in the dry and arid Sinai desert must have been thirsty work indeed. Where did the children of Israel get their water? Surely from the smitten rock in Horeb for the Psalmist tells us, "He opened the rock, and the waters gushed out: they ran in the dry places like a river." (Psa. 105 v 41). Psalm 78 v 15 also confirms this fact. Now the apostle Paul tells us in 1 Cor. 10 v 4, "that rock was Christ.", the smitten rock from whence the water flowed. Remember our initial question, 'Where did the water for the laver come from?' - the answer, from the smitten rock. Here is a wonderful lesson and one that answers a puzzling text in John's gospel chapter 19 v 34, "but one of the soldiers with a spear pierced His side, and forthwith came there out blood and water.", not just blood but also water for the laver must be filled. There must not only be the cleansing by the blood but provision for the constant washing of the Lord's people on their journey home. How the little details of the Word of God link up if we only have eyes to see them, eyes that must be opened by the Holy Spirit.

# CHAPTER TWELVE

# The Tabernacle Entrance

"I am the door." (Jno. 10 v 9)

We now come to the tabernacle proper, the tent. See illustration three. Pause a moment at the entrance for no man but the priest may go in here. We have a curtain supported by five pillars, and note that it does not say, "Its pillars five and its curtains five" for there is no free pillar on which to hang the fifth curtain – no, here we have one curtain supported by five pillars. It is not the same size as the gate which was twenty cubits by five, although it has the same area being ten cubits by ten cubits. The colours and material are the same as the gate – obviously it is setting forth the same glories but the difference is in the number of pillars and the size. The gate had four pillars and was wide, far wider than was really necessary for the job it had to do. The picture presented to us was the gospel in all its glory and width, "by me if any man enter in he shall be saved" (Jno. 10 v 9). The entrance to the tent is completely different. Its width is adequate but its height is more than adequate. No man ten cubits high is going to enter in here. It is higher than he can ever need or even reach. What are its lessons? It was in the gate that the four pillars spoke to us of the four evangelists, those who presented the wonderful gospel story in its fourfold aspect. Now we have five pillars and it may be a strange coincidence, but it may also be the foreknowledge of God and the mighty working of His Holy Spirit, for there just happens to be five writers of the epistles, Paul, Peter, John, James & Jude. Does not the contention as to who wrote the epistle to the Hebrews take on a new dimension? Little does it matter what modern scholarship says in the face of internal evidence such as this, – another caution, beware of man's learning. How many Bible Schools and

Colleges there are. There were none in the early church yet it grew both in size and in knowledge. How were those early Christians taught? They neither went to Bible Schools nor did they attend seminars. They forsook not the assembling of themselves together, (Heb. 10 v 25) but talked about the things of the Lord. They listened, and not content with listening they went back and consulted the scriptures, even as the men of Berea who were counted more noble than the men of Thessalonica because "they received the word with all readiness of mind, and searched the scriptures daily, whether these things were so." If we adopt this approach to the Word of God we shall find things therein that only the Spirit of God can show to us, giving the "light of the knowledge of the glory of God in the face of Jesus Christ." (2 Cor. 4 v 6). Give heed to Peter's warning, "Ye therefore, beloved, seeing ye know these things before, beware lest ye also, being led away with the error of the wicked, fall from your own stedfastness. But grow in grace, and in the knowledge of our Lord and Saviour Jesus Christ." (2 Pet. 3 vv 17 & 18). There are no short cuts. Taking our Bibles night and morning and reading a set portion taken from a calendar or prayer guide may be good, but it is not really the way to grow. Remember that one of the requirements of a clean animal was that it must "chew the cud". How true this is for us. Not only must we take in a portion of the Word of God as our food but we must also "chew the cud", ruminate on it, join the psalmist when he describes the blessed man in Pslam 1 v 2, "But his delight is in the law of the Lord; and in His law doth he meditate day and night." We may argue that we cannot see the wonderful things in the Word that some great teachers see. First of all remember that teaching is a gift, given of God. Secondly, remember that we will never understand the mysteries of God by man's wisdom. The fact that a man is a professor, a doctor, a scholar in this world's schools, or that he has half of the alphabet behind his name or nigh blasphemous titles such as reverend or very reverend (surely only one is to be revered and that is God) before his name, none of these things qualify a man in God's school. We listen to those who have the gift of teaching but we have either got to reject that teaching or else absorb it by careful examination asking God to show us wonderful things from His Word and claiming the Lord's promise in John 14 v 26, "But the Comforter, which is the Holy Ghost, whom the Father will send in my name, He shall teach you all things.", but we cannot claim this promise unless we fulfill the conditions laid down before this in John 14 v 23, "If a man love me, he will keep my words:" (go and wash in the laver) "and my Father will love him, and we will come unto him, and make our abode with him." As they say in Yorkshire, "Think on't". Go away and chew the cud.

Go through this curtain with reverential fear. Only priests are allowed in here, and make sure you have washed your hands and your feet at the laver. Consider this entrance with its appropriate "I am". "I am the door". We may well ask, "Where does it lead?". The Lord says in John 14 v 6, "No man cometh unto the Father, but by me." The Lord had been telling His disciples that He must go away, but He also told them that He was coming again to receive them to Himself. He was going to prepare a place for them in glory, telling them that, "In my Father's house are many mansions." You do not understand how there can be many mansions in a house? – neither do I. We are so limited that even God cannot explain heaven to us. Constantly the Holy Spirit tries to convey to our limited minds the glory that is to come. How wonderful are the words of Ephesians 2 v 7, "That in the ages to come He might show the exceeding riches of His grace in His kindness toward us through Christ Jesus." Chew the cud.

Not only is He the way, but He is also the truth. Call to mind how that when the Lord was in the judgement hall before the Roman governor, Pilate, that troubled man turned to the Lord and asked that most pertinent question, "What is truth?", poor puzzled man. Before him stood the one who proclaimed "I am the truth". The apostle Paul tells us that there are many voices in the world today, and who can tell which one is speaking the truth. (1 Cor. 14 vv 6-11). Which ones are telling the truth? Even those things that were taught as true in schools are questioned and often accounted unreliable. What shall a man believe as true? Says the Lord to us, "I am the truth.", and John in the opening chapter of his gospel says, "and we beheld His glory . . . full of grace and truth." (Jno. 1 v 14). Note the setting for this comment. John has been describing the Lord as The Word who was from the beginning. There are many, many difficult things in the Word of God. No man understands it all. We are, every one of us, still learning. It must be so if the Word is infinite and we are finite, but we press on, He is the Truth, and we can understand how that even the apostle Paul craves after that knowledge, "That I may know Him, and the power of His resurrection, and the fellowship of His sufferings, being made conformable unto His death." (Phil. 3 v 10). Do we understand that fully? No, and perhaps we never shall this side of the glory. Nevertheless we can see something of the wonder of it. Pause if you will and chew the cud a little. Selah!

"I am the Life." What a claim, the beginning of all things (Jno. 1 v 1), the upholder of all things by the word of His power (Heb. 1 v 3). "In Him was life; and the life was the light of men." (Jno. 1 v 4). These scriptures could be multiplied time and again. He was the author, the embodiment of life. Look back to the brazen altar, "The good shepherd giveth His life." "I lay down my life . . . I have power to lay it down, and I have power to take it again." (Jno. 10 vv 17 & 18). Who can fathom this, "The Lord of life to death made subject"? How was this to be accomplished? "Without shedding of blood there is no remission." (Heb. 9 v 22). "Yes, Christ the Son of God must bleed, if sinners must from sin be freed." As we said earlier, tread carefully. If you have met the requirement of a priest and washed your hands and feet at the laver, then come inside and look upon holy things, but before doing so let us consider the tabernacle proper, the tent.

# THE TENT

"AND THOU SHALT MAKE BOARDS FOR THE
TABERNACLE OF SHITTIM WOOD STANDING UP"
(Exod. 26.15)

Ten boards have been removed from the front of the model and
four of the bars cut away to show "the middle bar in the midst of
the boards" reaching "from end to end" (Exod. 26.28). Note also
the five pillars supporting the entrance curtain, the four pillars
suporting the cherubim embroidered vail and the sockets of
silver waiting to receive the ten boards that have been removed.

# CHAPTER THIRTEEN

# Of Boards and Curtains

The curtain that we have just considered not only formed the entrance to the tent but it also constituted the whole of the eastern wall. The other three sides were formed of boards with curtains and coverings laid over them.

We are told in Exodus twenty-six and verse sixteen that the length of each board was to be ten cubits and each board was to be one and a half cubits wide, but it does not tell us the thickness. Once again we must do a little mathematics. Moses was told to make twenty of these boards for the south side. Twenty times one and a half (the width of each board) gives us thirty cubits. That is fine for we need twenty cubits for the length of the Holy Place and ten for the length of the Holy of Holies., giving us thirty cubits in all. Now for the complication, the back of the tent or the western end. Moses is told in Exodus 26 v 22 to make six boards for this. Six times one and a half (the width of each board) equals nine cubits, but we know that the Holy of Holies and the Holy Place were both ten cubits wide. Do we? Perhaps we've been reading too many commentaries. Commentaries are good, they help us and give us the benefit of the study and understanding of brethren who have trod the pathway before us, but they are not inspired like the Word of God. Nowhere in Exodus twenty-six or thirty-six are we told the width of the tent. We know the height of the most Holy Place must have been ten cubits for that was the length of the boards. Knowing the total length of the sides of the tent to be thirty cubits (twenty boards of one and a half cubits each) we can deduce from the curtains as we shall see later that the vail was suspended twenty cubits from the front of the tent therefore we know that the Holy Place was twenty cubits long and thus the Holy of Holies must have been the other ten cubits in order to make thirty in all. So we now have the Holy of Holies measuring ten cubits high and ten cubits long but no measurement of its width. Somehow, something tells us that this width must be ten cubits in order to make the Holy of Holies, where God is to dwell among His people, foursquare. We have an indication that this should be so for in Solomon's temple the oracle or Holy of Holies was foursquare being twenty cubits by twenty cubits by twenty cubits. (1 Kings 6 v 20).

Now let us return to the western end of the tent. We have, in verse twenty-two of Exodus twenty-six, six boards and six times one and a half equals nine cubits – one cubit short of our ten. Read on a bit. "And two boards shalt thou make for the corners of the tabernacle" (v 23) "And they shall be eight boards" (v 25), so that we have six boards plus two corner boards, giving eight boards. Now eight times one and a half equals twelve cubits. We've overshot the mark, we need a width of ten cubits, but walls need to have thickness. Now suppose these boards were a cubit thick, then we could butt the side walls (i.e. the north and south walls) against the back wall (i.e. the west wall) and this would give us an internal measurement of ten cubits wide and thirty cubits long, while the external measurement would be twelve cubits wide and thirty-one cubits long. (I recall the words of my old Bible Class leader, "The Bible wasn't written for lazy people", how right he was). The test for these assumptions will be in the fitting of the curtains.

May we suggest that these boards are a picture of each individual believer being held together to form one whole dwelling place, a portable temple, for that is what the tabernacle really was, and the apostle Paul tells us in 1 Cor. 3 v 17, "Which temple ye are" and in case that is not sufficient he repeats this statement in his second letter, "Ye are the temple of the living God." (2 Cor. 6 v 16). It is worth having a closer look at these boards. First of all they were heavy and cumbersome, ten cubits long, one and a half cubits wide and very, very thick, one cubit (18"). Obviously it was not the intention to portray the saints as being "thick" yet how true it is. The risen Lord on the way to

Emmaus reproved the two disciples, "O fools, and slow of heart to believe . . ." and the apostle Paul chides the Hebrew christians, ". . . seeing ye are dull of hearing . . . and are become such as have need of milk, and not of strong meat." (Heb. 5 vv 11 & 12). Doubtless this was not intended but it is a lesson that we do well to heed. What is certain is that these planks were heavy and in this respect all were equal. It must have taken the children of Israel all their strength and cunning in order to get these boards standing upright and it would have been impossible for the boards to remain upright in the shifting sands of the desert unless a secure foundation had already been provided. The lessons come gushing out. Not only must the trees be cut down, then shaped and smoothed, aye and even covered with gold, but they must be stood upright. The salvation of a soul is only the commencement of the business. What effort must be expended to make the boards stand upright in the temple. The evangelist is very important but so is the pastor and the teacher, those who with skill and patience nurse the newborn babe and bring it to maturity. Remember Mephibosheth, Saul's son, to whom David would show kindness. His nurse saved him from death but she dropped him afterwards and for ever after he was lame in both his feet. Evangelism is essential but so are the other gifts in the church so that the boards can be upright. How can they stay upright? They need a firm foundation and they got it. Two sockets of silver were to be set under each board. These sockets were to weigh one talent each, about a hundredweight. (Exod. 38 v 27). Forty-eight boards (twenty on the north side, twenty on the south and eight on the western end) each board with two sockets and that equals ninety-six sockets, ninety-six hundredweight, and four for the veil makes one hundred, or nearly five tons of silver, surely the most costly foundation for a building that was about thirty-one feet long and twelve feet wide.

The meaning of the silver is obvious. It was the redemption price that had to be paid for an atonement for the souls of the children of Israel. It was a small amount and the rich man was not allowed to give more or the poor man less. We often stress that there is nothing to do for salvation and in one sense this is perfectly true, the Lord has done it all. There is, however, the other side of the coin. The sinner must see his need of redemption, it is the same for all men and he must accept this fact and build on it. To this end Moses had to furnish each board with two tenons, or as the margin has it, two hands, how lovely. These tenons were to engage in the pre-set sockets of silver. What does it all mean? The sockets, the basis for the boards standing upright were the silver redemption and atonement money. This is our sure anchor or foundation and Paul tells us "For other foundation can no man lay than that is laid, which is Jesus Christ." (1 Cor. 3 v 11). The two tenons or hands on the boards seem self-explanatory, they were for engaging into or holding on to the sockets of silver, the foundation which is Jesus Christ, but why two sockets? Some have seen in them the death and resurrection of the Lord, but His birth, life and ascension are surely just as necessary in the foundation. What two things form the basis of our salvation and redemption? We would enumerate many but have we any guide in scripture? Consider again the foundation that has been laid. What does it say? There can be no other foundation laid than Jesus – no. Then the Christ? - no. That foundation must be twofold, Jesus the Son of man, Christ the Son of God. This surely is the solid foundation to which we must cling with both hands if we are to remain upright in the temple, for all other truths and teaching spring from this dual character of the Lord, "Verily God, yet become truly human."

How interesting that the vail only has one socket of silver for each pillar. "And thou shalt hang it (the vail) upon four pillars ... upon the four sockets of silver". (Exod. 26 v 32). Wonder why? Dare we say it very reverently indeed that, unlike us, the Lord does not need to hang on with both hands to the truth of his deity and His divinity. His glory is apparent in the vail, the "blue and purple and scarlet and fine twined linen of cunning work: with cherubim." (Exod. 26 v 31), but all of this glory presents His flesh (Heb. 10 v 20). This is the basic foundation of our redemption, that the Lord became flesh, the one essential foundation – only one socket for each pillar. This is surely the reason for the reversion to four pillars. If we return to the gate we recall that it had pillars four and sockets four, because it told the wondrous gospel story of God coming down to earth and taking human form. When we proceeded to the door of the tent we beheld five pillars with sockets of brass representing the writers of the epistles, the sure counsels of God showing forth the Lord's glory. The vail reverts to the four pillars for this is the wondrous message, even of the bare-floored Holy of Holies, that redemption rested secure on the foundation that God has been manifest in flesh. Reckon that if you or I had designed the tabernacle we would have given each vail pillar two sockets of silver just to make them extra secure. What fools we are! Redemption is as secure as God Himself.

Doubtless the boards would remain upright if the two tenons fitted firmly in the silver foundations but something else is necessary. These boards have got to line up one with another, they cannot be just a row of free standing boards, they have got to be walls, each board held in correct relationship with its fellow, and how is this to be accomplished? By the insertion of gold covered bars of shittim wood. There were five of these bars to each side and they all located into rings of gold except for the middle bar on each side which shot through the boards from one end to the other. Various suggestions have been made concerning the meaning of these sets of five bars that held the boards securely together. Some have seen in them the gifts enumerated in Ephesians 4 v 11, apostles, prophets, evangelists, pastors and teachers. If that is a satisfactory solution well and good but in 1 Cor. 12 v 28 we are told of eight gifts given to the church. Admittedly some of these are no longer operative, comes to that, neither are the apostles and prophets which are counted in the first five.

May we suggest that there were not just five bars holding the walls in alignment but fifteen, five along each side and five at the back. Now consider the apostle's discourse on love in 1 Cor. 13 and we will find that he enumerates fifteen qualities that love possesses.

> 1. Love suffereth long.
> 2. Love is kind.
> 3. Love envieth not.
> 4. Love vaunteth not itself.

5. Love is not puffed up.
6. Love doth not behave itself unseemly.
7. Love seeketh not her own.
8. Love is not easily provoked.
9. Love thinketh no evil.
10. Love rejoiceth not in iniquity.
11. Love rejoiceth in the truth.
12. Love beareth all things.
13. Love believeth all things.
14. Love hopeth all things.
15. Love endureth all things.

If these aspects characterised each one of us believers how firm the local assembly would stand, how we would line up with every one of our brethren, but what of the middle staves, those that go right through the centre of the boards? Here we could insert the whole of Ephesians chapter four but perhaps odd excerpts will suffice, "forbearing one another in love; endeavouring to keep the unity of the Spirit in the bond of peace" (vv 2 & 3), "but speaking the truth in love, may grow up into Him in all things, which is the head, even Christ: from whom the whole body fitly joined together and compacted by that which every joint supplieth, according to the effectual working in the measure of every part, maketh increase of the body unto the edifying of itself in love" (vv 15 & 16), "for we are members one of another" (v 25). Selah! think of that and doubtless other scriptures will come to mind.

So much for the boards except that two are noted for special mention, not really as though they stand out above all others for they are singled out in verse twenty-three of Exodus twenty-six as "two boards shalt thou make for the corners of the tabernacle", but shortly afterwards they are included with the other boards, "and they shall be eight boards, and their sockets of silver, sixteen sockets" v 25, that is two corner boards and six ordinary boards forming the west side of the tabernacle. There is no extra glory attached to these two boards, no extra gold, no ornamentation, just ordinary boards, standing upright like pillars, indeed the root of the word pillar means to stand up or to stand firm, – no show, but how important, for these two boards are to be "coupled together above the head of it into one ring: thus shall it be for them both; they shall be for the two corners." (Exod. 26 v 24). Now whether this means that a separate ring went over the corner pillar and the plank next to it to fasten them together top and bottom, or whether it means that the corner boards were just fastened to the back and sides by any appropriate means so that the tabernacle now became one ring with boards on three sides and the curtain on the fourth, is perhaps not quite clear, but having made a model for photographic purposes, we did find that although in the northern, southern and western walls the boards were held together firmly to form a solid structure in each case, yet, nonetheless, the back or western wall could tend to separate itself slightly from the side walls. If, however, a fastening was made top and bottom, the structure became very firm and immovable. This leads us to think that when Moses was told to fasten the corner boards "to one ring" the reference was to the perimeter of the tabernacle building rather than to some sort of ring structure at each of the rear corners.

The Hebrew word used for ring here, (as in all the other references to ring in the Old Testament,) is TABBAATH and its strict interpretation is a signet ring, that is a ring with a seal that can be impressed in wax to show ownership or invest authority.

In Gen. 41 v 42 "Pharaoh took off his ring from his hand, and put it upon Joseph's hand" thus investing Joseph with the authority to seal things pertaining to Pharaoh. What a wonderful picture of the Lord. The Father has vested all authority in Him, authorising Him to stamp as His own all whom He will. This applies not only to the individual but also to the local assembly and to the assembly universal.

If our understanding of "they shall be coupled together above the head of it into one ring, thus shall it be for them both" is correct, that the ring referred to is the complete perimeter of the tent with twenty boards on the north and south sides, eight boards on the west and the entrance curtain on the east, then what a wonderful picture this idea of a signet ring presents to us.

The thought of the local assembly composed of separate boards (individual believers) joined fitly to each other by the external bars (the bonds of love) and held even firmer still by the centre bar that passes through their midst (the love of Christ); all of this structure bearing the authority, the stamp and the impression of the royal signet, displaying His authority, His character and His likeness.

The thought of the signet ring is further illustrated in the New Testament in Luke chapter fifteen. The prodigal decides to return home and ask to be made as one of his father's hired servants, but the father issues the instruction that a ring is to be placed on his hand, thus signifying the authority that was vested in him as a son and not a servant.

What is clear is that the corner boards were securely fastened to the sides and back at the top and the bottom. What can this mean? We have already suggested that the boards represent the individuals believers, fallen humanity, (the wood) smoothed and shaped and made to stand upright. Their foundation is firm in redemption, or rather in a redeemer, they are held together in bonds of love and they are covered with a glory of which only God and the priests can see anything, for the boards were only visible in the holy places. In every assembly of the Lord's people there are those who act as pillars or corner boards, fastened to the rest of the boards at the top and at the bottom, ministering to the needs of the saints spiritually (top) and physically (bottom). These brethren are not clad in sumptuous attire, they are just boards, the same as their brethren, helping to form a dwelling place that God may dwell among them. Why should not these corner boards, these pillars, have an additional glory, a bit more gold than their brethren? God's rewards are not given in this life, God's rewards will be given after we get home.

There were many pillars in the tabernacle, fifty-six to support the perimeter curtains, four for the gate, five for the door, four for the vail and just these two at the corners, not even called pillars but possibly taking more strain than any of the others, the only instance in the tabernacle of two boards functioning as pillars. Wonder what their reward will be? Does Solomon's temple furnish a clue? "He cast two pillars of brass, of eighteen cubits high apiece: and a line of twelve cubits did compass either of them about" (1 Kings 7 v 15), "and he set up the pillars in the porch of the temple:" (v 21), and he gave names to the pillars, JACHIN – He will establish, and BOAZ – In him is strength Rather appropriate for corner boards, pillars of brass, solid, strong, with pomegranates of fruitfulness. Perhaps we ought to write about the temple sometime. Meanwhile let us return to the tabernacle.

# THE CURTAINS

"TEN CURTAINS OF FINE TWINED LINEN, AND BLUE AND
PURPLE AND SCARLET; WITH CHERUBIM OF CUNNING WORK
SHALT THOU MAKE THEM." (Exod. 26.1).
Represented by the coloured curtain.

"AND THOU SHALT MAKE CURTAINS OF GOATS' HAIR TO BE
A COVERING UPON THE TABERNACLE … AND THOU SHALT
DOUBLE THE SIXTH CURTAIN IN THE FOREFRONT OF THE
TABERNACLE." (Exod. 26.7-9).

One corner of the goats' hair curtain has been folded back to
reveal the inner curtain. Note the goats' hair curtain folded back
at the front of the tabernacle.

# CHAPTER FOURTEEN

# Curtains and Coverings

Four materials were used to cover the boards of the tent. The outer two are described as coverings and the inner two as curtains. As we have decided to work inwards on the tabernacle, from the curtains and gate, to the brazen altar and laver, through the Holy Place and into the Holy of Holies, let us follow the same procedure with the covers and curtains, working from the outside inwards.

It may well be that the two outer layers of the tabernacle are called coverings as distinct from curtains because they could be conceived as a tent-like structure with a pointed apex so constructed as to allow rain to run clear of the tabernacle building. We are told nothing of such a structure so there can be no lessons there for us. What we are told is that the outer layer, for which no size is given, was to be made of badger skins. There has been a certain amount of controversy as to whether these were  badger skins, or seal skins, or as Strong gives "a (clean) animal with fur, probably a species of antelope", so where do we go from here? We don't even know what we are talking about. Yes we do, we are talking about a covering that is indiscriminate, uninteresting, at best a drab brown colour. What a mass of contradiction this tabernacle is. We have about five tons of silver sunk underground where no one can see it, yet outside we do not even have an ornamented curtain, nor even rams' skins dyed red to give a bit of colour, just drab brown. Compare this with the mosques and churches of our day, understandable when we think that many of them do not teach the same truths as the tabernacle. How the nations round about must have looked in wonder and most likely ridicule. Consider what they must have seen of the tabernacle – a tiny little structure in the middle of a camp that stretched possibly two or three miles in each direction, a tiny little structure with a wall of white curtains around its perimeter and the only building inside, a drab brown tent. What a temple! This was not according to man's design, it was God-given, so with our Saviour and our salvation. Man's design is by works and show of goodness. God's design is by way of the cross. Man is hopeless, helpless, bankrupt spiritually and morally, the Saviour, a crucified outcast. How apt are Isaiah's words when we see the drab outer tent, "He hath no form nor comeliness; And when we shall see him, there is no beauty that we should desire him. He is despised and rejected of men." (Isa.53 vv 2 & 3). For those who have entered in at the gate, passed the brazen altar, washed their hands and feet in the laver and dared to enter the holy place and perhaps even the Holy of Holies; Ah! for these it almost hurts to pen these words, "He hath no form nor comeliness", for He is found to be "altogether lovely". (Cant. 5 v 16).

The next covering is of rams' skins dyed red, and hardly anybody is to see this because it is covered with the badger skins. God alone would know its full extent, hence no size is given, but if this were a tent-like covering then perhaps a priest or Levite might see something of it. Another puzzle. The ram is the animal that sets its mind on an objective, puts its head down and come what will it goes for that objective. This must speak to us of the eternal purposes of God. If God decides to do a thing, then do it He will – rams' skins, God's eternal purposes, but why dyed red?

There is a "law" among Bible students known as "the law of first mention". Oftentimes the first mention of a word or thing in the Bible gives a clue as to its subsequent meaning. Now the word "red" in the description of the covering for the tabernacle is exactly the same root as is used for "Adam" and "man" in Genesis one and two, and in these chapters it is repeated over and over again. Rams' skins – God's eternal purpose, dyed red – with regard to man. What is God's first mention of the word in His book? "Let us make man (red) in our image". (Gen. 1 v 26). This is what God set out to do. May we say it very reverently, "the ram's head is down". If God fails then Satan has won, but God will not, God cannot fail for finally, "when He shall appear, we shall be like Him; for we shall see Him as He is" (1 Jno. 3 v 2). God will have accomplished His purpose. But why should it be that few should see this bar Jehovah? Speaking as a man, it seems as though God must constantly remind Himself of His pledge. Man is so rebellious, so unworthy. We have an illustration of this in Noah, when the end of all flesh came before God, and also when Moses pleaded for the children of Israel after the matter of the golden calf. God's wrath waxed hot against the children of Israel and He suggested that He should consume them, but Moses reminded Jehovah of His promises to the patriarchs and politely said to God, "You can't do this to your people because of your promises." (Exod. 32 vv 9-14). Praise the Lord for the rams' skins dyed red, and may we offer a little prayer here? "Oh Lord, please don't forget to look often and long on that covering for we are such an unworthy and rebellious people. Amen."

Next we come to the first of the two curtains and this is made of goats' hair, not goats' skins. The word of God is rather emphatic on this, "And all the women whose heart stirred them up in wisdom spun goats' hair". Hallelujah for the sisters!! Yes, thank the Lord for them, but what does it mean, spun goats' hair? – something like cashmere, very soft, very fine, very expensive?

Let us start from the beginning. Why goats' hair? The goat is the sure-footed animal. Saul went "to seek David and his men upon the rocks of the wild goats." (1 Sam. 24 v 2). Not only are the purposes of God sure and certain (the ram) but every step is precise and secure. This curtain is not just goats' skin, it is goats' hair spun and woven, each thread woven with meticulous care, "line upon line; here a little, and there a little." (Isa. 28 vv 10 & 13). Few men could see anything of this curtain, God alone knew its full extent. Let us cast our minds back to the prophets, men who were clad in animals' skins summarised in the roll of faith in Hebrews 11 v 37 as "they wandered about in sheepskins and goatskins;". They may have been dressed in goatskins but their words, their prophecies were like spun goats' hair, very fine, very precious, very expensive. Even in the times of Samuel and Eli and his wicked sons it is recorded, "and the word of the Lord was precious in those days" (1 Sam. 3 v 1). Even so today, perhaps this is why the people perish because "there was no open vision" or very little vision of any sort and "where there is no vision, the people perish" (Prov. 29 v 18). Take heed to the goats' hair covering as representing the unfailing, certain purposes of God, every step sure, every prophecy carefully detailed. See in the rams' skins dyed red, the eternal purposes of God that must go through at all costs. See in the woven goats' hair that this is not as it were a blind dash but every step is precise and unfaltering. We shall return to the goats' hair curtain after we have considered the second curtain.

This inner curtain, the one that immediately covered the boards and formed the ceiling of the Holy Place and of the Holy of Holies was made of fine twined linen and ornamented with blue and purple and scarlet. This ornamentation is described as being "with cherubims of cunning work". Now this curtain (we speak of it as one curtain although it was made up of ten, joined together in two sets of five to make one whole) differs from the gate and the door in that it has the cherubim worked on it in the same way that the vail had, but it differs from the vail and also from the gate and the door, in that the order of the materials is different. In the gate (Exod. 27 v 16) and in the door (Exod. 26 v 36) and in the vail (Exod. 26 v 31) the order is blue, purple, scarlet and fine twined linen. In the covering curtain the order is fine twined linen, blue, purple and scarlet. Now why? Has God made a mistake? God makes no mistakes. Bear in mind that the tabernacle was a precise structure and Moses had to make it after the pattern shown to him on the mount. Why then this change of order? There can be no doubt that the gate is a picture of the Lord as the only way, the blue must come first for this was God manifest in flesh. The door sets forth Christ as being the only way of priestly approach, the priest must learn of Him and grow like Him. The vail, there is no difficulty here for we are told that this is His flesh. All of these have the blue first, these set forth the Lord of Glory in various aspects, but this great big curtain which forms the ceiling of the tabernacle, this begins with the fine twined linen and John says, "the fine linen is the righteousness of saints" (Rev. 19 v 8). How in harmony with the boards, if they represent the saints as forming the temple, is it not right that the ceiling should show the saints made like their Lord? This curtain was an immense affair made of ten smaller curtains each of which measured twenty-eight cubits by four. Translate that into feet and we have ten curtains measuring forty-two feet long by six feet wide. Translate this into yards (or metres, there is little difference) and we have ten curtains fourteen yards long by two yards wide. Think of it, one hundred and forty yards of material, two yards wide, all of which had to be spun and woven then embroidered. How the Israelites worked, and what happened to all of that work? Only about one quarter was to be seen inside the tabernacle, the rest was completely hidden from view. Wonder how many cunningly wrought cherubim there were on these curtains, hundreds? thousands?, who shall say, but this we do know, the greater part of them was hidden from view. Who or what are these cherubim? Patience until we come to the Mercy Seat.

The ten embroidered curtains, each measuring twenty-eight cubits by four were joined together in two groups of five giving two curtains each measuring twenty-eight cubits by twenty. Along one long edge of each of these two curtains fifty loops of blue were made, and these loops were buttoned together by golden taches to form one huge curtain measuring twenty-eight cubits by forty. This large curtain was draped over the boarded walls beginning from the front so that the join made by the blue loops and the golden taches would be twenty cubits from the front and as we are told that the vail was to hang from these taches (Exod. 26 v 33) we can conclude that the holy place was twenty cubits long, and as we have been told that the north and south sides of the tabernacle were each thirty cubits long (Exod. 26 vv 18 & 20) then the Holy of Holies must have been ten cubits long. After covering the Holy Place and the Holy of Holies, about half of the second curtain would be left over to drape over the back wall of the tabernacle (Exod. 26 v 12). Now let us look in detail and see how this curtain would lie. The curtain was forty cubits long, joined down the middle by the loops and taches. One short side (28 cubits long) was laid along the front edge of the tabernacle, possibly attached to the curtain and pillars that formed the door. The curtain was then extended over the tabernacle, the loops and taches forming the division between the holy and most holy places, and the balance of the curtain was allowed to fall over the back of the tabernacle.

Now we know that the north and south sides of the tabernacle were each thirty cubits long. We have deduced that the walls were one cubit thick, so thirty plus one cubit gives us the exterior measurement of the tabernacle. If we deduct this measurement, thirty-one cubits, from the length of the curtain, forty cubits, we are left with nine cubits to hang down over the back, but we are told that the boards that made up the walls were ten cubits long and therefore the walls must be ten cubits high. Our curtain is one cubit short in length for we only have nine cubits left to hang down the back. If only the tabernacle walls had no thickness at all, then the curtain would be just right. On the other hand suppose the back wall, which measured twelve cubits (six boards plus two corner boards (Exod. 26 v 22-25)) was placed inside the north and south walls so as to give overall external measurements of the tabernacle as thirty cubits long and fourteen cubits wide then our curtain would fit exactly lengthwise but it would give us a holy place of twenty cubits by fourteen, and a Holy of Holies nine cubits by fourteen, doesn't seem right somehow, the priestly nose is twitching (see chapter two).

Let us go back to our original assumption that the exterior measurements of the tabernacle were thirty-one cubits long by twelve cubits wide, that the walls were one cubit thick and lengthwise the curtain was one cubit short. Now consider the curtain's width, twenty-eight cubits.

We know that the height of the tabernacle was ten cubits and we have assumed that its external width was twelve. Two tens, the north and south sides, plus the width comes to thirty-two cubits, more than our curtain width of twenty eight cubits, or if our schoolmasters are to be believed, two cubits short on either side. What is the Holy Spirit saying to us? One thing is certain, that we are not to worry about being a cubit short in the curtain's length for no matter how we seek to rearrange the sides of the tabernacle the curtain cannot possibly be made to cover it completely. Just accept the fact that the curtain left a cubit uncovered at the back of the tabernacle and two cubits uncovered on each side.'

Let us look at the curtain that was woven out of goats' hair. This was made of eleven curtains each measuring thirty cubits long by four wide. The eleven curtains were fastened together into two large curtains made up of five and six. Each of these two curtains had fifty loops along one thirty cubit side and the two curtains were joined together by taches made of brass to give one large curtain measuring thirty cubits by forty-four cubits. Now this looks more interesting, it is larger than the embroidered curtain. We have an extra four cubits in the length and an extra two cubits in the width. Let us drape this goats' hair curtain over the tabernacle. Stop! Everything must be done according to the pattern that was shown to Moses on the mount. Lay our big curtain flat upon the ground, it is made up of eleven small curtains joined together in a five and a six. Now we have to take the last curtain on the six side and fold it back on itself, there goes our extra four cubits in length for our curtain will now measure ten curtains each of four cubits wide, with the last curtain on the six side being double. That's what it says, "And thou shalt couple five curtains by themselves, and six curtains by themselves, and shalt double the sixth curtain in the forefront of the tabernacle" (Exod. 26 v 9). This brings the length of the goats' hair curtain to exactly the length of the embroidered one. It's going to be a cubit short! True, but put it on over the other curtain, so that lengthwise all is now covered with goats' hair except one cubit at ground level at the back. How about the width? We have an extra two cubits to play with here for the embroidered curtain only measured twenty-eight cubits wide whereas the goat's hair one measures thirty, two cubits more, still too short because we were four cubits short on the embroidered curtain. Well, it's a help for we are now only two cubits short, one at each side. One at each side? – but that is the same as the back, so that this goats' hair curtain covers the tabernacle completely except for one cubit all round at the bottom. Wonder if this is right; have a look at the instructions, "And the remnant that remaineth of the curtains of the tent, the half curtain that remaineth" (i.e. after one curtain has covered the tabernacle as far as the vail and the other curtain has covered from the vail to the back) "shall hang over the backside of the tabernacle. And a cubit on the one side, and a cubit on the other side of that which remaineth in the length of the curtains of the tent" (Exod. 26 vv 12 & 13). The verse is not very clear but it certainly seems to mention a cubit on either side and in the length. What does it all mean?

Numbers play an important part in the understanding of scripture but we must not be obsessed by them for in these curtains we have every number except nine. There was ONE curtain of each type. There were TWO curtains in all and each curtain was divided into TWO by the taches, the first half of the goats' hair curtain was made up of six smaller curtains and six is made up of TWO times THREE. Every small curtain was FOUR cubits wide, that makes twenty-one FOURS, both curtains finished up with a length of forty cubits, that gives another twenty FOURS. The embroidered curtains were twenty-eight cubits long, that gives seven FOURS for each curtain, multiplied by ten gives us another seventy FOURS. We can find FIVE and SIX in the coupling of the small curtains together and SEVEN in a quarter of twenty-eight which is the length of the embroidered curtains. EIGHT crops up as being one fifth of forty which was the length of both large curtains. It would perhaps be possible to write a book on all the combinations and meanings of the numbers concerned but one thing is paramount, the number four is dominant. We have shown over one hundred combinations of this number and there are more if we look for them. Every woven curtain had to be four cubits wide. The Israelites had to make looms six feet wide and rattle away on these, perhaps non-stop night and day in order to make this vast amount of material. Whatever these curtains stand for they represent an immense amount of work and care. Now we have already pointed out that the number four is connected with the earth, but these curtains were not allowed to touch the earth at any point being at least one cubit short all round. Furthermore the only portion visible would be the ceilings of the holy places. As the boards represent saints standing firm in redemption surely the curtains teach the lesson of man being lifted from the earth, having a heavenly character as is emphasised by the blue and the loops of blue on the inner curtain, and the fact that it formed the ceiling. Fair enough for the embroidered curtain with its host of cherubim but what about the goats' hair that covered all?

We have already pointed out that the goats' hair speaks to us of the sure word of prophecy. The sure-footed goat, connected with the prophets in Hebrews eleven verse thirty-seven, not just the skins but the hair, as it were the message carefully woven, long, tediously and carefully, a heavenly message that must not be dragged in the earth, a hidden message, God alone knowing the full extent but maybe allowing the priest and the Levite to see something as it hung under the coverings. And why did the front curtain have to folded back? It was surely pointing us to the fact that some of these prophecies had already been fulfilled, promises made to the patriarchs of old. The curtain already being rolled back, a process that will continue until we reach the glory and God reveals the whole of His plans. Reckon this is why there is no curtained ceiling in Solomon's temple. How wonderful these pictures are. Selah! The goats' hair curtain was exactly covering the length of the embroidered one but being wide enough that no portion should be left uncovered.

However, we have not finished with these two curtains yet. Both are joined together with taches at exactly the same point, the junction of the Holy Place and the Holy of Holies, the join being effected in both cases by fifty taches. The inner curtain is joined with taches of gold. Here the saints are raised to the heights of glory, the ceiling, "it doth not yet appear what we shall be" (1 Jno. 3 v 2), "as is the heavenly, such are they also that are heavenly" (1 Cor. 15 v 48). We can almost hear the cherubim saying, – patience, wait for the mercy seat. The goats' hair curtain is joined by fifty taches of brass. Brass was the durable metal of the tabernacle, the metal that withstood the heat of the brazen altar that formed the foundations for the gate, that linked these prophetic curtains together sure and stedfast.

It is only by asking questions that we can possibly get any answers and here we raise another query, why fifty taches in each curtain?

Two occasions are closely linked with the number fifty. "Then shalt thou cause the trumpet of the jubile to sound on the tenth day of the seventh month, in the day of atonement shall ye make the trumpet sound throughout all your land. And ye shall hallow the fiftieth year, and proclaim liberty throughout all  the land . . ." (Lev. 25 vv 9 & 10). Now that seems interesting, for the one thing that was connected with the vail and the Holy of Holies was the day of atonement. Selah! and we will give our thoughts later.

The second occasion is detailed in Leviticus twenty-three verses fifteen to nineteen. The essential features are that fifty days after the feast of firstfruits, on the morrow after the sabbath, two loaves containing leaven were to be waved before the Lord. This was Pentecost, an Old Testament institution that did not just originate in Acts chapter two. It contains some remarkable elements. It was celebrated, not on the sabbath but on the morrow after the sabbath. Two loaves were waved before the Lord. The loaves contained leaven. Selah!

Now to return to the year of Jubilee, the fiftieth year of liberation. Why should this be connected with the day of atonement? The atonement was God's side of redemption. No one else was in the Holy of Holies except the High Priest, not even his sons, and even as the High Priest he was not allowed to look upon the sprinkled blood on the mercy seat, the smoke of the incense clouded his view. The blood was for God and God alone. "When I see the blood" (Exod. 12 v 13). This was the atonement, the covering. Sacrifices had been offered perhaps by the thousands during the year denoting man's acknowledgement that he was a sinner, that one must die in his stead, but all of these sacrifices were of no avail unless God looked upon the blood and was satisfied with what He saw. Consider all of the Old Testament saints. Right from the beginning, Adam and Eve had to have garments of skins, the blood had to be shed. Abel and all the patriarchs builded their altars and offered their sacrifices, the animal slain, the blood shed. How glaringly wrong was Cain's sacrifice, no death, no blood. The sacrifices and the flow of blood increased over the years with the Mosaic ritual. Although man did his part, keeping the ritual, shedding the blood, not one of these Old Testament saints could have any place in eternal glory unless there was a victim whose blood could cover from a righteous God's viewpoint, a day of atonement, a special day of atonement was necessary. Speaking as a man, and God often does this to us in His Word in order to help us understand, speaking thus, think of all those Old Testament saints, right from the patriarchs down to the humblest Israelite, having the faith that the blood would shelter them, claiming their salvation by faith, but awaiting that great day of atonement. Have you ever wondered why God had to wait fifty days before Pentecost? Look at these saints in the glory waiting for their salvation to be perfected. Perhaps Isaiah 61 vv 1 & 2 take on a fresh significance ". . . the opening of the prison to them that are bound (held); To proclaim the acceptable year of the Lord". The year of Jubilee indicated by the brazen taches, certain and sure, the fulfilment of prophecy, the goat's hair curtain. What hallelujahs must have greeted the Lord as He entered victoriously into the Glory. God could look upon the blood, not of bulls and of goats which could never take away sins, but on the perfect blood. Oh, how great was the peace that He made by the blood of His cross. (Col. 1 v 20). Well might the psalmist write:-

"Lift up your heads, O ye gates; and be ye lift up, ye everlasting doors; and the King of glory shall come in. Who is this King of glory? The Lord strong and mighty, the Lord mighty in battle." (Psa. 24 vv 7 & 8). What a volume of rejoicing, of praise and thanksgiving must have filled heaven that day, for here was the Lord, the victor over sin and death. Salvation was an accomplished fact. That chorus will only be exceeded by a greater one. What! greater than all these Old Testament saints shouting their adulation? Look lower down in the psalm. "Lift up your heads, O ye gates; even lift them up, ye everlasting doors; and the King of glory shall come in. Who is this King of glory? The Lord of hosts, he is the King of glory. Selah!" (Psa. 24 vv 9 & 10). The Lord entered heaven the first time alone as the victor, "The Lord mighty in battle". He enters the second time with a great company, the redeemed since Pentecost, "Who is this King of glory? The Lord of hosts". May we ask a very pertinent question? Will you be among that great company? His coming could be very near.

What about Pentecost? It is not our intention to study the feasts. Already this book is assuming a proportion never intended, but what a volume the priests, the feasts and the offerings would make. We will take the salient features of Pentecost as they affect the taches in the tabernacle. This feast was to be celebrated on the day after the sabbath. How this must have puzzled the thinking Israelite. Since the world was created the sabbath had been the day that was sacrosanct, so holy that death was the punishment for violation. Now God bypasses the sabbath, the last day of the week and tells Israel that this feast must be celebrated "on the day after the sabbath", on the first day of the week. This was to be a complete change, a new era. What was the significance of it being recorded on that great fulfilment Pentecost in Acts chapter two, "Others mocking said 'These men are full of new wine'" (Acts 2 v 13)? Certainly it was the men from all over Jewry trying to explain the wonderful events, but it also served another important function, it emphasised the time factor, for Peter in his reply said "for these are not drunken, as ye suppose, seeing it is but the third hour of the day", that would be nine o'clock in the morning and by then all these things had happened, but do not let us imagine that these things occurred at night when no one was about for the chapter begins, "And when the day of Pentecost was fully come," (Acts 2 v 1), so things have been turned completely topsy-turvy by this great Pentecost. It was the first day of the week which by then had been recognised as the resurrection day, for already Mary and other women had come to the sepulchre very early in the morning on the first day of the week. The risen Lord had twice appeared to the disciples on that day as they huddled together for fear of the Jews. No longer was it the era of the last day of the week, the sabbath, beginning at six o'clock in the evening, this was the new era, day, light, hope. The resurrection day, the first day of the week and its activities started early in the morning for those coming into this new age were "all the children of light, and the children of the day: we are not of the night, nor of darkness" (1 Thess. 5 v 5).

Two loaves with leaven had to be taken on the Jewish day of Pentecost and they had to be waved before the Lord on the first day of the week. Here was the full wonder and glory of Pentecost, two loaves with leaven, Jew and gentile even although both were sinners in God's sight as the early chapters of Romans points out, coming to the conclusion "For there is no difference: for all have sinned, and come short of the glory of God." (Rom. 3 vv 22 & 23). However now, at the great Pentecost of Acts two, where the gentiles are going to be brought in, where Joseph's branches are to run over the wall (Gen. 49 v 22) (how that goats' hair curtain is rolling back) Jew and gentile are to be made one and the point at which this is to happen according to the tabernacle is at the golden taches, at the vail, which Hebrews ten verse twenty tells us " : the veil, that is to say, His flesh." Now look at Ephesians chapter two verses fourteen and fifteen "For He is our peace, who hath made both one, and hath broken down the middle wall of partition between us; having abolished in His FLESH the enmity, even the law of commandments contained in ordinances; for to make in himself of twain one new man, so making peace." Selah! There is no need to elaborate.

We remarked earlier that the return of the Lord could be imminent. While it is perfectly true, and we must ever be mindful of the fact that "Of that day and hour knoweth no man, no, not the angels of heaven, but my Father only" (Matt. 24 v 36) yet we must remember that the Lord called the Pharisees and Sadducees hypocrites, because they could foretell the weather but not understand the "signs of the times". (Matt. 16 vv 1-4). The principle seems to be that we should have our eyes open to all the things that are happening around us, compare them with the prophecies in the Word, and although no man can tell the exact day and hour yet nevertheless we should be able to say our redemption draweth nigh. Right from the days of creation it looks as though man's tenure of the earth as we know it will be about six thousand years, the six days of creation then the millennium of rest. The Lord was born about the year 4,000 leaving 2,000 years to run. The good Samaritan gave the innkeeper two pence, enough for two days lodging. Some have seen in Hosea 6 v 2 "After two days will he revive us: in the third day he will raise us up, and we shall live in his sight." a picture of the Lord's return and the millennium to follow. As we look around the world today and see the state of things corresponding to the days of Noah, as we look at Israel and see her gathered in unbelief, what clue does the tabernacle hold? The veil, Pentecost, was twenty cubits from the front of the tabernacle. The rest of the tabernacle was ten cubits, exactly half. From the creation to Pentecost was four thousand years. Half of four thousand is two thousand, we are now in the twentieth century. "And that, knowing the time, that now it is high time to awake out of sleep: for now is our salvation nearer than we believed" (Rom. 13 v 11). Please read on in Romans thirteen and, Selah!

# CHAPTER FIFTEEN

# The Holy Place

The only metals that we have seen in the tabernacle so far have been silver and brass. It is not until we come to the entrance to the Holy Place that we begin to encounter gold and from there on the only metal visible is gold. The five columns at the entrance and the finely wrought curtain that constituted the door tell us what to expect inside, the glory that is to follow. Bear in mind that it is only priests, the sons of Aaron, who have access to the Holy Place. Unless we are priests we may be unable to see or understand the glories of that place. If we know the joy of that relationship, if we are conscious that we are sons of the High Priest let us linger at the door and give thanks "unto the Father, which hath made us meet to be partakers of the inheritance of the saints in light: who hath delivered us from the power of darkness, and hath translated us into the kingdom of His dear Son: in whom we have redemption through His blood, even the forgiveness of sins". (Col. 1 vv 12-14). If we know our qualification as "Aaron's Sons" let us enter the Holy Place, conscious of its sanctity and the dignity of our position. Some may once again be raising their eyebrows. Why refer to any saints as "Aaron's Sons"? We are the sons of God. (Rom. 8 v 14). True, how gloriously true, but it all depends on our appreciation of the meaning of the word "son". If we understand it in the modern sense as being the offspring of a union between husband and wife, then we must, in all honesty, agree with Rome and look for the Lord's mother, and Mary can be the only candidate. Before we run round to our local cardinal, (does that word or classification appear in the scriptures? You do the searching.) fall down and worship before a bejewelled and gold encrusted image of the Virgin, usually complete "with child", let us ask ourselves whether we have a right understanding of the word "son" as used in scripture.

The New Testament begins, "The book of the generation of Jesus Christ, the son of David, the son of Abraham." (Matt. 1 v 1), from which we conclude that Sarah was the mother of David, she being Abraham's wife, and the Lord's mother was . . . Michal? Abigail? or Bathsheba, to name but a few. Gets a bit involved and stupid and we trust you will not interpret it as nigh blasphemy. We are using this blunt, matter of fact reasoning to show that our modern understanding of "son" is not the way that it is used in scripture.

Repeatedly, in both the Old and New Testaments, we find genealogies with generations omitted, and even nephews and grandsons included, yet each one of them is described as "sons". What then are we to understand? It is abundantly evident that the chronicler is showing that these various descendants came from the same stock. Usually members of a family or lineage share some common feature. Even allowing for the immense amount of inter-marriage that has taken place between nations we still often look at a person and say, "typically German," or French, or perhaps more particularly Jewish. Hence in common parlance we have coined the phrase, "A chip off the old block", meaning, "like father, like son".

How does the Lord use this word? In Mark 3 v 17, we read that the Lord surnamed "James the son of Zebedee, and John the brother of James;" as "Boanerges, which is, The sons of thunder". Maybe the Lord is just giving us an insight into the characters of James and John. Might it not also be true that the Lord is showing us how the word "son" is to be understood? Let us put it to the test.

The seventeenth verse of Matthew chapter one reads, "So all the generations from Abraham to David are fourteen generations; and from David until the carrying away into Babylon are fourteen generations, and from the carrying away into Babylon unto Christ are fourteen generations." Long and wearying have been the controversies over these numbers of generations. Let us ask ourselves a simple question. If we solve these controversies

*159*

how will it glorify the Lord or bring blessing to His people? Do not these questionings rather savour of the warnings given both to Timothy and to Titus, that they were to "avoid foolish questions and genealogies" (1 Tim. 1 v 4; Tit. 3 v 9). So we see that all of the genealogies in the Bible are useless. How we jump to futile conclusions. God does not put anything in His Word that is not of profit. Of course there are wonderful lessons to be learned from all genealogies. We ourselves are seeking to profit from Matthew's genealogy and if you wish to pursue his genealogy further, ask yourselves why there are four women included, and why has one of these women lost her name and is only referred to as "her that had been the wife of Urias;". Seeking an answer to these questions can be profitable indeed, but trying to disprove the accuracy of Matthew's genealogy is decidedly unprofitable and destructive. Then why mention these three lots of fourteen generations each?

May we suggest that the Holy Spirit has carefully detailed the Lord's natural genealogy, not only that we can see who His actual father, grandfather etc. were, it does do this, but also to show that He was of the stock of Abraham and David. Could it not be that we are being told that physically the Lord bore the natural and national likeness of His forebears? He was a Jew and bore the characteristics of that race.

In verse seventeen, where we get the three contentious sets of fourteen generations, may we suggest that we are being taught (possibly among many other things) that not only is this one that is to be born the very embodiment of the Jewish race; He was the "son of", or like all of these naturally, but He will be the embodiment and fulfilment of the whole of their history and hopes.

The first set of fourteen generations takes us from Abraham to David. The promise made to Eve that her seed should bruise the serpent's head is taken up in Abraham for in his seed all the nations of the earth will be blessed. During that troublous period from Abraham to David we see this earthly promise gradually coming to a partial fulfilment. As we trace the sons (?) of Abraham through the servitude of Egypt across the wilderness, into the land, we see that this great people are steadily becoming a nation and this is brought into effect by David being set on the throne of Israel. The first fourteen generations gave us the seed coming to completion in the king. We therefore see that the Lord is the personification of this Seed. We are being told to have a look at this Son, He is like this Seed, He is this Seed.

The second division of fourteen generations takes us from "David until the carrying away into Babylon" (v 17). During this period Israel, as a nation, suffered a sad disintegration, not permanent but progressively severe. The kingdom was divided under Rehoboam, David's grandson (1 Kings 12) and the history of the kings both of Judah and Israel cannot, even with the kindest of intentions, be described as a success story. Right from the initial split under Rehoboam godly Jews must have been praying for Messiah. He did not come. Indeed things went from bad to worse until the mighty hand of Babylon took them into captivity. The end of Israel? No. God was chastening His people and using that mighty dictator, Nebuchudnezzar, to chastise the nation. Hitler was a babe when compared to Nebuchudnezzar for "whom he would he slew; and whom he would be kept alive" (Dan. 5 v 19) with no questions asked! Strange, yet wonderful, that the prophet Jeremiah should repeatedly describe this tyrant as "Nebuchudnezzar, the king of Babylon, my servant" (Jer. 25 v 9, 27 v 6, 43 v 10). This does not mean that God sanctioned the dictatorial actions of this potentate, but it does mean that God used this man's pride and aggression as an instrument to chastise His people, even although at a later date He took this same Nebuchudnezzar to task for lifting up his heart. Wonder if a modern Jeremiah would described Hitler as God's servant? Hold it, don't explode! God would never sanction Hitler's pride and arrogance. Hitler's basic sin was the same as that of the wayward farmer in Luke 12 v 18, saying in his heart, "I will pull down my barns, and build greater." and Hitler paid the price for his sinful pride, "thy soul shall be required of thee" (Luke 12 v 20). What a sobering thought. My brother, my sister, make sure that in your simple way you are not pulling down your barns in order to build greater. The maxim is, "seek ye first the kingdom of God" (Matt. 6 v 33). Now where does this leave Adolf Hitler?

How could a modern Jeremiah possibly describe this dictator as "God's servant"? In the same way as he described Nebuchudnezzar as God's servant. Nebuchudnezzar took the Jewish people into captivity, slaying many, destroying their homes and their cities, bringing them into a long period of servitude; what a servant! Yet he was, for unwittingly he was accomplishing Jehovah's eternal purposes.

How about our notorious Hitler, born Schickelgruber? A man who came from nothing, to be, for a time, the most powerful man in Europe, even as the latter day beast will be. Is it possible to describe A.H. as God's servant? Although the price paid was extremely high, one of the effects of Hitler's seeking to form his third Reich was that he drove thousands of Jews back to Palestine and in this way helped to found the new Jewish nation, even as the word of God had foretold. Learn another lesson. Although we may look upon the world at large and see the utter despair and pain brought about by sin's entry into the heart of man, in spite of all of the wars and rumours of wars, in spite of the famine and pestilence, God is still controlling the affairs of men, using even the wrath of man to praise Him (Psa. 76 v 10).

Part of that eternal plan vitally affects you and me. God tells us in His word that "we were chosen in Him before the foundation of the world" (Eph. 1 v 4) and that was a long, long time ago. Do you think that God has lost sight of His purpose? Never! Never! The plan is so great that it needs all history to bring it to completion and the crowning event in that history was that God came to earth as a man, an event which is summarised by the evangelist as the "four V's", the Virgin birth, the Virtuous life, the Vicarious death, and the Victorious resurrection.

The great event of the Lord's first advent has set the seal on the purposes of God with regard to the world, with regard to Satan, with regard to Israel and, wonder of wonders, with regard to you and me. If we are trusting in the Lord as Saviour there is only one thing that is now certain in our future. What is that? Death? No. The Lord may return for us. The thing that is certain is that one day, one glorious day, you and I are going to see Him face to face in all His glory. If our faith is in the Lord let this sear into our hearts. I shall be there, I shall actually see the King in

His beauty. What a day that will be.

*On that bright and golden morning when the Son of Man shall come*
*And the radiance of His glory we shall see*
*When from every clime and nation He shall call His people home,*
*What a gathering of the ransomed that will be!*

Excited? You should be. Let us now remind ourselves of something even greater. What? Greater than seeing the Lord in all His glory? Yes. You and I are not just going to scrape into heaven as sinners saved by grace. We are that now and we always will be, but God's eternal purposes are so grandiose, so enormous, so mind boggling. Listen to this, "when He shall appear, we shall be like Him; for we shall see Him as He is" (1 Jno. 3 v 2). What? Like the Lord in all His glory? If words have any meaning at all, that is what it says ... like Him for all eternity. Selah! Think of that. Please do, for this is a glory so superlative that no pen dare seek to describe. Now we can understand a little of what the apostle Paul was saying, "for I reckon that the sufferings of this present time are not worthy to be compared with the glory which shall be revealed in us" (Rom. 8 v 18). Take heart my fellow believer and remember that no matter how dark the clouds may be either internationally or even in our private lives,

*God is still on the throne*
*And He will remember His own*
*Though burdens may press us and trials distress us*
*He never will leave us alone.*

In all of this we see that the Lord is our Hope, just the same as He was to Israel during their servitude under Babylon. Referring to Jeremiah again, you know, that great prophet who described Nebuchudnezzar as God's servant, twice over in his prophecy he describes Jehovah as "The Hope of Israel" (Jer. 14 v 8 & 17 v 13). What a wonderful title. (I'm sorry but I can't help preaching to you. Is He your Hope as well?) So that in the second fourteen generations of Matthew 1 v 17 we could say that the Son was like the Hope of Israel. Indeed He was the Hope of Israel. At last we got there. Took us a long time but, we trust, time well spent for we saw some very important lessons.

The final fourteen generations in Matthew 1 v 17 takes us

from the carrying away into Babylon to the birth of the Christ, the Anointed, the Messiah. This last division is perhaps far easier for us to see for both of the other two "fourteens" are bound up in this. The one who was the Seed is also the Hope. "For all the promises of God in him are yea, and in him Amen," (2 Cor. 1 v 20). This One, this Son of Abraham, this Son of David, was not only like Abraham and like David after the flesh, that is, He was of their lineage, but He was also like the Christ, the Messiah, indeed He was the Christ, the long looked for Messiah.

Each of these three periods are of the same duration. That is what Matthew says and he was inspired by the Holy Spirit. You, with your secular learning, may choose to differ (may the Lord pardon your indiscretion). Matthew is emphatic. Fourteen generations each. All of equal length. What then do we learn from this? Perhaps that all are of equal importance! Is it not just as essential that Israel, and also we in our present age and dispensation, should realise and appreciate that the very first promise with any hope attached to it was made to Eve concerning her Seed. It was a comfort and a prospect for the woman who caused the fall of the human race. It was also a comfort and prospect for Israel and surely a comfort and prospect to us. Look at the second fourteen generations, the Lord as the Hope of Israel. Apart from the Messiah, Israel had no hope. Look at Israel today. Apart from the return of her Messiah, the nation has no real hope. How about you and me? Apart from the return of the Lord we have no hope, for if He does not come again as promised then the whole of the Word of God, in which you and I so fully trust, will be invalidated.

So Matthew 1 v 17 leaves us in practically the same position as the Israelites. They had the promise of the Messiah and they must wait for His first advent. We have the promise of the Lord from heaven. It is as firm and sure as the promise made to Israel, "He that shall come will come, and will not tarry." (Heb. 10 v 37). There are two texts that are repeated four times in scripture. The first is "The just shall live by (his) faith" (Hab. 2 v 4, Rom. 1 v 17, Gal. 3 v 11, Heb. 10 v 38) and the second, which is the one with which we are particularly concerned is, "Thou art my Son; this day have I begotten thee" (Psa. 2 v 7, Acts 13 v 33,

Heb. 1 v 5, Heb. 5 v 5). Here we go again! Argument, contention, division. When was the Lord Jesus begotten or born? Was He always the Son? Maybe at times we feel as though we could bang holy heads together. Yet it must not be, for love must characterise our attitude towards our brethren, "In this shall all men know that ye are my disciples if ye have love one to another" (Jno. 13 v 35). In this type of argument let us always ask ourselves, "Will the solution glorify the Lord or spiritually edify His people?" Will the question of the Lord's eternal sonship glorify Him if settled? No. If anything it could diminish Him. Will it spiritually edify the saints? No. If anything it could undermine their appreciation of the Lord and that is a terrible thing to do. The sensible course is for us to ignore these four repetitions of "Thou art my Son, this day have I begotten thee". No! No! No! We have already written that God does not put things into His book unless we are to learn from them. Because some brethren preach "Christ of contention" (Phil. 1 v 16) we must not let them rob us of any truths contained in the scriptures. Let us look at each of the four texts in turn.

The first is in Psalm 2 v 7. In this Psalm Jehovah sets fourth the confusion and disarray of the nations as they take counsel together against the Lord and His anointed. There can be little doubt that in its original application, ignoring for the moment any prophetic content, the Psalmist had David in mind, but we can see how inadequate David was to fulfil all of the promises and hopes expressed. As in so many of the Psalms, perhaps it would be true to say, in all of the Psalms, if we look for it, there is some exposition of "great David's greater Son", the Lord Jesus. This is perhaps most patently seen in Psalms twenty-two and sixty-nine, but it is there in some form or another in all of these writings, and Psalm 2 is certainly no exception. What is Jehovah's reaction to the counsels and rebellion of the nations? He is so certain of the result, it has already been decided in His counsels even before the world was, so that Jehovah does not even deign to stand up, He just sits back and laughs. More than once it is recorded that God laughs at the pride and rebellion of men (Psa. 37 v 13, 59 v 8,and if wisdom is counted as diety, Prov. 1 v 26). All of these references are in the Old Testament.

God does not laugh in the New Testament. When it actually came to the time for God to deal with sin and man's rebellion, and that involved the putting away of sin by the sacrifice of Himself (Heb. 9 v 26) there was no laughter of any kind. Although Calvary brought complete satisfaction and fulfilment to Jehovah, in a way that nothing else could, there was no aspect of it that caused God to laugh. Is this thought enshrined in the Preacher's words, "Sorrow is better than laughter" (Eccles. 7 v 3). Men of the world may laugh and jeer but the Preacher continues, "For as the crackling of thorns under a pot so is the laughter of the fool" (Eccles. 7 v 6).

Why does God mention this verse at all in the Old Testament? Surely it was not until the Lord was born of the Virgin Mary that God could point to Him and say that this is His Son. The words in Psalm two are certainly prophetic. A prophet not only foretold somewhat of the future, but this forth-telling was a part of the prophet's revelation concerning the mind of God to men. This prophetic psalm is really inviting us to understand more about God by looking at the father-son relationship even in the Old Testament. Can we justify this approach?

Start at the beginning in Genesis, where so many of God's lessons for us seem to commence. The promise was made to Eve through the serpent that the seed would be at enmity with Satan and finally bruise his head. (Gen. 3 v 15). That Eve understood this promise in this way is shown in the first verse of Genesis chapter four. Here we read that Eve brought forth her first born son and called his name Cain, which means "acquired". After Cain had slain Abel it seems as though Eve realised that Cain could not be the chosen seed or son, for he was so unlike his Father. It could not be Abel for he was dead, and therefore when "she bare a son, and called his name Seth" she was partially correct in her surmise that this was the promised son "for God, said she, hath appointed me another seed instead of Abel, whom Cain slew" (Gen. 4 v 25). So the first Old Testament lesson that we have to learn is that God's son is to be the child of promise.

Unfair criticism of the Word of God sometimes mocks and says that its content is mainly a list of "begets and begats". The answer to such criticism? Place a Bible in the critic's hand and ask for the evidence. It is not there. True there are several genealogies, although it is doubtful whether the ignorant critic would be able to find them, but the overall lesson that God is teaching by these family histories, even although there are many subsidiary lessons, is that a son is like his father and like all of his forebears. He comes from the same stock, even although it may take several generations to demonstrate the full corruptness and failure of that stock. This carping type of criticism reminds us again of the Preacher's thorns crackling under the pot (Eccles. 7 v 6) and God will not hold these men as guiltless when they appear before Him in the final assize.

We cannot dwell upon all, or nearly all, of the lessons of sonship as expressed in the Old Testament. Already we have wandered a fair way from the tabernacle but we feel that it is justified if we bear in mind the purpose of the wilderness shrine, "Let them make Me a sanctuary that I may dwell among them." God wants to dwell among His people today, and in the same way that He laid down exact conditions for the building of His sanctuary, so today, He lays down strict conditions if if He is to dwell among His people. If this work explains some of the difficulties of the tabernacle it has perhaps done well. If, on the other hand, it can teach some of these lessons that will enable God to dwell among His people today, it will have done infinitely better. If you find this portion irrelevant by all means skip a page or two but if you would "learn more about Jesus" then give heed to what follows.

To trace all of the lessons of sonship in the Old testament would be impossible and the attempt would be too much of a digression even for the present writer. Let us consider just one or two obvious examples and leave the others for your private study.

Jump over one or two chapters in Genesis and come to chapter twenty-two. This is indeed a chapter of father and son. We often refer to this chapter, it is so glorious, showing the Father and the son going, both of them together (emphasised twice in this chapter, vv 6 & 8) to the place of sacrifice. It tells how God will provide Himself a lamb. It shows how the Father laid on the Son the burden of humanity typified by the wood (v 6). It teaches us the lesson of substitutionary sacrifice (v 13) and a thousand and one other lessons, inexhaustible, unfathomable. Selah! "This is my beloved Son, this day have I begotten Thee."

Think farther on in the history of Isaac, the beloved son of his father Abraham. Many lessons here, but concentrate on the way the servant, a picture of the Holy Spirit, seeks a bride for his master's son. "And Isaac went out to meditate in the field at the eventide: and he lifted up his eyes, and saw, and, behold, the camels were coming." Selah!

On to Joseph, Jacob's favourite son, the gift of the coat of many colours, Joseph's dreams of the sun, moon and stars and also of the sheaves of wheat. Go over his life, His rejection, His being forgotten, His vindication, His glory. What a book should be written not on the vexed question of when and how was the Lord the Son, but on the wonderful bedrock truth that HE IS THE SON. "This day have I begotten thee." We must leave the Old Testament to your meditation, please meditate therein otherwise this book will not achieve its purpose. Let us turn to the New Testament and consider this only begotten Son of the Father.

The first time that our text appears in the New Testament is in Acts. 13 v 33. Here the apostle Paul addresses his sermon to the Jewish people that were in Antioch in Pisidia, commencing thus, "Men of Israel, and ye that fear God, give audience" (v 16). The verses that follow are entirely Jewish in their context and point out that although Israel had rejected the Lord, the leaders had unwittingly fulfilled the eternal purposes of God. This passage shows us that the Lord is the subject of all Old Testament prophecy. We see, therefore, that Acts chapter thirteen is the complement and completement of Psalm two for both of the scriptures centre on the statement, "Thou art my Son, this day have I begotten Thee". Psalm two gives us the prophecy, Acts thirteen the fulfilment. We can therefore bracket the Old Testament and New Testament scriptures together under the heading of "The Prophet".

Hebrews chapter one next draws our attention. Verse five

reads "For unto which of the angels said He at any time, "Thou art My Son, this day have I begotten Thee?" One of the aspects of the Hebrew epistle is to show the superiority of the Lord in every direction and over all things. In this first chapter the Lord is being set forth as the Eternal creator (vv 10-12) and concludes with the Son being set at God's right hand in glory, supreme over all, waiting for His enemies to be made the footstool for His feet, reigning supreme, God's King, so that here the Holy Spirit is bringing forth the son to us as "King'.

On to chapter five in the Hebrew epistle, and here is the last reference to the text, "Thou art my son, this day have I begotten Thee" (Heb. 5 v 5). Here the apostle is setting the Lord forth as being superior to any other high priest appointed from among men. He is the High Priest who endures forever, "Thou art a priest for ever after the order of Melchisedec" (v 6). Thus we see that the Holy Spirit is here presenting the Son as the great "High Priest".

Looking then at these four references to the text, "Thou are My Son, this day have I begotten Thee" (or brought Thee forth), we see that Psalm two and Acts thirteen present the Lord as Prophet, Hebrews one as King, and Hebrews five as Priest. What a Book! What a revelation!

Before we leave this Sonship question, note one other thing. This text is mentioned four times. What a coincidence (or is it?) that, as we have seen, four is the number connected with the earth. But surely, the Lord is being presented as the son of God, "Thou art my Son". True, but do not lose sight of the basic truths of our faith. "Other foundation can no man lay than that is laid, which is Jesus Christ" (1 Cor. 3 v 11). Jesus the obedient Son of Man. Christ – the anointed Son of God.One of Newberry's little notes helps us here. In Leviticus chapter one when God is detailing His requirements for the burnt offering, which was to be entirely for Himself, the Word reads "If any man of you bring an offering unto the Lord, ye shall bring your offering of the cattle, A SON OF THE HERD (Newberry), and of the flock." (Lev. 1 v 2). Even in this sacrifice which is to be entirely for Jehovah, we must not lose sight of the fact that the Lord was not only the Son of God, but also "a Son of the herd and of the flock", truly the Son of Man. So in our four texts, the Lord is presented pre-eminently as the Son of God but the Holy Spirit gives us this gentle reminder, a four times repetition, four the earthly number per-taining to man, the Son of God yet always the Son of Man. Selah!

Learn two lessons in the practical understanding of the scriptures. First of all never attempt to split the Godhead into individual personalities. "I and my Father are one" (Jn. 10 v 30). Secondly, never attempt to measure the things of eternity with the measures of time. In our environment and thinking we are dominated by time. Everything has a beginning, a duration and an end. Eternity has no beginning and no end, it simply is.

In our study of the tabernacle we left ourselves standing outside the Holy Place whilst we discussed our right of entry. Aaron and his sons alone could enter here. If we are priests and share the likeness or character of our Great High Priest, then we may enter and understand some of the things that we see. Do not think for one moment that when we say we should be like Him, that we are suggesting that we should be perfect. That must wait till the glory. Rather let us examine ourselves and ask whether the people in the world round about see anything of the priestly character of the Lord reflected in us. How about our fellow saints? How often we hear great students and expositors of the Word described as lacking in love, or grace, or humility. Ah! how often indeed. Our Great High Priest was characterised by these things. How much of a "son" are we? If we are not "Aaron's sons" we shall understand little of what follows.

We slip past the entrance curtain which falls into place behind us, for the things that we see are not for profane eyes. The air is heavy with the smell of incense, and a scene of wondrous glory meets us. We find ourselves in an oblong room, twenty cubits (30 feet) long and ten cubits (15 feet) wide. As the curtain has closed behind us we are in a silent world, we might almost adapt the words of the hymn, "Closed the door, we leave behind us, toil and conflict, foes and strife." There is no window in this room, the only light comes from a lampstand which has seven lamps burning to our left as we come in but close to the curtain at the far end. This curtain is wonderful, being more elaborate than the curtain of the door that is behind us for it is ornamented with cherubim. This is the first time that we have met these creatures and we shall deal with them in greater detail when we finally come close to them and see them on the Mercy Seat. For now we will leave them, and concentrate our attention on our immediate surroundings. Behind us we have the entrance curtain. In front of us, twenty cubits away, at the far end we have the other glorious curtain called the Vail. The two side walls gleam with solid gold, except that we know that they are not solid for they are wood covered with gold, and are made of planks. Each plank is one and one half cubits wide, ten cubits (15 feet) high and a cubit thick. The ceiling is of similar design to the Vail being ornamented with cherubim. How many? We do not know, the Holy Spirit does not tell us, perhaps more than we can number. Who can conceive of a more glorious room, gold and embroidery of blue and purple and scarlet and fine twined linen everywhere, and, as we have said, the air heavy with the smell of incense, not any incense, but an incense specially compounded, and for any man to attempt to make any like it invited the death penalty.

How about the floor? Just the bare desert. How incongruous, all this lavishness and wealth, all this skilled work. What architect has been so remiss, could not the children of Israel afford carpets? Yes. carpets would have been no problem for the people had to be restrained from giving of their substance for this tent, and as God was the architect there must be a reason for the bare earth floor. Call to mind again the purpose of the tabernacle, "That I may dwell among them". (Exod. 25 v 8). God coming down to earth – to earth. No floor coverings. How stark and clear God makes His lessons at times.

What furniture have we in this Holy Place, this room twenty cubits by ten cubits? Just three items (all of which will be dealt with separately later). As we have seen there is the lampstand with its seven lamps on our left, in front of the Vail. On our right there is a small table measuring 2 cubits (3 ft.) by one cubit (1 ft. 6 ins.) and one and a half cubits high (2 ft. 3 ins). It being the sabbath there are on the table twelve loaves sprinkled with frankincense and an assortment of utensils. JND translates the relevant passage, "And thou shalt make the dishes thereof, and cups thereof, and goblets thereof, and bowls thereof, with which to pour out: of pure gold shalt thou make them." (Exod. 25 vv 29 & 30). What do we want cups and goblets and bowls for if we only have bread on the table? ... later. In the centre and immediately in front of the Vail is a tiny little altar, one cubit by one cubit and two cubits high. It is so small that it only has two rings,one each at opposing corners, in order that it might be carried on staves, whereas the table, called the table of shewbread, has four rings, one at each corner, just below the border but at the top of the legs. Why these simple meagre furnishings, for although they are elaborate and wonderful in themselves they are lost in so vast a room? Why these wonderful walls and beautiful ceiling yet a plain earthen floor? Do not the words of the apostle Paul as he writes to the Romans send a trembling thrill up our spines, "that He might make known the riches of His glory on the vessels of mercy, which He had afore prepared unto glory, EVEN US, whom He hath called." (Rom. 9 vv 23 & 24). Having set the background, let us consider each of the articles of furniture in turn.

# CHAPTER SIXTEEN

# The Lampstand

"I am the light of the world." (Jno. 8 v 12 & 9 v 5)

It may perhaps seem strange to equate "I am the light of the world" with the lampstand, remembering that we are now in the Holy Place where only the priests are allowed to come. The world outside cannot see the light of the lampstand and therefore the text seems inapposite. Consider the phenomenon of light. It has much in common with water in that it will fill any space into which it is introduced, provided that the water or light supply is sufficient. This is one of the reasons why water is such a lovely picture of the Holy Spirit. Not only can it cleanse a man but it can also fill him. No matter what his colour, his social background, his wealth or poverty, no matter what his 'shape' he can be filled with the Holy Spirit. Light differs dramatically in characteristic from water in that, for light to be present, it must either have a source or be reflected from a source. We cannot take an empty box into a brilliantly lighted room, close the box and take it to an adjoining darkened room, open the box and expect light to come out. If there is no light source then there is no light. If on the other hand, we could arrange a mirror at the correct angle to the light source we might be able to transmit light from a brilliantly lit room into one that is dark.

The apostle John makes a clear statement in the first chapter of his first epistle and verse five, "This then is the message which we have heard of him, and declare unto you, that God is light." In the spiritual world God is the source of light, therefore when the Lord Jesus said, "I am the light of the world", He was not claiming that He was glowing like a torch but that He was the spiritual light of the world. Not only did He use the divine title 'I Am' but He also used the divine character as being light, showing in an indirect manner that although He was essentially man, He was also God. We have already written that light must have a source, and as far as the world is concerned that light source is the Lord. You will note that at the heading of this chapter we have given two references, Jno. 8 v 12 and Jno. 9 v 5. Look at the latter scripture in full, "As long as I am in the world, I am the light of the world." Does this mean than that as the Lord Jesus is no longer visible on earth, He is no longer the light of the world? No, it certainly does not but note Matthew 5 v 14. The Lord Jesus is talking to his disciples, not the general public, not just believers, but disciples, those who not only believed on Him but also followed Him, and He says, "Ye are the light of the world." Let us look at the picture from the beginning.

The day that Adam sinned in the Garden of Eden darkness fell over this world. No longer was God resident among men, the Light had gone. This was why God was giving Moses such explicit instructions with regard to the tabernacle "that I may dwell among them". God was determined that His full character of light should once again shine in its full glory among men. One thing stopped this, something introduced by Satan through Eve and passed on to Adam – Sin. Until sin could be dealt with righteously, justly, and effectively, light could not be restored to this world. Even as sin and death reigned from Adam till the coming of the Lord, so darkness reigned over the entire world, a spiritual darkness complete and absolute that contained no gleam of light other than that which centred in His Son. For about four thousand years God looked down upon mankind and saw no man who was not in darkness, until one glorious night was shattered by light and angels appeared to certain shepherds as they watched their flocks in the darkness and were surprised by the shining of the glory of the Lord. The darkness was broken, what a night that was for mankind, how aptly the hymnwriter has put it, "The hopes and fears of all the years are met in thee tonight." Forty long centuries God had looked down upon this world. More than once He had been tempted to wipe man from the face of the earth because the imaginations of his heart were only evil continually, but God had declared that He was going to make man in His own image, and that decision had to be implemented. Yet for all those long centuries God could only look down on sin and death and darkness until, in the fulness of time, God sent His own Son who, "being found in fashion as a man, He humbled Himself, and became obedient unto death, even the death of the cross." (Phil. 2 v 8). God could now look down upon this darkened world and see one ray, one source of light. No wonder God repeatedly says, "This is my beloved Son.".

That the Lord Jesus is the only light of the world is made abundantly clear in scripture. All light must emanate from Him. He must be the source, but the Lord Jesus is no longer physically present in this world. Men cannot see Him even although He is the source of all spiritual light, but what they do see is the reflected light while He is away, therefore the Lord tells His disciples "Ye are the light of the world", a light that does not come from themselves, as the apostle Paul puts it, "For ye were sometimes darkness, but now are ye light in the Lord: walk as children of light." (Eph. 5 v 8). Present day disciples of the Lord Jesus have been brought face to face with Him, made to sit with Him in heavenly places, made as it were to enter into the Holy Place and come right into His presence, to see and handle things unseen, to look at the lampstand and be in contact with that light, "For God, who commanded the light to shine out of darkness, hath shined in our hearts, to give the light of the knowledge of the glory of God in the face of Jesus Christ". (2 Cor. 4 v 6). If that light shines in our hearts while we are in His presence in the Holy Place, then when we go out into the world our faces will shine, even as Moses' did, a reflected light because men will see that we have been with Jesus. Outside of the Holy of Holies, the lampstand was the only item of furniture that was made entirely of gold. The rest were either brass, wood overlaid with brass, or wood overlaid with gold, but here we have something that is solid gold, and beaten gold at that. It was not a lightweight structure as it weighed a talent, or about a hundredweight. The description given is fairly clear although not as clear as that received by Moses, for Exodus 25 v 40 tells us that an exact pattern was showed to him on the mount. From what we can gather, the lampstand had a central stem with a lamp on the top. In this stem were four bowls or containers shaped like almonds and above each bowl was a knop or knob (JND), which would have been rather like the capital on top of a column except that the column continued through the three lower capitals and terminated below the top one, so that we have a straight stem with four almond shaped bowls, showing like bumps in the stem, the top bump being at the top of the stem. Above each bump was a collar or knop ornamented with an almond blossom. Indeed the whole collar may have been shaped like one bloom. Six arms or branches extended from the sides of the central stem. The branches were arranged in pairs, three on each side, and each pair of branches rested on the top of the lower three knops. In his margin, Newberry points out that the word branch suggests a cane, that is, a hollow tube. The lampstand was to be fed with oil beaten out of the olive and it was to be kept burning continually. Each branch of the lampstand had three almond shaped bowls, together with the almond flowered knops. Seeing that there are such a large number of bowls, four in the main stem and three in each of the six branches, giving twenty-two in all, and seeing that the branches are likened to hollow canes, we may assume that all of the bowls were interconnected, the branches receiving their supply of oil from the main stem by way of the bowls located immediately below each branch junction. The oil was stored in the almond shaped bowls in each branch so that the supply of oil was always adequate.

We could just as easily have used the lampstand as an illustration of the text, "I am the vine, ye are the branches." (Jno. 15 v 5), in the same way that we could apply the text "I am the way" to practically every item in the tabernacle. We cannot, indeed we must not, limit the application of scriptures relating to the persons of the Godhead. We must visualise Calvary as the place where the Lord died, and rightly so, but we must never forget that the Father and the Son went "both of them together" to the place of sacrifice. To say that the brazen altar exclusively represents "The Good Shepherd" would be wrong for, as we shall see, this 'Good Shepherd' also made provision for the sheep to feed, as at the table of shewbread, so that, although we allocate one specific 'I am' to each of the characteristics of the tabernacle we in no wise limit the application of such a title.

There is no wood in the lampstand. It is of pure beaten gold and in one piece. As the lampstand is the only source of light in the Holy Place it must speak to us of the Godhead, hence no wood, for wood speaks to us of humanity. Nevertheless, notice that there are four bowls in the stem suggesting the supply of divine power to mankind, four being the number of the earth.

The decoration and part of the structure of the lampstand seems to be characterised by almonds and almond blossom. In Ecclesiastes 12 the wise preacher is describing the weaknesses of old age, using such expressions as "when the keepers of the house shall tremble", signifying the arms, and "the strong men shall bow themselves," speaking of the legs. He continues in verse five, "and the almond tree shall flourish", suggesting to us the white hair of the old man being like an almond tree in flower. How wonderful this picture is when applied to the lampstand, the flower speaking to us of many years, but the fruit suggesting to us youthful and fruitful bearing. How like the one who is described as "The Ancient of Days". Compare this with the description of the risen Lord given in the first chapter of Revelation. "His head and His hairs were white like wool, as white as snow" (v 14). Here is the almond blossom, the wisdom of the ages, but lest we should think that the vigour has departed John goes on to say, "and His eyes were as a flame of fire.", the energy and radiation of eternal youth.

Great play is made of the fact that the lampstand is to be made of beaten gold, in the same way that the oil is to be "pure oil olive beaten for the light, to cause the lamps to burn continually." (Lev. 24 v 2). From this we learn that in order for the lampstand to shed forth its light, both the lampstand and the oil must be beaten. Dare we, with very great reverence, suggest that the bringing of the Light of the World to mankind was a costly thing for the Godhead? We know that the Lord suffered more than any man for never was any sorrow "like unto my sorrow, which is done unto me." (Lam. 1 v 12). Not only were there the terrible sufferings of the Lord on the cross, and who can attempt to describe those, but right from His birth he bore the burden of humanity, He saw and shared in the suffering that permeated mankind. Think of that awful verse in Jno. 11 v 35, "Jesus wept". How often we tell the children that it is the shortest verse in the Bible, but perhaps it is the longest in its implications. The Lord of Glory, on earth as a man, and so much a man that He cries. Impossible! It cannot be! Yet, says the scripture, "Jesus wept". "Surely He hath borne our griefs, and carried our sorrows."(Isa. 53 v 4). Ponder that pathway, 'uncheered by earthly smiles, that led only to the cross.' Ponder the wonder of that last supper, the going across the "brook Cedron, where there was a garden, into the which He entered." (Jno. 18 v 1). Ponder the events in that garden, the loneliness, the failure of the disciples to watch, the coming with swords and staves, the traitor's kiss ... Gethsemane, can I forget? Ponder the judgement hall, the smiting, the spitting, the pulling out of His beard, the bruising, the crown of thorns and the buffetting reed. Ponder the crucifixion. A place too holy, too terrible perhaps to write about in detail. 'Alas, and did my Saviour bleed, and did my Sovereign die? Would he devote that sacred head, for such a worm as I?' Beaten gold? How wonderful, but look at the beaten gold, what glory. "The head that once was crowned with thorns is crowned with glory now." Look upon the lampstand and see the wonder shining in that light, then consider that awful tragedy, "And this is the condemnation, that light is come into the world, and men loved darkness rather than light, because their deeds were evil." (Jno. 3 v 19).

The Son suffered that man might be redeemed, but how about the Father? Sufficient to say that God gives us the picture of Father and Son, and always remember this, it was GOD who so loved the world that He sent His only begotten Son. Sometimes we tend to visualise God as the distant, offended God, thirsting for vengeance, like some grey bearded old man sitting in the heavens with a big stick in His hand waiting to clobber the guilty sinner. It is not like that. It was the Father who sent the Son. It was God who so loved. Was it an easy thing for the Father to spare His Son from His side, the One who was daily His delight?

These are depths into which we cannot enter. We can see them in shadow and in type in the beaten gold. And what about the third person of the Trinity, the One who supplies the power for the light? The work of the Holy Spirit is hidden all the time, "thou hearest the sound thereof, but canst not tell whence it cometh, and whither it goeth." (Jno. 3 v 8). We cannot see the oil in the lampstand but we can see the light. One thing we are told about the oil, it was "pure oil beaten".

Why did the lampstand have seven lamps, although they are referred to as one lamp in Lev. 24 v 2? (JND). May it not be to link this marvellous source of light with that shown by the assemblies during the Lord's rejection? If we look at the early chapters of the Revelation we find there seven lampstands with the risen Lord in the midst, and we are told "The seven lampstands which thou sawest are the seven churches." Now if the Lord is in the midst of the lampstands then the bulk of the light from those lampstands must fall upon Him. What a lesson. The prime objective of the assembly should be to throw light upon the one "who hath delivered us from the power of darkness, and hath translated us into the kingdom of his dear Son" (Col. 1 v 13). The secondary objective of the lampstands was to shed the remainder of the light to the world round about.

Only two items of furniture in the tabernacle had no provision made for their transportation. Every item except the laver and the lampstand was equipped with rings through which staves were inserted so that the sons of Kohath could carry them during their wilderness journey. Were the lampstand and the laver to be left behind? Certainly not, for with the lampstand at least, Moses was given instruction to fasten it to a pole for carrying. And the laver? We are told nothing about that, no details whatsoever. How elusive that laver is, no shape, no dimensions, no details as to how it was to be carried or even whether it was to be carried. Now we know full well that God does not forget to insert things in His Word, and we also know from experience that if something is omitted there must be a good reason for it. Now here is a problem. No rings on the lampstand; no rings on the laver, and indeed no instructions at all as to how the laver was to be carried. Wonder why?

The laver was filled with water and the lampstand was filled with oil. Both oil and water are used in scripture to typify the work of the Holy Spirit, that blessed third person of the Trinity, so powerful, yet always in the background. Surely the lesson must be this. You and I cannot carry the Holy Spirit round where we wish. He must take the lead and we must follow. Remember that great man in the Old Testament about whom we read so little, but what little we do read is so pregnant with meaning. This man of faith "pleased God" (Heb. 11 v 5). What a wonderful attainment, and we read of Enoch in Genesis 5 v 24 that "he walked with God: and he was not; for God took him." The event is wonderful in itself for although it only occupies one little verse in Genesis 5 yet it gives us a glorious picture of the Lord taking home His church before the punishment and tribulation comes. In Enoch's case he was taken before the flood. In the Church's case we shall be taken home before the tribulation. We must return to the tabernacle. How does the translation of Enoch have any bearing on that? Note the exact words, "He walked with God." Note the order, it does not say, 'God walked with him'. He walked with God. God must take the lead and Enoch must follow. We cannot carry God around with us, taking Him where we want to go. God must take us, we must be led by His Holy Spirit and go where He dictates if we, like Enoch, are to please God. Now we can understand why the laver and the lampstand had no carrying rings, and this is emphasized in the case of the laver for, as we have seen, the laver speaks to us particularly of the Holy Spirit. Pause a moment to look at the overall picture of the courtyard. First of all we have the tabernacle, the tent where Jehovah dwelt, speaking to us of the Father. Then we have the laver with all the mysterious, nebulous, yet powerful symbolism of the Holy Spirit, and finally we have the brazen altar, the place of sacrifice where the lamb was a continual sweet smelling savour, obviously speaking to us of the Son, the stamp of the ever blessed Trinity impressed firmly on the tabernacle.

Light is part of God for John has already told us that "God is light", unfathomable, unknowable in all its fulness. We can see a rainbow where white light is split up into its various colours. Spectacular! glorious! but we only see part of the glory for there are limits at both ends of the spectrum that the eye cannot see, the infra red and the ultra violet. In like manner, no matter what glories we see in the Godhead and perhaps especially in the Son, who was God manifest in the flesh, we shall never see it all, there will still be fresh wonders, throughout eternity, for we are promised that in the ages to come He will show us the exceeding riches of His grace. (Eph. 2 v 7). When God fitted this earth for man's occupation the first thing that He caused to happen was light to shine out of darkness. "And God said, 'Let there be light'." (Gen. 1 v 3). The last thing that God does in His book is to take away the lampstand as it has fulfilled its purpose and God shines forth in all His radiance. "And there shall be no night there; and they need no light of a lamp, neither light of the sun; for the Lord God giveth them light: and they shall reign for ever and ever." (Rev. 22 v 5 (Newberry note)).

The three items in the Holy Place, the lampstand, the table of shewbread and the altar of incense, are identified together in that during the porterage of the tabernacle through the wilderness they were each covered with a cloth of blue before being covered with badger's skins. Blue as we have already seen, typifies heavenly things, and as we consider the furnishings of the Holy Place we are reminded of the Lord's words to Nicodemus in John 3 v 12, "If I have told you earthly things, and ye believe not, how shall ye believe, if I tell you of heavenly things?". The understanding of things in the tabernacle becomes more and more difficult as we proceed towards the Holy of Holies. Indeed it must be so in our Christian experience. We cannot expect the newly converted man to understand in any degree the deep things of Christ. All who have had any dealings with those who have had the joyful experience of knowing that their sins are forgiven are conscious of the lack of understanding of the 'new born babes'. Oftentimes it is a wondrous miracle to see growth taking place. Recognising these facts the apostle John says, "I write unto you, LITTLE CHILDREN, because your sins are forgiven you for His name's sake." (1 Jno. 2 v 12). Peter takes up the theme, "as newborn babes, desire the sincere milk of the

*181*

word, that ye may grow thereby:". We do not reach maturity overnight in the things of the Lord. It is a process of growing, even as the progression through the tabernacle. There were the children of Israel, seeing only the door, the way in; there were the Levites who went into the tabernacle courtyard but could not touch the holy things, even when it came to carrying the tabernacle they were not allowed to handle or even look upon the holy things; then there were the priests, those who had a fuller knowledge of the ways of Jehovah, these could enter the Holy Place and in fear and trembling handle and minister the holy things.

How can we, sinners of the gentiles, once so very far away from God, hope to understand the secrets of the Holy Place? Only one way, only one source of light, the curtain has closed behind us blotting out the natural illumination, the only light must come from the lampstand. It is not without significance that in the first chapter of John's gospel we have the opening verses "In the beginning was the Word, and the Word was with God, and the Word was God. The same was in the beginning with God." Here we have it, the almond tree is in full bloom, the Ancient of Days. John then goes on to equate this Word with life and light, saying, "In Him was life; and the life was the light of men. And the light shineth in darkness:" (Jno. 1 vv 4 & 5). If we wish for any light in the Holy Place it has got to come from the lampstand. Forget about the natural light. Ignore the dictates of the professors or scholars of this world. Let the curtain fall and just look at that light as being the Word of God. Read carefully the first chapter of the first letter to the Corinthians. Here Paul says, "hath not God made foolish the wisdom of this world? . . . the foolishness of God is wiser than men . . . God hath chosen the foolish things of the world to confound the wise; and God hath chosen the weak things of the world to confound the things which are mighty . . . that no flesh may glory in His presence." In the light of the lampstand let us proceed and consider the table of shewbread. Should you find the lessons being taught are hard to grasp, should you even think that these things are beyond your comprehension, do not despair, we are all continually growing in that gracious knowledge of our

Lord Jesus Christ. None of us knows it all. No ordinary priest could go into the Holy of Holies. No man can fully know God. Even the High Priest who went into the Holy of Holies was prevented from looking upon the Holy Presence because of the cloud from the incense, but the one who is our great High Priest, the Lord Jesus, says, "neither knoweth any man the Father, save the Son, and he to whomsoever the Son will reveal Him." (Matt. 11 v 27). It is a long and slow process. Many lessons have to be learned on the pathway, but the end, EVERLASTING GLORY.

# CHAPTER SEVENTEEN

# The Table of Shewbread
"I am the the Bread of Life." (Jno. 6 v 35)

The table of shewbread consisted of a small table measuring two cubits in length and one cubit wide (36" x 18"). It was made of shittim wood and covered with gold, this latter factor making it one of the "heavenly things", while the wood reminds us that the table could not be provided unless the Lord had taken humanity upon Himself. This distinguishes the table from the lampstand. As the light of the World His down-stooping was not necessary for the Light was "in the beginning". As far as we can judge it followed the conventional design of an ordinary table with a leg at each corner. The top had a border of a hand's breadth which would make it appear that the top was a handbreadth thick. In most modern tables a drawer would be inserted in this border but the table of shewbread was plain. At the top of each leg, just by the border there were four cast golden rings through which staves made of wood and covered with gold could be inserted during porterage.

In common with the grate in the brazen altar and the mercy seat in the Holy of Holies, the table of shewbread was one and a half cubits high. One other feature that it shared with three other items of furniture was that it had a golden crown, edge or ledge on its upper perimeter. On this table twelve pierced loaves were placed and arranged every sabbath, and these loaves were for the priests to eat. Newberry points out in the margin that the word used for these loaves means "pierced loaves", suggesting to us the fact that even during the heat of the oven they did not rise, giving us a picture of the Lord in His humility, and this is something on which the priest can feed, gazing upon every facet of that One. Sometimes we hear brethren quoting Psalm 139 vv 23 & 24, "Search me, O God, and know my heart: try me, and know my thoughts: And see if there be any wicked way in me.", and applying it to themselves. What hypocrisy! No priest, however good and perfect in his walk can pray that prayer unless he shelters under the imputed righteousness of Christ, but with the Lord, how different. Even Satan came and found nothing of sin or pride in Him. Ponder these loaves, the fine flour, the piercing, the fierceness of the oven and the sprinkling with the frankincense. This is your food, this is your portion as a priest.

How are we to understand the heavenly things? Call to mind that in this tent-room measuring ten cubits by twenty cubits (15' x 30') and characterised by gold there was no natural light. All of the illumination had to come from the lampstand and as we have seen this light is identified with the Word. Let us then examine the table of shewbread in the light of our guide book, the New Testament. Firstly we should note that the crown with which the table was surmounted bears no connection to a royal diadem. Much has been made about the crowns on the ark, on the altar of incense and on the table of shewbread extolling the wonders of their having crowns of glory. This is not the understanding of these crowns, indeed JND translates the word as 'border'. On each of the three items that had this crown or border, something had to be placed. In the case of the ark it was the mercy seat. The altar of incense obviously had the incense placed on top, while the table of shewbread, as the name implies, displayed the twelve loaves, so that, instead of crowns or borders speaking to us of regal glory they rather seem to indicate the security of the items placed thereon. There was no chance of anything falling off, so that the shewbread is secure and firm on the table.

It is important that we should distinguish between the Lord's Table and the Lord's Supper. The Lord's Table is that provision that is made for us, both spiritual and temporal, as we journey home. It is something that we are constantly at and that we never leave. Mephibosheth gives us a wonderful picture of this, and the ninth chapter of the second book of Samuel closes with these words, "for he did eat continually at the king's table" even although he was lame on both his feet.

The Lord's Supper is something completely different. This is for the Lord, the request being "this do in remembrance of me" (1 Cor. 11 v 24). This is why the apostle John, under the guidance of the Holy Spirit, makes no mention of the breaking of bread and the drinking of the cup at the last supper lest we should confuse it with John chapter six where it is a question of feeding on Him at the Lord's table. The distinction is clearly shown in 1 Cor. 10 (the Lord's Table) and 1 Cor. 11 (the Lord's Supper).

How often do we hear brethren quoting from the Song of Solomon, "He brought me to the banqueting house, and his banner over me was love" (S of S 2 v 4) and applying this almost exclusively to our gathering together to remember Him. It may be a nice sentiment and doubtless on these occasions we are very conscious of the Lord's presence in a very special way but, brethren, we do not come to feed and to get from that remembrance, we come to give, to remember Him. It does not matter how smug and glowing we feel, the major question is what does the Lord receive? That you will get a blessing is beyond doubt. Learn a lesson from the woman who came and anointed the feet of the Lord. This type of event is recorded in all four gospels. Luke is perhaps the most graphic. Here was a woman who was a sinner with no worthiness of her own but one to whom the Lord had forgiven much. She does not come to get food from the feast, she comes with but one purpose, to worship and pour out her heart, weeping and kissing the Lord's feet and wiping then with her hair. She did not come to get but to give. Possibly it did not occur to her that the whole house would be filled with the fragrance but that is what happened. Possibly it is also correct to assume that all in that house would leave with the distinctive odour lingering about them. How about you and me? When we gather to remember the Lord do we come to partake of a feast? Surely we come as sinners saved by the Lord himself and bring our box of ointment, our worship, very precious in the Lord's sight. Perhaps we feel unworthy to anoint His head (and who does not) but we fall at His feet and anoint Him, breaking our alabaster box of ointment. It is for Him. This is our objective. But who does not know the unique wonder of remembering Him?

How can we go from such a gathering without the fragrance of that worship lingering about our person so that men can know that we have been with Jesus.

Do not let that which has been written about the banqueting house rob you of any blessing concerning our gathering together to remember Him. There is a closeness and an intimacy in the remembrance of the Lord that is unequalled. Simply let us ask ourselves this question, when we leave that morning meeting do we also leave His banqueting house? Is His banner of love no longer over us? Surely we must agree that we need the food of the Lord's provision every hour of the day and that banner of love, dare we step from underneath it even for a single instant? Rejoice and feed at the King's table continually and on the first day of the week gather to give and thus remember Him.

The sixth chapter of John's gospel contains a wonderful discourse on the Bread of Life, a discourse so wonderful, yet so alarming that "From that time many of His disciples went back, and walked no more with Him." (v 66). We said this was going to be difficult. These men were not just believers, they were actually disciples but the discourse of John six was just too much for them to understand. Call to mind that only the priests were allowed into the Holy Place. If we are to understand the table of shewbread we must be not only a believer, not only a disciple, but a priest. The atmosphere of the Holy Place is heavy with the smell of incense, speaking to us of worship, not being able to understand perhaps all that is implied but, nevertheless, in the light of the Word understanding something of the deep things of Christ. Maybe for years we have imagined that we are feeding on the Lord, maybe in part we have been, but have we ever considered the subject in depth? This feeding is entirely on Him. "Whoso eateth MY flesh, and drinketh MY blood, hath eternal life." (Jno. 6 v 54). Every evangelist is excluded, no pastor has a place, even the teacher, although he can help to supply the food, cannot be that food. The apostle Paul was surely at the shewbread table when he wrote, "That I may know Him, and the power of His resurrection, and the fellowship of His sufferings, being made conformable unto His death." (Phil. 3 v 10). Oh, how we dwell on the feeding on the bread. How we love to sing, "I'm feeding on the living bread", but what about the blood? The chorus writer switches from the blood to "the fountain head", going from John six back to John four. The Lord said we must drink His blood, otherwise we have no life in us. Strong words. No wonder the Jewish disiples turned back from following Him. All their lives they had been taught that they must never drink the blood of animals, it was strictly forbidden in their law, yet here is this man, this prophet, who although He can do miracles as they have already seen, now He tells them that they must drink His blood. Impossible, it cannot be. How difficult are these heavenly things. Come closer to the table of shewbread. Not only are there twelve loaves upon it but also Moses was told, "And thou shalt make the dishes thereof, and cups thereof, and goblets thereof, and bowls thereof, with which to pour out" (Exod. 25 v 29 (JND). Now we cannot eat bread from a goblet, and bread cannot be poured out. (Are your priestly garments shewing, or do you feel that it is time to leave the Holy Place and settle for being a Levite?) Whatever could the priests have drunk at the table of shewbread? Have a look at the twenty-eighth chapter of Numbers. Here Jehovah is detailing the burnt offering that is to be offered on the brazen altar. Together with the morning and evening lamb a tenth part of an ephah of fine flour was to be offered and a fourth part of an hin of wine for each lamb. This would be about five pints of wine a day with, on the sabbath, a double portion. (vv 9 & 10). What happened to this wine? "In the sanctuary shall the drink offering of strong drink be poured out to Jehovah." (v 7) (JND). Where in the sanctuary could the drink offering be poured out? Certainly not on the lampstand for five pints of wine a day would extinguish the lamps. Neither could it go on on to the altar of incense for with reference to that altar the Word says, "Ye shall offer no strange incense thereon, nor burnt sacrifice, nor meat offering; neither shall ye pour drink offering thereon." (Exod. 30 v 9). How gently does the Lord lead us along. How easy it would have been for the Lord to have instructed Moses that the drink offering was to be placed on the table of shewbread. No, God tells him that it is to go into the sanctuary, but it cannot go on the lampstand, and we can imagine Moses looking round and asking himself whether it should go on the altar of incense, but God tells him that this must not be, and we, together perhaps with Moses, look at the table of shewbread, and lo, bowls, goblets and cups. What do we do as priests? We try to understand what God is telling us. We are not told that the shewbread was made from the fine flour offered on the brazen altar, but we are told that the wine came from that altar. What was the height of the table of shewbread? Just one and a half cubits. What was the height of the grating upon which the sacrifice rested? Just one and a half cubits. Coincidence, or part of the divine plan? My priestly brother, start feeding. All that we know of Him that will make our souls fat has its origin in that sacrifice at Calvary. Eating His flesh we can understand as typifying our feeding on Him through His Word. This is made obvious and clear by the twelve loaves but what about our drinking His blood? This is obscure and difficult. We are not told that there was anything to drink on the table of shewbread, yet it is there by implication, so what are we to understand? Before seeking to unravel this problem let us return to the loaves. Much has been made of there being twelve, perhaps representing the twelve tribes, one for each tribe. Maybe, but the tribes are outside the sanctuary, this has only to do with the priests, Aaron's sons. Turn to our guide book again. John chapter six has been the basis for our understanding of the 'Bread of Life' Any indication there? Look at verse sixty-seven, " 'Then said Jesus unto the TWELVE, 'will ye also go away?' " Just a strange coincidence that twelve should happen to be mentioned in this connection, or is the Lord saying that the feeding on Him can only be experienced by the true and close disciple. Rather a searching thought. Ponder over the Lord's words to the woman of Samaria, "But the hour cometh, and now is, when the true worshippers shall worship the Father in spirit and in truth; for the Father seeketh such to worship Him. God is a Spirit: and they that worship Him must worship Him in spirit and in truth." (Jno. 4 vv 23 & 24).

The multitudes would have understood the Lord's reference to the manna, this was the food of the people in the wilderness, and here before us as we examine the tabernacle is the wilderness. The people receive their daily portion from Him. It does not fail all the time that they are wandering and until they reach the promised land. The Lord's Table is sufficient for them, but here we are going beyond the manna. We are in the confines of the Holy Place, only priests are allowed here and they are few and far between, only two to begin with in addition to Aaron the High Priest. Call to mind the other occasions when the multitude was fed, not this time in the wilderness of Sinai but in the desert and wilderness of Palestine. On one occasion the Lord fed four thousand people and on the other five. This was surely proof that whenever the Lord saw fit He could produce bread from nothing. Why then did He instruct the disciples to gather up fragments, and what were those fragments going to be used for? There seems to be no other reason than that the disciples would eat them. Food, unappreciated by the multitudes, discarded and left. Their appetite had been satiated, but this was to be the disciples' food. What, left-over scraps that were reckoned as of no account by the multitudes? The Lord later asks His disciples how many baskets of left-overs they took up after each of the miraculous feedings and they replied that there were seven on the one occasion and twelve on the other. Matthew and Mark record the seven baskets while all four evangelists record the twelve, therefore we must conclude that the twelve were the most important. Then why mention the seven? It is generally accepted that the number seven speaks of that which is perfect in the sight of God, thus we could conclude that these baskets of scraps were not unwholesome in the sight of the Lord, they were food of a special nature, food that the multitude did not appreciate. But why the twelve baskets and why are these mentioned in all four gospels? They must be important. This was food set aside exclusively for the twelve, as it were a basket each. Compare this with the tabernacle. The multitudes, not just four or five thousand, but a couple of millions, had their daily food provided by God, their manna, but within the sanctuary there was food set aside for the priests. Sumptuous food? Rich fare? It would not have been so in the eyes of the multitude for the twelve loaves of the shewbread were pierced, dry, unleavened bread, in itself completely unpalatable. They could not have been delicate little loaves for each one contained two tenth deals of fine flour. (Lev. 24 v 5). They must have been thick heavy loaves for twelve of them to be placed on the table in two rows, so that each loaf must have been about six inches in diameter in order to fit into the length of the table which was two cubits long (36"). They must have been quite thick and dry, especially as they had to remain on the table for a week before they were eaten. Poor priests. Wait a moment. Remember the cups and the goblets on the table of shewbread and the wine that came from the morning and evening sacrifice? The bread, washed down with the wine would be extremely palatable, food not for the multitude but for the priests. If you consider yourself to be in any wise a priest, ponder the food for your provision. Not the savoury spiced meats of the world, not even the normal food, the manna of the saints, but something that can only be eaten in the sanctuary with the world shut outside, the only light being the Light of the World, the air heavy with incense suggesting the worship and praise of the priest. The food? Ah yes! Made from fine flour, flour that had been ground between the upper and nether millstone, fine flour with no lumps or coarseness, speaking to us of the perfect human life of our Lord. It is not for us to detail all the qualities of that fine flour. If you are a priest you will find food here that even the believer does not appreciate. He cannot see the value of that food, the discarded morsels. Look again at the loaves, pierced so that there is no 'pride' in them and then subjected to the heat of the oven. If you are a priest you can feed here. It would be wrong for us to attempt to go further into the details, the food must be yours. It is not for profane eyes to see, and you, my fellow priest, will not be able to see it, you will not be able to take of that food unless it is mingled with the wine that comes from the continual sacrifice. Let us have a look at the wine.

The very mention of wine or strong drink is sufficient to send some brethren into a state of paranoia. Surely we must look at the problem in the light of the Word. That the abuse of wine or strong drink is very wrong indeed, there can be no doubt, especially in a believer and more especially in a priest. If we look closely it would appear that the over indulgence in wine was the root cause of the deaths of Nadab and Abihu when they offered strange fire before the Lord, (Lev. 10 vv 1-5), for immediately afterwards God instructed Aaron, "Do not drink wine or strong drink, thou, nor thy sons with thee, when ye go into the tabernacle of the congregation, lest ye die:" and the reason is a very strange one, for the Lord goes on to say, "that ye may put difference between holy and unholy, and between clean and unclean." (Lev.10 vv 9 & 10). Now obviously Aaron is being instructed to differentiate between two things. First of all it is between the holy and the unholy. May we suggest, in view of what has been written before, that Aaron is being told to make a marked difference between wine that is drunk as an ordinary beverage (the unholy) and that which has been sanctified and is to be drunk as a drink offering in the Holy place (the holy). He must also differentiate between the clean and the unclean, the emphasis being laid on wine being used for a right and lawful purpose (the clean) and wine being used to excess whereby man is made exceedingly unclean.

That wine is spoken of as being potentially dangerous there can be no doubt. Noah, Lot and many others serve as examples of excess. Wine is also described as a mocker, (Prov. 20 v 1), but the view that we take must be balanced for the same writer who described wine as a mocker also tells us that 'wine maketh merry' (Eccles. 10 v 19) and after the Nazarite was released from his vow, the instruction is 'after that the Nazarite may drink wine.' (Num. 6 v 20). All of these instances and quotations come from the Old Testament, where it appears that drinking wine was permitted but excess was condemned for excess often led to dire consequences. Let us now look at wine in the New Testament.

That wine as an alcoholic drink was one of the staple drinks of the country of Palestine there can be little doubt. The 1978 edition of the Newberry Bible has a section at the end headed 'Aids to Bible Study' and under wine we read 'This was the produce of the fruit of the vine, and occasionally of the pomegranate and other fruits. Sometimes it was drunk in an unfermented, but, more generally, in a fermented state, after the lees had been drained off. It is associated among the gifts of God with "corn and oil', and it appears along with them as one of the distinctive products or benefits of settled agricultural life." Most of the Bible encyclopedias seem to agree with these sentiments. Now the first miracle that the Lord performed in Cana of Galilee was to turn water into wine. Here was a village wedding, possibly with hundreds of guests and gatecrashers, in a country, not where prohibition was the practice but where one of the staple drinks was wine and intoxicating wine at that. Can you imagine such a gathering being served with lemonade or fruit juice? The wine ran out and the Lord turned a very great deal of water into a very great deal of wine. It is an insult to any man's intelligence to suggest that at a village wedding anything other than wine, in the accepted sense of the word, was served, and note the reaction of the governor of the feast. We are explicitly told that he did not know where it came from (Jno. 2 v 9) but he actually called the bridegroom, this was not just a chance remark but a calculated conclusion, and almost reprimanding him by saying, 'Every man at the beginning doth set forth good wine; and when men have well drunk, then that which is worse: but thou hast kept the good wine until now.' (Jno. 2 v 10). If this were un-fermented fruit juice what difference would it make whether the good juice was served first or last? On the other hand, as the governor seems to imply, if the wine was alcoholic, then the more men drank the less discriminating they would be.

That the Lord Himself drank wine is apparent from the accusations made against Him in Matt. 11 v 19 and Luke 7 v 34, "Behold a gluttonous man and a winebibber." Surely these men knew the difference between fruit juice and wine. The accusation was obviously false being a blatant case of hyperbole but the Lord does not refute the charge that it was wine that He was drinking. Remember the story of the good Samaritan in Luke 10. When he tended the wounded men he poured in oil and fruit juice? No, he poured in oil and wine.

Now let us come to the epistles. Nowhere is the drinking of wine forbidden. On the contrary Timothy is told to 'Drink no longer water, but use a little wine for thy stomach's sake and thine oft infirmities.' (1 Tim. 5 v 23). It may well be, as some assert, that the water where Timothy lived was impure, although Paul does not tell us this, but what he does tell Timothy is that he should use something that must be taken with restraint, and if he does so his health will most likely improve. We must ask ourselves whether such a cautious piece of advice would be put forward by the apostle if he meant just fruit juice. This appears to be the only positive instruction to anyone concerning the use of wine.

It is apparent that the early church used wine, as we know it, to celebrate the Lord's Supper, for in 1 Cor. 11 the apostle Paul chides the saints for abusing the remembrance of the Lord and treating it as a love feast, leaving some saints hungry and some in an inebriated condition (1 Cor. 11 v 21). The apostle does not reprimand the saints for drinking wine but rather for their lack of order and summarizes his rebuke in the closing verses of the chapter, 'Wherefore, my brethren, when ye come together to eat, tarry one for another. And if any man hunger, let him eat at home; that ye come not together unto condemnation.' (1 Cor. 11 vv 33 & 34).

Further guidance concerning wine is afforded in the qualifications for both elders and deacons in 1 Tim. 3 v 3 and 3 v 8 and again repeated for bishops in Titus 1 v 7. The meaning of the word here is 'one who is constantly alongside wine' or in modern language, a tippler. What then should be our attitude towards wine?

The Christian pathway does not consist of a series of 'thou shalts' and 'thou shalt nots'. This was the dictates of the law, although some brethren seem to delight in promulgating their own opinions and forbidding certain things and allowing others. Do not imagine that Christianity is a lax pathway, it is not, but it is not governed by legal restrictions but by a law of love that requires a walk of godly self-control. There are so many things in our lives that in themselves are neutral, neither good nor bad, and these things affect all of our five senses. Take our eyes, they can look upon all manner of pornography, on television, in daily papers, in books or even in life round about. On the other hand we can fill our vision with those things that are beautiful, the glories of nature wherein we see the wondrous hand of our creator God. We can use those eyes to read and our range can extend from the filth of the most lurid novel, to the holy occupation of reading the word of God. Similarly our ears can be utilised to listen to some programmes on the radio that contain blasphemy and filthy talk, on the other hand they can be employed listening to the expositions of the Word or playing their part in holy conversation. The third chapter of the epistle of James gives us the state of that little member, the tongue, and he shows us the two ways in which our tongues can be used, giving as a summary, ' Therewith bless we God, even the Father; and therewith curse we men, which are made after the similitude of God.' (Jas. 3 v 9). There is more harm brought into the world by sex than by wine or any other cause, and sex possibly involves all of our senses. When we consider the ruined lives, the illegitimate children, the distraught parents, the awful diseases including the terrible onslaught of AIDS we are faced with the complete disintegration of all moral fibre. What then does a Christian do, shut his eyes, plug his ears, cut out his tongue and refuse to have children? No, the answer is that the believer has always and in everything, to exercise godly self-control, something that we cannot do in our own strength. We need, indeed we must have, the cleansing and keeping power of the Holy Spirit. Why then do we have to isolate wine from the rest of our daily living? Should it not rather come under the heading of those things  that the apostle Paul deals with in Romans chapter fourteen where he begins, 'For one believeth that he may eat all things: another, who is weak, eateth herbs. Let not him that eateth despise him that eateth not; and let not him which eateth not judge him that eateth;' (Rom. 14 vv 2 & 3). Further down the chapter the apostle tells us that we should consider our brethren and not put a stumbling block in their pathway. From this it would appear that we must not force our views and lay down laws one for the other.It may be perfectly right and proper for one brother not to touch wine. If a brother finds that he has a weakness in that direction or if he has had an experience of the evils of excessive drinking that has seared itself into his mind, then that brother is to be lauded for refraining from ever touching strong drink. If a brother finds that he can use wine as part of his normal eating and drinking and not go to excess or become addicted then he is in a different category.

GOD'S SANCTUARY

The greater problem is how not to give offence to our brethren. We can find those who hold all sorts of extreme views and are sincere in them. The apostle refers to those who will not eat meat, so then we must all be vegetarians. Some brethren find music to be a snare, so we must not listen to music. When radio first came on the scene many brethren held up their hands in horror quoting the advertisement of Ultra Radio, 'Brings the world into your home' and almost quoted this as chapter and verse. In many circles radio is no longer looked upon as solely the work of the Devil even although some of the programmes would never have been countenanced by men of the world in an earlier generation. Much attention now focuses on television. We can hear and let our imaginations run riot but we must not look. Some brethren decry the reading of anything except the Word, and may be they are right, but where, oh where, do we draw the line?

All of the cases mentioned above present us with problems and exercises, and each one of us has got to examine each problem and somewhere along the line, according to our understanding of scripture and the mind of the Lord we have got to decide at what point we draw the line in each case. Having drawn that line, how do we avoid giving offence to our brethren? Take the thorny question of drinking wine. Maybe our conscience is clear. Maybe we can keep the mocker in place and instead receive its benefits, but what of my brother? It would be wrong for me to produce wine with a meal if I were entertaining a brother who regarded wine as best left alone. It would also be wrong of me to expect that brother to produce wine for me if I visited his house, although how gracious and understanding that would be. Likewise it would be wrong from my brother's point of view for him to condemn me if I felt free to take wine in moderation, and the last word, moderation, is certainly the dominant factor.

Let nothing that has been written encourage or entice anyone to drink wine. Unless our consciences are perfectly clear we should and must abstain, and if ever we find that there is a danger of taking wine to excess remember that this is contrary to the mind of the Lord for it spoils our service for Him and renders us unfit for use either as an elder or a deacon.

Wine and blood are sometimes connected together in the scriptures. Isaiah 63 tells of One whose clothes are red from treading in the winepress and likens the stain to the blood of the people sprinkled upon His garments. In Revelation chapter 19 we have One who treads the winepress of the wrath of Almighty God and His vesture is dipped in blood. Perhaps of greater importance and significance is the fact of the Lord taking the cup at the last supper and telling His disciples that this wine represents His blood. It is useless for brethren to say that we do not know what was in that cup, for as the Lord took it He said, 'I will drink no more of the fruit of the vine, until that day I drink it new in the kingdom of God.' (Mark. 14 v 25).

The blood seems to be Jehovah's portion. The children of Israel were forbidden to eat blood in any form and so strong is this prohibition that the apostles and elders bring it into the New Testament in Acts 15 v 29 saying to the early church that they lay upon them no greater burdens than are necessary, among which are "that ye abstain from meats offered to idols, and from blood . . .".

The blood has a special significance for Jehovah and its uniqueness is clearly shown in Leviticus 17 v 11, "For the life of the flesh is in the blood: and I have given it to you upon the altar to make an atonement for your souls; for it is the blood that maketh an atonement for the soul.", and we should remind ourselves that it was the blood upon which God looked when He passed through the land of Egypt slaying the firstborn, 'When I see the blood I will pass over you' (Exod. 12 v 13). Whatever did the Lord mean in John chapter six when He told His disciples that unless they drank His blood they had no life in them?

Somehow we automatically skirt round the drinking of His blood. We do not do it intentionally but we seem to be able to understand the eating of His flesh, the feeding on Him. Maybe we cannot comprehend it fully but we can see a vestage of truth in it. When we come to the drinking of His blood, however, we tend to think of the water of the well in John 4 or the living water of John 7, but we do not seem to come to grips with drinking His blood. That this has nothing to do with the remembrance of the

Lord is at once apparent, for there is no thought of remembrance in John chapter six. This is a question of food and drink for the disciple, perhaps even more exclusive than that for at this time all of His disciples left Him because of the difficulty of this drinking of His blood, leaving only the twelve, the close disciples.

Come back to the Holy Place, to the table of shewbread. Here is the food for the priest, the loaves of the shewbread. We have begun to see some of the lessons of these loaves. We have begun to feed, but we cannot enjoy that food, we cannot appreciate it in any wise unless we have the wine taken from the sacrifice, the wine speaking to us of His blood. But how? The blood was primarily for God, 'When I see the blood'. Unless God has looked upon the blood there is no redemption. Unless the sacrifice of Calvary has been accepted by Him it is of no avail to us. God has accepted that sacrifice, He has looked upon that blood, He has passed over us in His slaying. Because God is satisfied with the sacrifice of Calvary, because that shed blood has been presented before Him even as the blood of the bullock and the goat were presented on the day of atonement, God looks upon the blood and sees that which brings complete satisfaction to Him. Here is the Son, the one who perfectly displayed the character of God when He walked among men. Here is God's perfect servant (the bullock) doing the Father's will even to the extent of laying down His life, nay, more than that, even to the extent of being made sin in order that sinners might be made righteous. Here is the Messiah, the Hope of Israel, fulfilling all of the ancient prophecies (the sure-footed goat). Writing in language that we as mere men can understand, God looks upon and holds forth the Lord saying "This is my beloved Son in whom I am well pleased" (Matt. 3 v 17, 12 v 18, 17 v 5; Mark 1 v 11, 9 v 7; Luke 3 v 32, 9 v 35). "No man knoweth the Son but the Father" (Matt. 11 v 27). The truth of this scripture is shown in the sixteenth chapter of Matthew. Peter has just declared that the Lord is 'the Christ, the Son of the living God' and he is then told that this revelation came from no other source than God, "flesh and blood hath not revealed it unto thee, but MY Father which is in heaven" ( Matt. 16 v 17). So with us. The first revelation that we are given is that the Lord has made "peace through the blood of His cross"

(Col. 1 v 20). This brings satisfaction and assurance to us. God then wishes us to progress in this revelation of His Son that we might become priests Godward, that He might take us into the Holy Place where only priests can enter, and bid us share in some small measure God's appreciation of His Son. Taking us in to eat of the shewbread, ah! and wonder of wonders to drink of that wine of the drink offering, speaking of the blood shed. Potent food and still more potent drink. Was this not why Nadab and Abihu died before the Lord? Read the story in Leviticus chapter ten and note the sequel in vv 8-11. Is this not why Aaron and his sons are told that 'Thou and thy sons and thy father's house with thee shall bear the iniquity of your priesthood' (Num. 18 v 1, see also Exod. 28 vv 38 & 43). What does this mean? Simply that Aaron and his sons are to bear the responsibility for offences against the sanctuary. Aaron, you and your sons must learn the lesson of Nadab and Abihu, if not, your lives also will be forfeit.

How careful we should be that as priests we do not count the blood of the covenant, wherewith we are sanctified, an unholy thing (Heb. 10 v 29). Note the warning that follows, "It is a fearful thing to fall into the hands of the living God" (Heb. 10 v 31). Spoken primarily to believers!!!

In this Age of Grace the sinner cannot wash himself in that blood. The Lord does it all, so that when we are gathered home we shall sing with the apostle John, 'Unto Him that loved us, and washed us from our sins in His own blood' (Rev. 1 v 5). It is the Lord who does the washing in His own blood. On to chapter five and join the song of the four living ones and the four and twenty elders, 'for thou was slain, and hast redeemed us to God by thy blood' (Rev. 5 v 9). He has done the redeeming by His blood. Here comes that contentious brother again. Do not condemn him, he is doing the right thing by examining the scriptures. Look at Revelation chapter seven, 'These are they which . . . have washed their robes, and made them white in the blood of the Lamb' (Rev. 7 v 14). Who does the washing in the blood? Not the Lord. Who then? Always be careful in quoting part of a text. You will notice that we have inserted a series of dots in the middle of this quotation. What has been missed out? '. . . came out of the great tribulation and . . .' Ah! these saints do not belong to the Age of Grace. The Church has been taken home. Now the saints must do something for their salvation. They must refuse to have the mark of the beast upon their foreheads and this would virtually spell isolation and death. They've got to do the washing, in much the same way that the Old Testament saints had to offer continual sacrifices for their cleansing. Salvation before and after the Church period was not of grace but of doing. This is clearly shown by the Lord when he answered the lawyer who tempted Him in Luke 10 vv 25-28. 'This DO and thou shalt live'. Why? The Lord had not yet died. Compare this with the similar question raised by the Philippian jailer in Acts sixteen, 'Believe on the Lord Jesus Christ and thou shalt be saved'. Nothing to do – only believe. Do we ever thank God that we have been born in this wonderful Day of Grace? Let us make sure that we do not abuse the privilege and tread the blood of Christ underfoot. On you, my fellow priest, is laid the iniquity of the holy things. What a sobering thought. Selah!

Now the picture that is being given to us in John six and given in type in the table of shewbread is that although God has accepted that blood, although His holiness is satisfied, yet it is requisite that the priest should drink it, that is, appropriate it to himself, not just as the multitude who could look upon the blood at the gate of the tabernacle but as a priest in the Holy Place, as he eats the shewbread he may know Him . . . and the fellowship of His sufferings, – difficult lessons, difficult to see, and how difficult to write about. These things belong to the sanctuary.

Before we leave the table of shewbread let us look at an important event in which the shewbread figures prominently. We refer of course to the incident recorded in 1 Samuel 21 vv 1-6 where David is fleeing for his life from Saul and in his extremity he calls upon Ahimelech, the priest, to give him the shewbread that he and his followers might eat.

That this was a flagrant violation of God's law seems obvious for this bread was only for the High Priest and his sons. Why then was David not punished? We read that Uzzah was slain by the Lord when he simply put forth his hand to steady the ark as it wobbled unsteadily on the ox cart. (2. Sam. 6). David not only touched the shewbread but actually ate it.

Strangely enough (or perhaps not so strange when we remember that this is God's book and He is continually teaching us lessons) this incident is referred to in all of the synoptic gospels (Matt. 12 v 4, Mark. 2 v 26, Luke. 6 v 4) and in every case the Lord does not condemn David but rather commends him and uses the incident to show that 'the Son of Man is Lord also of the sabbath'. Why was David not punished? Are there further lessons that we should learn?

If we read the account in 1 Samuel twenty-one we find that David must have come to Ahimelech either late on Friday night or early on Saturday morning. The reason for this conclusion is that the loaves of shewbread were due to be replaced with those hot from the oven. (J.N.D.'s translation makes this a little clearer). This is born out by David's remarking that the bread was in a manner common, it having fulfilled its purpose of being food for the priests. They had eaten their fill. Now we can see why David asked for the five loaves that were under Ahimelech's hand. The priests had eaten seven loaves and the shewbread was due to be replaced by another twelve new loaves, hot from the oven. The hunger of the priests had been satiated. It was no longer a crime for holy men (1 Sam. 21 v 5) to eat the remainder. Any further lesson for us? There must be! If we are priests, the Sons of Aaron and have entered that sacred and holy place where the Lord is all and in all, where there is no light other than the 'Light of the World', if we have eaten our fill of the shewbread, and the loaves were of such a size that there was always some over, Selah!, then it is right and proper that as priests we should tell holy brethren of the wonders and glories of the person of the Lord even although they may not yet be able to enter into the holy place. Please remember that in this context we are not talking about any one particular sect, denomination, or non-denomination, but we are talking of every saint, no matter how feeble their faith and understanding, wherever there is trust in the Risen Lord. All do not go into the Holy Place. Those who do, having eaten of that Holy Food, distinct from Manna, and having been filled by eating His flesh and drinking

His blood, when they come out of the sanctuary they should allow those holy brethren who have a need and are hungry to share some of the marvels of the feasting on Him, to have their hunger met, not by entering into the holy place but by the priests bringing the remainder of that food out to them.

When we are first converted to Christ we know little more than the fact that He died for us and our sins are forgiven. We begin to eat the manna and to grow. We have crossed the Red Sea and our wilderness journey has begun. Gradually we learn that not only has Christ died for us but we must die with Him. We cross the Jordan and begin to fight the battles in the land. It is during this period in our spiritual history that brethren who have progressed further in the things of the Lord tell us of the glories and wonders of the person of the Christ, feeding us some of the shewbread left over and slowly we begin to function not only as priests manward but, having grown more like our Great High Priest, we begin to function as priests godward and enter that realm where we feed on His flesh and drink His blood, where our food is not only what He has done for us in providing for the wilderness journey typified by the manna but we now feed on what He is in Himself. We begin to know Him and the power of His resurrection and the fellowship of His suffering. We enter as priests godward into the Holy Place where all is of Him.

# CHAPTER EIGHTEEN

# The Altar of Incense
"I am the vine, ye are the branches." (Jno. 15 v 5)

We now come to the last item of furniture in the Holy Place. It is situated in the centre, right in front of the vail and is made of shittim wood overlaid with gold, teaching us once again that although this altar has the appearance of Godhead glory, nevertheless it could never be unless God had been manifest in the flesh and walked here in a path of humility that led only to the cross. Although we are not told the actual size of the lampstand we are told that it was beaten out of a talent of gold, and therefore it seems safe to assume that the altar was the smallest item in the Holy Place. As an altar it was tiny being only one cubit square (18" x 18") yet it was higher than the grate in the altar and higher than the table of shewbread, its height being two cubits (30"). Presumably it was a square box with a crown or border round the top edge. We have already noted that these crowns have little to do with regality or glory but are retaining edges in order to ensure the safety of that which is placed upon it.

There are two oddities about the altar of incense. First of all it only had two rings into which the carrying poles were to be inserted, one ring on each of the two diagonal corners. (Exod. 30 v 4). How odd! If it had four rings, one in each corner, surely it would have been more stable when it was carried. As it is, with a ring at each of only two corners, it will tend to sway on its poles, yet the instruction seems very clear, only two rings, why? Had there been four rings, one in each corner, the poles would have been about 18" apart, just a nice width to fit on an average man's shoulders, and as the altar was not very big and therefore could not have been very heavy, surely this would have been the ideal arrangement, one man in front and one man behind, nice and neat and tidy. This is not what Jehovah tells Moses, and no matter how sensible the four rings may seem to Moses, he has got to obey the divine instruction, two rings and two rings only.

How often are we reminded that God's ways are not man's ways. As there were only two rings on the altar, on diagonally opposite corners, then it must mean that the altar had to be carried diagonal-wise between the two poles. This would mean that the altar would no longer fit comfortably on the shoulders of two men for the poles would now be about 25" apart, the obvious inference being that although the altar was not heavy in man's eyes, yet God required four men to carry it because although small it was very weighty before God.

The other odd thing about the golden altar is the fact that it had four horns, one on each corner. Now the only thing to be offered on this altar was the special incense, the instructions to Moses being, "Ye shall offer no strange incense thereon, nor burnt sacrifice, nor meat offering; neither shall ye pour drink offering thereon." (Exod. 30 v 9). The instruction is very clear and precise, incense and incense only, and that must be made to a special prescription. Now we cannot tie incense down to the horns of the altar. It has already been pointed out that the horns, even on the brazen altar, must have been symbolic, and we endeavoured to show that the cords that bound the burnt offering to the altar were invisible cords, speaking to us of those cords that bound the Lamb of God to that awful tree. Now what are we going to bind to the horns of this altar, even in symbolic form? My priestly brother, prepare for a shock and do not run away, for it is you and I who must be bound on to this altar, if we are to fulfil our priestly function to the full. "But", we may cry, "I am too big to go on to an altar just 18" square." Then, my brother, you are not ready for the cords. Call to mind the words of the Baptist, "He must increase, but I must decrease." (Jno. 3 v 30). Until we become small, and very small, before the Lord we are not ready for the golden altar. Until we see that we are nothing and He is everything, until we almost say in our hearts, "It had been better, Lord, that I had gone to a lost eternity than that You should have endured the humiliation, the pain, and the degradation of the cross." When we reach that stage, how we fall at His feet and say from the depths of our hearts, "But Lord, how thankful I am that You did it", we are half way on to that altar, becoming very small indeed, no matter how we have served Him down here. No matter how good a Christian we may think we are, we realise that all our righteousnesses, yes all our righteousnesses, not our bad deeds, are as filthy rags in the sight of a thrice holy God. How small we become, how insignificant, how great He becomes and how glorious. Take heart, my brother, the altar on which we are being bound is gold covered. We are in the place of glory.

This altar is the smallest of the measured items in the tabernacle, yet having the highest operative surface, higher than the table of shewbread, higher than the grate in the brazen altar, higher even than the mercy seat. Here is priestly food, it will not be appreciated by any but priests, even the Levites were not allowed here. Ponder this in your heart, the altar of incense although so very small has the highest operational surface. There are things about which it almost seems a profanity to write, things which the average believer may not see, and even as the apostle, when he was caught up into the third heaven and heard "unspeakable words" and saw indescribable things, (2 Cor. 12), so sometimes it is possible for us to see things in the scripture that are best kept for our private meditation.

Perhaps we shall come to appreciate the golden altar more if we consider the incense that was to be offered thereon. As a background to this may we remind ourselves of some of the things that are recorded as sacrifices of the saints in our guide book, the New Testament. "Ye present your bodies a living sacrifice, holy, acceptable unto God, which is your reasonable service" (Rom. 12 v 1). "The sacrifice and (poured forth) service of your faith" (Phil. 2 v 17). "I (Paul) have all, and abound: I am full, having received of Epaphroditus the things which were sent from you, an odour of a sweet smell, a sacrifice acceptable, well pleasing to God" (Phil. 4 v 18). "By Him therefore let us offer the sacrifice of praise to God continually, that is, the fruit of our lips giving thanks to His name. But to do good and to com-municate forget not: for with such sacrifices God is well pleased" (Heb. 13 vv 15 & 16). Here we have the thought of the Vine and the branches. The objective of the Vine and the branches is to bring forth fruit and, says the apostle Paul, one of the fruits that we can bring forth continually is the fruit of our lips. "Ye also, as living stones, are built up a spiritual house, an holy priest-hood, to offer up spiritual sacrifices, acceptable to God by Jesus Christ" (1 Pet. 2 v 5) (Newberry). Broadly speaking a sacri-fice demands an altar. We cannot occupy the brazen altar for this is the one sacrifice for sins for ever. True we must reckon that we died with Him but ours was in no wise a sacrificial death for sin. The Lord was alone and unique in this respect. His was the larger altar, His was the sacrifice that the Levites could see and smell, His was the sacrifice that the children of Israel could glimpse through the door, this was the sacrifice, the odour of which permeated the camp. This was the sacrifice where the blood of all the other sacrifices must be poured, unique, large, constant. Even in writing of that altar we have difficulty dragging ourselves away, the wonderful glory of Cavalry; but there is another altar, a lot smaller, but how precious in the sight of Jehovah, situated right in the centre of the vail, filling the Holy Place with a fragrance with which none other can be compared. Consider this fragrance. Consider this incense.

Exodus chapter 30 v 34 tells us that there were four com-ponents in the sacred incense, stacte, onycha, galbanum and pure frankincense, four, once again this number connected with the earth. Surely this incense is worth examining in greater detail if we would understand anything of the import of the Altar of Incense.

All incense, all worship, must ascend to the Father as a reflection of the Son. We have nothing in ourselves that can in any wise be acceptable in His sight, but if that worship arises because "we have obtained an inheritance (in Him), being predestinated according to the purpose of him who worketh all things after the counsel of his own will: that we should be to the praise of his glory" (Eph. 1 vv 11 & 12), then there will arise a special fragrance to the Father, distinct from the sweet savour of the burnt offering for that is the unique Lamb of God, but as a result of that sacrifice many sons have been brought to glory, offering "the sacrifice of praise to God continually, that is, the fruit of our lips giving thanks to His name" (Heb. 13 v 15). This is perhaps difficult for us to understand as we seek to fathom what is "the riches of the glory of HIS inheritance in the saints." (Eph. 1 v 18), remembering the words of Moses, described as a song in Deut. 31 v 30, "For the Lord's portion is His people; Jacob is the lot of His inheritance. He found him in a desert land, and in the waste howling wilderness; He led him about, He instructed him, He kept him as the apple of His eye." (Deut. 32 vv 9 & 10).

Consider the first ingredient of the sacred incense, stacte. The word means a drop or tear, especially that which is squeezed out. Crying in the New Testament is difficult to understand, it always seems to raise the question, "why". The Lord wept at the tomb of Lazarus, why? Many of us never get further than remarking that the event contains the shortest verse in the Bible. How superficial. How irrelevant. Why did the Lord weep? Think of what was happening. Here was the Lord of glory, the one who had everything and could do anything, standing as a man upon earth and weeping. How can it be and why? Was it because Lazarus was dead? Seems strange if the Lord knew He was going to bring him back to life. Was it because He saw the sorrow of Martha and Mary? But the Lord knew that He was going to turn this sorrow into joy. Did it go deeper than these things, beyond Martha and Mary whom He loved? Did the Lord see the whole misery of the human race who through fear of death was all its lifetime subject to bondage? Did the Lord see beyond the immediate resurrection of Lazarus that this poor man and his sisters had got to go through this suffering a second time? Face to face with death did the reality, as a man, come upon Him that He must go into death? These and perhaps many another question arises in our minds. Perhaps we do not understand at all, perhaps it was a combination of all of these suggestions, who can say. One thing we know, the tears fell, Jesus wept.

How about the woman who was a sinner in Luke 7 v 37-end?

Was it her sins? Was it her love? The Lord alone knew and it was acceptable to Him.

What of the great drops of sweat that fell like blood to the ground in Gethsemane's garden? Who shall enter here? None could, none dared, for He went a little further.

If you are a priest, if you have entered the Holy Place and eaten the priest's food in the light of that golden lampstand, let the drops of stacte fall, What do they stand for? The forgiveness of your sins? The glory into which you are being brought? The unfathomable love of your Saviour and the price paid for your redemption? Let the queries rise, let the tears fall, let a fourth part of your worship be the stacte.

Next we come to the onycha. Not liking the idea of an unclean shellfish some have tried to interpret it as a lion. Lions do not give off a sweet fragrance when burnt but the onycha, the unclean mussel of the Red Sea, does. What a lesson. There is nothing in ourselves that brings joy to the Lord, but what wonder, what glory there is in a sinner saved by grace. We were certainly unclean fish with the wrath of the Red Sea rolling over us, but He took that which was unclean, that which had no hope, that which was lost in the depths of hell and lifted it to the highest heights of glory. Let the sweet fragrance rise, but it can only rise if the mussel is burnt. He must increase, I must decrease.

Of all of the spices of the east who would choose galbanum as the third ingredient of the holy incense, for galbanum is a gum that exudes from a tree and has a disagreeable odour, but it has the amazing property of enabling a perfume to retain its fragrance longer. What is it that makes the odour of this incense linger? What is the eternal factor that will take this fragrance through time into eternity? "Unto Him that loved us and washed us from our sins in His own blood . . ." for time and all eternity, a sinner saved by grace. Nothing sweet smelling in the sinner but how the "saved by grace" makes the fragrance linger eternally, "that in the ages to come He might show the exceeding riches of His grace in His kindness toward us through Christ Jesus" (Eph. 2 v 7). What a prospect! What a thrilling prospect! Ponder it and let the incense rise.

What of the last ingredient, the frankincense? Frankincense is white, pure, it is an incense in its own right. Stacte, onycha and galbanum are only each mentioned once in scripture and that is in the verse under consideration (Exod. 30 v 34), whereas frankincense is first mentioned here and goes right on to the last book of the Bible. We speak quite reverently when we ask what constituent of our worship and sacrifice of praise is pure, unsullied, having a fragrance that is entirely acceptable in itself yet can take of the other ingredients and combine them into the perfect and acceptable whole? Call to mind the Lord's words in John 4 v 24, "God is a Spirit: and they that worship Him must worship Him in spirit and in truth." Without the frankincense the stacte is meaningless. The tears, whether of joy or sorrow, in themselves are ineffective and unacceptable. Remember Esau "for he found no place of repentance, though he sought it carefully with tears" (Heb. 12 v 17). How about the onycha? The fact of our being sinners under judgement on its own is of little use. Does the galbanum fare any better? Because we are "stinking" sinners in itself adds nothing to the incense, but merge them all together with the life giving power of the Holy Spirit, not just the adding of the frankincense, this is essential, but the whole lot burnt upon the altar of incense, fire being a further picture of the Holy Spirit in action, consuming the dross and turning that which was for destruction into the glory of the Lord. Truly, "He brings a poor vile sinner into His house of wine," but even more than that He finds His portion, His chief delight in gazing upon His people, so that Solomon, a type of the bridegroom, can say to the Shulamite (the female version of Solomon and a picture of the bride), "Return, return, O Shulamite; Return, return that we may look upon thee." (Cant. 6 v 13). Can we now see, perhaps dimly, why the altar of incense is higher than the grate of the larger altar, or the table of shewbread? This is the culmination of all. This is that which brings joy and satisfaction to the Lord, "who for the joy that was set before Him endured the cross, despising the shame, and is set down at the right hand of the throne of God." (Heb. 12 v 2). This in no wise exalts us as though we have effected this great glory. Our only contribution is the fact that we are sinners in need of a Saviour. Just to be saved from hell and given a place in one little corner of heaven would indeed be marvellous grace and mercy, but to be raised to such heights of glory that the Lord should delight in us and make us like unto Himself, what shall we say? Just let the incense rise and the worship flow. We'll never understand or fathom the love of God for us.

> *Far beyond all human comprehension,*
> *Measured by an infinite dimension,*
> *Wonderfully broad in its intention,*
> *Is the wondrous love of God.*

Perhaps it would be arrogant and proud but speaking as mere humans, wouldn't it be marvellous when we get home in glory, to turn to one of the mighty angels and ask, "Does the Lord love you enough to die for you?". Wonder what he'd say? "Perish the thought, such things should not be mentioned" or "I just don't know". How unfortunate for the angels, "They know not Christ as Saviour but worship Him as King", whereas we can say, "the Son of God, who loved me, and gave himself for me" (Gal. 2 v 20). How wonderful to be the recipients of such love. No wonder the hymnwriter could write.

*"What will it be to dwell above and with the Lord of Glory reign?"*

Let the incense rise for ever and ever "Unto Him that loved us, and washed us from our sins in His own blood, and hath made us kings and priests unto God and His Father; to Him be glory and dominion for ever and ever" (Rev. 1 vv 5 & 6). Let those amens begin now and never ever cease.

And so we leave the altar of incense, set in the middle of the Holy Place, having, together with the table of shewbread, a crown round about, for none of this incense must fall to the ground, and we are confronted with the vail, all that separates us from the Holy of Holies.

# CHAPTER NINETEEN

# The Veil
"I AM." (Jno. 18 v 5)

The entrance to the tabernacle was at the eastern end. Three sets of curtains barred access to the Holy of Holies. The first set was the gate, the second the door to the tent and the third was the veil. Each of these sets of curtains had the same area. The gate was five by twenty cubits giving one hundred square cubits and the door and the veil were each ten by ten cubits giving again one hundred square cubits, giving us the lesson that whether it be an initial approach to God, our instructions as priests or our entrance into His very presence there is that aspect of the Lord wherein He is "the same yesterday, and today and forever" (Heb. 13 v 8). The gate is low and wide, clearly proclaiming that "whosoever will may come". The door is foursquare telling us that we are approaching that which is perfect and as priests we are the only ones allowed to enter here, and the veil is not only foursquare but has the additional ornament of cherubim about which we shall devote a whole chapter when we come to the Ark and the Mercy Seat.

Like the gate, the veil is supported on four pillars, indeed it is characterised by the number four in the same way that the gate is. The gate has four curtains, four pillars and four details of its construction, blue, purple, scarlet and fine twined linen. The veil is foursquare, has four pillars for support and is also made of blue, purple, scarlet and fine twined linen. We have described these qualities in detail when dealing with the gate but we must certainly ask ourselves why this similarity between gate and veil. The gate presents the Lord as man's approach to God, showing God in a way that man can understand. "God was manifest in the flesh" (1 Tim. 3 v 16). Now we have no difficulty in knowing what the veil represents for our guide book tells us plainly in Hebrews chapter ten verse twenty "... the veil, that is to say, His flesh", another aspect of that body. Note that it is described as "His flesh", no bones, for later on in Herod's temple this veil is to be rent from top to bottom and even in type no bone must be broken.

Some have laid hold of the fact that certain manuscripts omit "broken" in 1 Cor. 11 v 24, "Take eat; this is my body which is broken for you". Certain manuscripts also omit "Take eat" (See Newberry's notes). These brethren may have a point but somehow the breaking of that loaf does seem suggestive. Wonder whether "broken" should be in or no. It is largely due to the statement that the apostle John gives in his gospel (Jno. 19 vv 33-37) quoting from various Old Testament scriptures, Exodus 12 v 46, Numbers 9 v 12 but mainly from Psalm 34 v 20 that we realise the importance of the Lord's body remaining intact especially the legs, for is it not true that the two malefactors, together with each one of us, walked this earth along a very sinful and wayward path? Our legs deserve to be broken, but the Lord? – perfect, never putting one foot wrong, never speaking one word that should not have been said, never withholding a single sentence that would show the love and character of God. "This man hath done nothing amiss" (Luke 23 v 41), in word or deed or walk. His legs must not be broken.

Now turn to Lamentations chapter three and verse four, "My flesh and my skin hath He made old; He hath broken my bones" What!!! Let us write that again, "He hath broken my bones". What is happening? If the soldiers had broken the Lord's legs would John have quoted Lamentations chapter three? The word of God is not like that, it is sure and stedfast. What then can be the answer? Turn on a chapter in Lamentations and you will find this quotation "Her Nazarites were purer than snow, they were whiter than milk, they were more ruddy in body than rubies," (Lam. 4 v 7). Now the word translated "body" in this passage is exactly the same word (estem) as is translated "bones" in chapter three, so that it would be perfectly correct to translate Lamentations 3 v 4 as "He hath broken my body". To be fair it should be pointed out that the word in Psalm 34 v 20 from which John quotes is also etsem, but let us bear in mind that although no actual bone was broken, the breaking of His body did entail the dislocation of His bones for Psalm 22 v 14 tells us "And all my bones are out of joint;" and again in verse 17 "I may tell all my bones:". Surely, although no actual bone was broken, His body, as such, was broken. Now, how about 1 Cor. 11 v 24? In view of the expressiveness of the loaf we prefer to leave "broken" in.

So the veil is quite easy to understand for our guide book tells us that it represents His flesh. Nothing in the Word of God is entirely simple. We are dealing with the things of eternity. Our finite minds will never fully encompass the infinite, but oh the thrill and joy of seeing something in the Word of God for the first time. Even the gospel is like this, all our gospel hymns and all of our evangelists tell the wondrous simple story "Whosoever believeth in Him should not perish, but have everlasting life." (Jno. 3 v 16). Simple? – could not be simpler. Now examine the full text in all its greatness:

| | |
|---|---|
| *For God* | *the greatest person* |
| *So loved* | *the greatest love* |
| *The world* | *the greatest mass of people* |
| *That He gave* | *the greatest action* |
| *His only begotten Son* | *the greatest gift* |
| *That whosoever* | *the greatest opportunity* |
| *Believeth in Him* | *the greatest simplicity* |
| *Should not perish* | *the greatest certainty* |
| *But have everlasting life* | *the greatest possession* |

Now analyse each one of these "greatests". "For God", our Bible begins "In the beginning God . . .", eternal, being before the beginning; we're out of our depth already. The Word of God is simple yet profound. So it is with the veil. It represents His flesh. That is a simple statement. Now attempt to consider it in depth.

The tabernacle was primarily intended for Israel. It was to be constructed so that Jehovah could dwell among His people yet no one could approach Him except the High Priest once a year on the Day of Atonement, and the final barrier that prevented even the priests from entering fully into His presence was the veil and that, so the guide book says, is His flesh. Even in its travels the Ark had to be covered with the veil.

The one thing that prevented the Israelites from understanding the import of all the sacrifices, the tabernacle, the Feasts of Jehovah and all of the Mosaic ritual was this one fact, they could not comprehend or contemplate a Messiah who could suffer at the hand of Jew and gentile and be rejected and crucified. We must not blame the Israelites, it was impossible that it should be otherwise. It was the final straw, God being manifest in flesh (the veil), a suffering Messiah that prevented them, and again we repeat, it could not have been otherwise, from understanding the types and pictures as we see them today. Do we ever thank God that we have been born in this wonderful day of grace?

Even when the Lord was here upon earth and they saw the miracles that He did it was incredible that this was the veil that was to be rent in order to make open the Holy of Holies. They knew this man, He was the carpenter, His mother and His brethren moved freely among them, the veil that was actually amongst them still barred the way. Is it not so with Israel today? Scriptures like Isaiah 53 are interpreted as representing the nation of Israel as Jehovah's servant. The prophetic psalms are understood as simply being the sufferings of David and the other psalmists. Had the Holy Spirit not opened our eyes we could never have looked inside that veil. How many professing Christians simply see the Lord as a good man, even a perfect man, but beyond that little or nothing.

The veil in the tabernacle was never rent from the top to the bottom yet there are indications to show that we are to understand that in type it was. What a puzzler this simple veil is.

That at one time Moses went beyond the veil into the Holy of Holies seems fairly certain for in Exodus 25 v 22 we read "And there I will meet with thee, and I will commune with thee from above the mercy seat, from between the two cherubims which are upon the ark of the testimony, of all things which I will give thee in commandment unto the children of Israel". We do well to note the full import of this instruction for Jehovah says to Moses "I will meet with thee by appointment" (Newberry), not just at any time, and when you keep that appointment I will commune with thee "of all things which I will give thee in commandment unto the children of Israel". In other words these were not occasions when Moses could dash in and out of the Holy of Holies for a quiet chat as it were but these were appointments of Jehovah when He would give Moses further commandments concerning His requirements from the children of Israel. Indeed we might wonder whether Moses actually went into the Holy of Holies for in describing the altar of incense God instructs Moses to beat some of the incense very small "and put it before the testimony in the tabernacle of the congregation (not the Holy of Holies) where I will meet with thee". Perhaps Moses could have heard the voice coming from the mercy seat without actually looking thereon. This almost seems to be borne out by Numbers 7 v 89. "And when Moses was gone into the tabernacle of the congregation (not the Holy of Holies) to speak with Him, then he heard the voice of one speaking unto him from off the mercy seat that was upon the ark of testimony, from between the two cherubims". Certainly in Exodus 29 vv 42 & 43 we read ". . . at the door of the tabernacle of the congregation before the Lord: where I will meet you, to speak there unto thee. And there I will meet with the children of Israel." So this must have been at the very gate of the tabernacle.

Perhaps the sequence was that Jehovah gave Moses extra commandments from between the cherubim making these commandments as it were "ex cathedra" from the very seat of God. Having given these commandments Jehovah tells Moses that He will now meet with him at the gate of the tabernacle and in Leviticus 16 v 2 Jehovah seems to tell Moses that while he was about it "Speak unto Aaron thy brother, that he come not at all times into the holy place within the vail before the mercy seat, which is upon the ark;" (not much ambiguity there) "that he die not:", telling Moses, at the same time, to impress the importance of this upon Aaron by gently reminding him of the death of his two sons. (Lev. 16 v 1).

However we interpret these scriptures it seems pretty obvious that none was allowed into the Holy of Holies save Aaron and that once a year, and Moses did not go before the mercy seat asking God for anything and even although the veil has been rent, neither can we.

Most of us have been brought up to understand the Mercy Seat as a place to which we can flee with all the difficulties of life, our schoolday problems, our exams, whether we should go to university and which one, what girl or boy we should marry, what good job we should get, what nice house we should buy, etc. etc. In fact we tend to regard the Mercy Seat as a sort of heavenly supermarket with no check-outs. Did Moses use it like that, or Aaron, or the children of Israel? Then why should you or why should I?

Hymnbook theology says,

> *Ah, whither could we flee for aid*
> *When tempted, desolate, dismayed?*
> *Or how the host of hell defeat,*
> *Had suffering saints no Mercy Seat?*

Whither indeed!! Should we not pray about all the little details of our lives? Certainly we should but not at the Mercy Seat, it is only the blood and the incense that belong there. But, we may remonstrate, at this time the veil of the tabernacle was not rent in twain. True, in reality it was not, but our guide book tells us to reckon that it was. Look at Hebrews chapter nine. Here the tabernacle is being described and to make sure that we understand that this is the tabernacle in the wilderness the writer points out that the ark contained the tables of the law, Aaron's rod that budded and the golden pot of manna (v 4), whereas when the ark was in the land, the pot of manna and Aaron's rod had been removed. (1 Kings 8 v 9).

The first few verses of Hebrews chapter 9 contain some strange revelations. Having established in chapter eight that he is speaking about law and covenants, he continues this theme into the first verse of chapter nine. This is all about the law, about a new covenant, about a Mercy Seat or propitiatory, about a great High Priest who has gone into the very presence of God with the blood of atonement, and because He has gone there, and because that blood is acceptable in God's sight, then we have these facts as an anchor of hope on the wilderness journey "which hope we have as an anchor of the soul, both sure and stedfast, and which entereth into that within the veil;

whither the forerunner is for us entered, even Jesus, made an high priest for ever after the order of Melchisedec"; (Heb. 6 vv 19 & 20), the kingly priest, one who not only presents the blood of cleansing but one who also requires a throne as king.

Back to Hebrews chapter nine and verse two and here we have the holy place described "wherein was the candlestick, and the table, and the shewbread". What about the altar of incense? Look in verse four. Here the Holy of Holies is described, "which had the golden censer, and the ark of the covenant." But the Holy of Holies only contained the ark, why the censer? Does it not suggest that the veil has been rent? No longer is the incense outside the veil but carried inside so that in chapter ten and verse nineteen it is recorded, "Having therefore, brethren, boldness to enter into the holiest by the blood of Jesus, by a new and living route (not a door) which he hath consecrated for us, through the veil, that is to say, his flesh". We are then told what that way or route is "Let us draw near with a true heart in full assurance of faith". Here is the start of the road. One of the most oft repeated texts in the Bible is "The just shall live by faith". Here we have the gate of the tabernacle, the truth of the gospel which we lay hold of by faith. "Having our hearts sprinkled from an evil conscience". Go on past the brazen altar where we see the lamb of God taking away the sin of the world, on to the laver where we have "our bodies washed with pure water" and as priests we enter the holy place and none but priests can enter here.

Another remarkable feature in Hebrews nine is the reference to two veils (v 3). The priests pass the first veil, and none but they can pass, but are confronted by the second veil which they cannot pass until it is rent in twain. But what about the first veil that is still intact? Only as priests can we go forward. This has to do with the holiness and sanctity of God. Nothing came in here except the blood and the incense. How restrictive. Can I not come near and make my request known to God? Not at the Mercy Seat. You need grace as well as mercy. "For the law was given by Moses, but grace and truth came by Jesus Christ". (Jno. 1 v 17). Our great High Priest is ordained after the order of Melchisedec – the King Priest. He needs not only a Mercy Seat on which to perform His priestly office but He needs a throne from which He can dispense grace and truth. "Let us therefore come boldly unto the throne of grace that we may obtain mercy and find grace to help in time of need." (Heb. 4 v 16).

To understand this more fully it is necessary to consider our pathway as pilgrims in the wilderness and soldiers in the land. We shall therefore have to consider the veil and the Mercy Seat together for they are intimately connected although we shall deal with the ark and the cherubim under separate headings.

CHAPTER TWENTY

# The Veil and The Mercy Seat

Two very similar events occurred in the history of the children of Israel. On leaving Egypt they crossed the Red Sea on dry land. On entering the land they crossed Jordan on dry land. Both equally wonderful and marvellous events. We can understand that when the Red Sea was crossed the children of Israel were jubilant, "Then sang Moses and the children of Israel this song unto the Lord, and spake, saying, I will sing unto the Lord for He hath triumphed gloriously . . ." (Exod. 15 v 1). Yet when, some forty years later, the flooded Jordan (Josh. 3 v 15) was crossed and the water "rose up upon an heap" (Josh. 3 v 16) until the people were clean passed over, there was no singing or rejoicing.

First of all note a remarkable common factor in both events. In Exodus fourteen where we have the story of the crossing of the Red Sea we get the expression "the midst of the sea" repeated five times (vv 16, 22, 23, 27 & 29).

In Joshua chapters three and four where the crossing of the Jordan is recorded we get the expression "the midst of Jordan" mentioned five times (ch. 3 v 17, ch. 4 vv 5, 8, 9 & 10). Now here is a remarkable fact. In Exodus we read "and the children of Israel went into the midst of the sea" but we do not read of them coming out. The last thing we read is "But the children of Israel walked upon dry land in the midst of the sea" (Exod. 14 v 29). Of course they came up out of the midst of the sea but the Holy Spirit does not record it, only by inference. Now when we come to the crossing of Jordan the entrance of the children of Israel into the midst of the river seems to be suppressed whereas the coming up out of the river is emphasised very much (Josh. 4 vv 16, 17, 18 & 19). It looks almost as though we are to understand the picture as if the children of Israel went into the midst of the Red Sea and came up out of the midst of Jordan. In other words this is two aspects of one and the same event.

It was impossible for the Israelites to be in two places at once. They could not cross the Red Sea and enter the wilderness and at the same time cross Jordan and enter the land. Therefore in their history the one event had to follow the other whereas in our experience it is possible for us to be in the wilderness one day and in the land the next and perhaps back in the wilderness the day after. Let us consider each event.

The children of Israel were massed on the shores of the Red Sea. Behind them, and intent on pursuit were the Egyptians complete with chariots and armour ready to take them back to the slavery of Egypt. What they needed was a saviour of some kind although the position seemed desperate. God was their saviour and He caused a strong east wind to blow all night and parted the Red Sea in front of them. All that the Israelites had to do was go over as fast as they could and when the last one was over and the Egyptian host tried to follow the waters returned and Pharaoh's host was engulfed.

No wonder the children of Israel sang and their song was directed, not to Moses, he was only the servant, but to the God of their deliverance. "The Lord for He hath triumphed gloriously". Ask an Israelite where his enemies were and he would tell you that they were dead upon the sea shore. Ask him how many he killed and he would tell you not one. The Lord has done it all.

This corresponds to our salvation. We have been delivered from Satan's bondage, the world is behind us, we are journeying towards a land of promise and the Lord has done it all. The picture is of the Lord dying for us, He did it all. No wonder the children of Israel sang, no wonder we rejoice in our new found salvation. But that rejoicing is ephemeral, the wilderness is before us. There is no escape for there are lessons that we must learn on the journey that we cannot learn elsewhere. Beware of the "Glory, hallelujah" Christians; they're still on the bank of the Red Sea; they know nothing of the journeying for that journey is rough. Look at the children of Israel. No one over twenty reached the end of that journey except Caleb and Joshua. Food was short, water was short. The people were discouraged and murmured. God had to punish and chasten them. Bitter were the lessons they were taught. So bitter that they wanted to go back to Egypt but that was impossible, the Red Sea was back in place again. Whether they liked it or not they were Jehovah's people. God provided food for them and gave them water from the rock but they lusted after the flesh, the cucumbers, the melons, the leeks, the onions and the garlic of Egypt. Nothing wrong with these foods, perhaps they are among the most health giving foods for the natural man. The trouble was that they were Egypt's food. They could not go running to the Mercy Seat and ask for these things and neither can we on our wilderness journey. We cannot ask God for a better car, a new house, a handsome husband etc, these are Egypt's food. The Lord will provide that which is good for us. A hard lesson, an almost impossible lesson and there is many another like it on the wilderness journey. The answer is obvious and easy, we'll join the "hallelujah Christians". We'll stay by the Red Sea. If you're really saved you won't; read Hebrews 12 vv 5-8. If you're a son then God will correct and chasten for He's a good father and He wants to perfect us that we might show forth His praise and that He might bless us with all spiritual blessings. We might say in our hearts that we will not go into the wilderness. If you belong to the Lord you have no option for the Lord himself "was in all points tested like as we are" (Heb. 4 v 15) yet He came through that testing without sin, but what does Mark 1 v 12 & 13 say? "And immediately the Spirit driveth him into the wilderness. And he was there in the wilderness forty days, tempted of Satan;" There He was tempted with the world when the devil took Him up into an exceeding high mountain and showed and offered Him the glory of the things of the world (Matt. 4 v 8). He was tempted with the flesh for when He was hungry Satan suggested that He should satisfy that hunger by turning stones into bread (Matt. 4 v 3). He was tempted by the devil challenging His authority to be the Son of God (Matt. 4 vv 5 & 6). "It is the way the Master went, should not the servant tread it still?"

There is only way out of the wilderness, learn its lessons and become a good soldier of Jesus Christ ready to go into battle in the land, but always remember this, even while you are in the wilderness there is that knowledge that Jehovah is in the midst of His people. The pillar of cloud by day and the fire by night are unmistakable, resting above the Mercy Seat, acting as an anchor for the soul and a constant hope "Which hope we have as an anchor of the soul, both sure and stedfast, and which entereth into that within the veil; whither the forerunner is for us entered, even Jesus, made an high priest for ever after the order of Melchisedec". (Heb. 6 vv 19 & 20).

We now come to the crossing of Jordan. It is often pointed out that contrary to what some hymnologists and songwriters assert, Jordan is not a picture of death and Canaan is not a picture of heaven. This is only a half truth. Jordan is a picture of death, not of physical death but rather the mortification of the old nature and Canaan is not a direct picture of heaven but rather that realm in the heavenlies where "we wrestle not against flesh and blood, but against principalities, against powers, against the rulers of the darkness of this world, against spiritual wickedness in high places." (Eph. 6 v 12), and the apostle says that to do this we must put on the whole armour of God, not part of it. If one item is missing then we are vulnerable. There is only one place where we have no armour and that is on the back. There can be no running away, there is no armour against that, we will be struck down. Tempting as it is we must not enter into the details of the Christian warfare. Already we have wandered perhaps too far from the tabernacle. Let us then pick out the salient features concerning the crossing of Jordan as they throw light on the veil and the Mercy Seat. Note first of all that the children of Israel are kept at a distance from the Mercy Seat (Josh. 3 v 4). The ark was still the evidence of the presence of Jehovah in the midst of His people. The next thing to note is that each tribe was identified with a man (Josh. 4 v 2). Next, each of the twelve men were to be identified with a stone (Josh. 4 v 3). Twelve stones were to be taken out of the midst of Jordan and set up on the bank as a testimony to the fact that the children of Israel had crossed Jordan. Joshua also took twelve stones and put them into the midst of Jordan.

What is the picture? Every tribe identified with a man. Every man identified with an old stone and a new stone taken up out of Jordan and a testimony established. Is there not a distinct parallel here with Romans chapter six? "Buried with Him (the stones were put where the priests' feet rested) (Josh. 4 v 9) by baptism into death:" "raised up from the dead by the glory of the Father, even so we also should walk in the newness of life etc." (Rom. 6 v 4).

The Red Sea was a picture of Christ dying for us, Jordan is a picture of us dying with Christ. A painful process, no singing, we've got to be equipped as soldiers. The discipline, although motivated by love, is strict. Have a look at the next chapter, chapter five and verse two, "Make thee sharp knives, and circumcise again the children of Israel the second time".

Having reckoned the old nature dead, mortifying his deeds (for we will not get rid of him this side of the glory) we are in a position to fight the battles in the land. As long as we are obedient we shall triumph in the most wonderful and extraordinary ways (Jericho). If we disobey, then it's failure for us and also for our company (Ai). How does this affect us and help us to understand the Mercy Seat? During the wilderness journey the pillar of fire and the cloud stationary above the ark are our sure hope and and stay but we cannot get near for our thoughts and minds are occupied often with the things of Egypt. Sometimes the Lord will listen to our rebellious cries and our lusts but the things of Egypt always bring sorrow in their train. It was so with the Israelites and so it will be with you and me.

Have a look at someone who has crossed the wilderness on a long and painful journey. The story is told in 1 Kings chapter 10. A queen came from a great distance; the Holy Spirit, through Matthew and Luke (Matt. 12 v 42: Luke 11 v 31) describes her journey as from "the uttermost parts of the earth", and in Acts chapter eight we read of a fellow countryman of hers, the Ethiopian eunuch, and Phillip was sent to the way that ran from Jerusalem to Gaza "which is desert" and if we trace the route from Ethiopia to Jerusalem we find that best part of it is wilderness and desert. Why then did this woman cross this inhospitable land? She had heard of a King, not a priest, but a king who excelled all others and she was therefore prepared to go through the wilderness, doubtless learning many hard lessons on the way but coming at last to the temple? No! To the Mercy Seat? No! but to a throne. She had passed through the wilderness. Was it worth it? Read 1 Kings 10. What sort of throne was this? "And Solomon told her all her questions ..." (v3). "And King Solomon gave unto the queen of Sheba all her desire, whatsoever she asked, beside that which Solomon gave her of his royal bounty" (v 13). How shall we describe that throne? Shall we settle for a throne of grace? "Let us therefore come boldly unto the throne of grace, that we may obtain mercy (not only mercy but grace) and find grace to help in time of need". (Heb. 4 v 16).

Let us not imagine that the throne excels the Mercy Seat. We cannot approach the throne until we learn the lesson of the Mercy Seat. The Mercy Seat shows us what we are saved from, the law and all of its penalties. The throne shows us what we are saved to, our inheritance in glory.

We have only dealt with the Mercy Seat as connected with the veil. Let us go inside the Holy of Holies and we shall see the Mercy Seat as connected with the ark.

# CHAPTER TWENTY-ONE

# The Ark and The Mercy Seat
## "I AM."

As we pass through the veil you will have noticed that at the heading of this chapter we put the title "I AM". Perhaps this makes an eigth I AM but really it is the embodiment of all. This was the name by which Jehovah chose to reveal Himself to the children of Israel in Exodus 3 vv 14 & 15, "I AM hath sent me unto you . . . the Lord God of your fathers, the God of Abraham, the God of Isaac, and the God of Jacob hath sent me unto you." Small wonder that the place that we now enter is called the Holy of Holies.

Here is the ark, a chest or box measuring one and one half cubits wide, one and one half cubits high and two and one half cubits long. It was made of shittim wood and completely covered inside and outside with gold. As we come closer and enter into the most holy place so the full understanding of what is before us becomes more and more difficult. Many books and articles have been written about the Ark, the Mercy Seat and the Cherubim but the subject has never been, and can never be exhausted. We only understand and see a little part for so great is the One of whom it all speaks that the Holy Spirit records in Matt. 11 v 27, "No man knoweth the Son, but the Father". This does not mean that we should cease to think or ponder about Him for we often draw attention to the apostle Paul's words, "That I might know Him", but what it does mean is that even the greatest apostle could not comprehend the Son, so great is He. When the Lord asked Peter in Matt. 16 vv 15-17 to identify Him, Peter said, "Thou art the Christ, the Son of the living God", and the Lord's response was, "Flesh and blood hath not revealed it unto thee, but my Father which is in heaven". There is no other way of knowing anything about the Son except by revelation. How often does theological scholarship fall down on this, accepting the wisdom of the world in its efforts to understand "Christ the power of God, and the wisdom of God" (1 Cor. 1 v 24). Let these thoughts then act rather as pegs upon which you can hang your own experience and understanding. Maybe some of the pegs you will reject. It matters little so long as it serves to magnify Him.

One of the most important features of the Ark was the crown of gold, "And thou shalt make upon it a crown of gold round about" (Exod. 25 v 11). After the dimensions and the material this is the first detail to which we are directed. May we again draw attention to the fact that these crowns on the ark, the altar of incense and the table of shewbread, were not diadems or regal crowns but were mouldings or edges erected round the top circumference of the article concerned in order to prevent anything placed thereon from falling or becoming dislodged. The table had the shewbread upon it, the golden altar was for the unique incense. How about the ark?

Nothing small like the incense, nothing multiple like the loaves but one solid slab of gold that completely covered the ark and was held firmly in position by that crown of gold. This was the propitiatory or mercyseat made of pure gold – no wood, because Jehovah must look upon that blood as ". . . the blood of Christ, who through the eternal Spirit offered himself without spot to God," (Heb. 9 v 14). We are taken back into a realm that we cannot understand, "the eternal Spirit", when the Lord said, "Lo I come to do thy will, O God" (Heb. 10 v 9), "The lamb slain from the foundation of the world" (Rev. 13 v 8), not in AD 33 or thereabouts but in the beginning when God created the heavens and the earth. Selah! Think about that! and we are lost in the eternal counsels and purposes of God. One thing we do know for certain. That lid, that covering, that Mercy Seat is firmly held in position by the crown round about. But it was not only on the Mercy Seat that the blood had to be put by the High Priest on the day of atonement, it also had to be sprinkled before the Mercy Seat. "And he (Aaron) shall take of the blood of the bullock, and sprinkle it with his finger upon the mercy seat eastward; and before the mercy seat shall he sprinkle of the blood with his finger seven times" (Lev. 16 v 14). "Then shall he kill the goat . . . and do with that blood as he did with the blood of the bullock" (v 15). The blood must be sprinkled on the earth, but so also has been the blood of many of the Lord's servants. "For they have shed the blood of saints and prophets, and thou hast given them blood to drink; for they are worthy." (Rev. 16 v 6). But the Lord was no ordinary prophet (Acts 7 v 37) and the Lord was no ordinary servant (Isa. 52 vv 13-15). Let us take a brief look at the High Priest as he comes into the Holy of Holies on the day of atonement.

Moses is told to tell Aaron that he must only come into the Holy of Holies once a year. A gentle reminder concerning the death of his two sons (Lev. 16 v 1) emphasises the sanctity of the occasion implying that Aaron was walking a tightrope of death if he put one foot wrong. Furthermore he was not even to be allowed to look upon the mercy seat "and he shall put the incense upon the fire before the Lord, that the cloud of the incense may cover the mercy seat that is upon the testimony, that he die not" (Lev. 16 v 13). No eye may look upon that blood. It is for Jehovah alone, "When I see the blood, I will pass over" (Exod. 12 v 13). Now observe carefully what Aaron has to do. He has to take "a young bullock for a sin offering, and a ram for a burnt offering". (Lev. 16 v 3). Now the bullock was the serving animal in Israel, it drew the carts and pulled the plough. The ram is the animal that once it sets its mind on a target is blind to all other considerations and goes through come what may, hence the battering ram. May we suggest that these characteristics are reflected in the various sacrifices. Aaron must take the blood of the bullock, in his case to make an atonement for his own sins and the sins of his house. Now we must make ourselves perfectly clear here in order that we should not be misunderstood. Let us state categorically and clearly that the Lord was absolutely and perfectly sinless. Peter, the man of action, says, "He did no sin" (1 Pet. 2 v 22), Paul, the man of the intellect, says He "knew no sin" (2 Cor. 5 v 21) and John, the man of the heart, says, "In Him is no sin" (1 Jno. 3 v 5). Let there be no doubt about this. "For such an high priest . . . is holy, harmless, undefiled, separate from sinners, and made higher than the heavens" (Heb. 7 v 26). We trust we have made that perfectly clear, but . . . as the willing servant of Jehovah – the blood of the bullock – He takes primarily Israel's sins and bears them as His own. This is part of the message of Isaiah 53 for God raises the subject of His servant in chapter 52 and continues, "Surely He hath borne our griefs, and carried our sorrows" (v 4) "And the Lord hath laid on Him the iniquity of us all" (v 6) "And He bare the sin of many" (v 12) and the apostle Peter takes up this same scripture in 1 Peter 2 vv 24 & 25, "who His own self bare our sins in His own body on the tree . . . by whose stripes ye were healed" and Paul appears to go even further when he says, "For he hath made Him to be sin for us, who knew no sin, that we might be made the righteousness of God in Him" (2 Cor. 5 v 21). As the hymn writer says, "He took my sins and my sorrows and made them His very own". Who can imagine the spiritual anguish of the Lord when in effect He said to His Father, "Take the sins of Barabbas and if needs be put these to my account" and the thief on the cross "add these thereto" and your sins my brother, my sister and mine also which are weighty enough in themselves – "Oh what a load was thine to bear alone in that dark hour, Our sins in all their terror there, God's wrath and Satan's power." Selah! Think of that.

The lessons of the mercy seat are many and varied. None will ever fathom them all this side of the glory and perhaps it will take all of eternity to understand all of its teaching. Surely one of the greatest truths concerns the "ark of the covenant" (Num. 10 v 33, 14 v 44, Deut. 10 v 8, 31 v 9, 31 vv 25 & 26, etc. etc.) and the expression is also taken up in the New Testament (Heb. 9 v 4). God is a covenant-making God. He made a covenant with Noah that He would not flood the world again (Gen. 9 vv 8-11). God made a covenant with Abram, promising his seed a great inheritance (Gen. 15 vv 18 & 19). He established this covenant with Isaac (Gen. 17 v 9) and remembers this covenant in Egypt when "God heard their groaning, and God remembered his covenant with Abraham, with Isaac, and with Jacob". (Exod. 2 v 24). All of these covenants were one-sided, God undertaking to bless without any obligation on the part of man.

Now God brings in a new covenant, one in which He will confer enormous blessings upon Israel but in return there must be complete obedience otherwise the dire consequences of Leviticus 26 would fall upon the people – and they did. But even then Jehovah remembered His former covenants to Jacob, Isaac and Abraham (Lev. 26 vv 40-45). This covenant of the law is the most stringent of all of the Old Testament covenants. The apostle Paul points out, in the early chapters of the Roman epistle, how that it is binding upon both Jew and Gentile for says he, "there is no difference; for all have sinned, and come short of the glory of God." (Rom. 3 vv 22 & 23). The tables of stone, the ten commandments, written by God's own hand spell the death sentence for every man, woman and child, an eternal death sentence for twice over in the Old Testament God says "the soul that sinneth it shall die" (Ezek. 18 vv 4 & 20) and the New Testament endorses this thought saying "the wages of sin is death" (Rom. 6 v 23). The inference is obvious. Are we, each one of us, going to die? Then in God's sight we have broken this great covenant, we are sinners and eternal death is our due. Now look again at the "ark of the covenant". The Lord Jesus fulfilled the law, met every requirement, and speaking as a man it is as though He contained it within Himself even as the tables of the law were contained in the ark and finally He put the lid on it and sealed it with His blood, so that God (in type) could not see or look upon the tables of condemnation. He had to look upon the "Propitiatory", the "Mercy Seat" and that was sprinkled with the blood of the new covenant, and we call this to mind when we remember the Lord, "This cup is the new covenant (testament) in my blood" (Luke 22 v 20).

Return again to the High Priest on the day of atonement. He had to dip his finger in the blood of the bullock and sprinkle it upon the mercy seat eastward. In order to sprinkle the blood from his finger the High Priest had to fully immerse that finger. It was not just a question of wetting the point and wiping it on the mercy seat, the blood had to be running off of his finger so that he could sprinkle it. He had to sprinkle it eastward upon the mercy seat. What does all of this teach us? That the High Priest had to be fully identified with that blood, that the supply was plentiful and sufficient, but why eastward? The gate of the tabernacle was at the eastern end, therefore the entrance to the holy place and also into the Holy of Holies must have been from the east. In entering the most Holy Place and approaching the ark, the high priest must have been travelling away from the east and facing west. It follows that as the High Priest was facing west, if he sprinkled the blood on the mercy seat eastward he must have been drawing his finger towards himself, thus further identifying himself with the blood. What does our guide book say? "Who bore our sins on the tree"? No! "Who His own self bore our sins on the tree"? No! "Who His own self bore our sins, in His own body on the tree" Yes! The double identification, "His own self", "His own body" – the high priest, his finger steeped in the blood ("His own self"), drawing his finger towards himself ("His own body"). But the lessons do not stop there.

The High Priest had also to sprinkle the blood seven times before the ark, once on the mercy seat then seven times on the earth. We have already seen how this can teach us the lesson that the blood was not only that of the Son of God but also the Son of Man. This is the day of atonement, the root of the word is "to cover with pitch", to seal it up, to make expiation or to cancel. Nothing to do with "at one ment", another of these incorrect clichés, but rather a wiping out of things that were wrong so that a holy God could dwell in the midst of His people. Let us go back to the beginning. Adam sinned and so death passed upon all men. To expiate this the last Adam must die and His blood be presented before Jehovah as the continual evidence of His death. The blood must be sprinkled once upon the mercy seat. But Adam did not die physically for some hundreds of years. The first man to die was murdered. Cain rose up and slew his brother Abel and the accusation that God levelled against him was "The voice of thy brother's blood crieth unto me from the ground". God cursed the ground first of all because Adam sinned (Gen. 3 vv 17 & 18) then He cursed the ground again because "it opened her mouth to receive thy brother's blood". The prime reason for capital punishment in the Bible was not the principle of "an eye for an eye and a tooth for a tooth", that came later. The prime reason was given to Noah, "Whoso sheddeth man's blood, by man shall his blood be shed: for in the image of God made He man." (Gen. 9 v 6). Violence to the image meant an affront to God himself. Think of all the blood that has been spilled and soaked into the earth since then. All the violence among men, all the wars, all the exterminations in concentration camps, blood! blood! blood! spilled upon the earth and every drop an affront to the Creator. This must be atoned for if a Holy God is to put His foot upon the earth and dwell among His people. But how? The blood of bulls and of goats could not avail, they only give us a type, "But," says the writer to the Hebrews, "Ye are come . . . to Jesus the mediator of the new covenant" (there it is, the old covenant has been fulfilled, annulled, and is safely locked within the ark) "and to the blood of sprinkling" (seven times before the mercy seat) "that speaketh better things than that of Abel" (Heb. 12 vv 22-24). Abel's blood cried for vengeance but the Lord "made peace through the blood of His cross, by him to reconcile all things unto Himself; by Him, I say, whether they be things in earth, or things in heaven" (Col. 1 v 20). "Full atonement can it be? Hallelujah, what a Saviour".

The blood of the ram that Aaron took is not sprinkled on and before the ark. The ram here is to be a burnt offering, wholly for God, that God may see the eternal purposes being carried out in full perfection. In spite of Satan's efforts to thwart the divine will, right from the garden of Eden to the cross of Calvary, God's purposes, His plan has never wavered and the ram is offered as a burnt offering, wholly to God, a sweet-smelling savour of the one who "set His face to go to Jerusalem" (Luke 9 v 51).

*"Unmoved by Satan's subtle wiles or suffering shame and loss;*
*That path uncheered by earthly smiles, led only to the cross".*

But what of the goat? One of the two goats was to be the scapegoat, the other Aaron was to "kill the goat of the sin offering, that is for the people, and bring his blood within the veil, and do with that blood as he did with the blood of the bullock, and sprinkle it upon the mercy seat and before the mercy seat" (Lev. 16 v 15).

Now the goat is the sure-footed animal and tells us that not only are the purposes of God certain and sure (the ram) but that each step will be meticulously carried out. The process is crystal-lised in John 10 and thirty-five "the scripture cannot be broken" and time and time again in the gospels we read "that the scripture might be fulfilled" (Jno. 13 v 18, 17 v 12, 19 v 24, 19 v 28 and simi-lar such phrases). This is the sure-footed goat, and its blood must be taken into the holiest for not only is the atonement made by Jehovah's servant (the bullock) but by His obedient servant, the one who fulfilled the law in every detail. The bullock was for the High Priest and his household, perhaps speaking to us primarily of the Jewish nation. The goat was for the people, "whosoever will". The purpose has been meticulously carried out and "He which hath begun a good work in you will perform (or perfect) it until the day of Jesus Christ" (Phil. 1 v 6).

One other interesting feature about the ark is the rings and staves. Moses was told to cast four rings of gold, one for each corner of the ark and through these rings staves were to be put in order that it might be carried. How long were the staves and along which sides of the ark did they run, the short sides or the long sides? Most illustrations show them on the long sides which means that in transit one of the cherubs would be travelling backwards – somehow that hardly seems right (the priestly nose again). We only find part of the answer in the book of Exodus. How like the Word of God that is. We do not find the whole of the story of creation in Genesis chapter one but we find an odd verse here and there which helps us to understand the whole. How apt were the Lord's words, "Search the scriptures" (Jno. 5 v 39), and it was the obedience to this command that made the Jews of Berea more noble than those of Thessalonica and led to their belief in the apostles' message. (Acts 17 vv 10-12).

Now we know that the Holy of Holies was a cube ten cubits by ten cubits by ten cubits. We also know that the staves were not to be taken from the ark (Exod. 25 v 15) and therefore in order to fit into the most Holy Place the staves could not have been more than ten cubits long, but they could have been a lot shorter.

Now this selfsame ark was carried into Solomon's temple and the ark ceased from its travelling and came to rest and the staves were drawn out. We then read this cryptic verse, "And they drew out the staves, that the ends of the staves were seen out in the holy place before the oracle, and they were not seen without: and there they are unto this day" (1 Kings 8 v 8). Obviously things are going to get a bit complicated, so stick with it.

We know that Solomon made two large cherubim that spanned the oracle or most holy place (1 Kings 6 vv 23-27) and he set these "in the midst of the house" (1 Kings 6 v 27). Now when the ark was brought in it was placed "under the wings of the cherubim" (1 Kings 8 v 6), therefore the ark must have been placed in the centre of the Holy of Holies. Which way round was it to be? With the short side facing the entrance, or the long side?

The day of atonement still had to be celebrated every year and therefore the High Priest would have to approach the ark in order to sprinkle the blood of the bullock and the goat on the mercy seat. If the ark was end-on to the entrance the High Priest would not be able to go straight ahead and perform this task because one of the cherubs on the mercy seat would be in the way, and in view of the fact that the High Priest could hardly see where he was going because of the smoke from the incense (Lev. 16 v 13) it would seem logical and sensible to assume that the ark was placed crosswise in the oracle, that is with its long side parallel to the entrance. Now we know that the oracle was twenty cubits by twenty cubits by twenty cubits (1 Kings 6 v 20). Let us return to our cryptic verse in 1 Kings 8 v 8, "And they drew out the staves that the ends of the staves were seen out in the holy place before the oracle, and they were not seen without: and there they are unto this day". Now visualise this sequence of events. The ark is in the centre of the oracle and therefore there is slightly less than ten cubits between the front of the ark and the entrance, to be exact it would be nine and one quarter cubits, (half of the oracle, ten cubits, less half of the ark, three quarters of a cubit). Suppose the staves were ten cubits in length, just long enough to fit into the Holy of Holies in the tabernacle, and the staves were fixed in rings on the short side of the ark, that is at right angles to the entrance and we wished to withdraw those staves. All would go well until we came to the last three quarters of a cubit for we should find that we have run out of space between the front of the ark and the entrance (9¼ cubits). We therefore poke the ends of the staves out past the entrance and having cleared the rings in the ark we bring them back in again and lay them on the floor beside the ark where the High Priest will not be in danger of tripping over them on the day of atonement. Now take our cryptic verse, "And they drew out the staves, that the ends of the staves were seen out in the holy place before the oracle (that is as they were clearing the rings on the ark) and they were not seen without; (that is they were taken back and laid beside the ark) and there they are unto this day." (1 Kings 8 v 8). It took a lot of explaining but we got there in the end. Now what useful information does this tell us?

Firstly the staves ran along the short sides of the ark and not along the longer sides as they are usually shown. Hence one cherub did not have to travel backwards but they were both travelling sideways on equal terms with their faces towards the mercy seat. Secondly that the staves would have been two and a half cubits apart and therefore it would not have been practical for just two Levites to carry the ark because the rings being about one and a half cubits from the ground (2'3") it would be necessary for the ark to be carried at shoulder height and no Levite was two and a half cubits broad (3'9"), showing once again that God regarded these things as weighty matters irrespective of what man may think. Thirdly the poles being about ten cubits long would ensure that even the Levite should not come too near the ark, always there was the distance for the Kohathite, because these things were most holy. (Num. 4 v 15, Josh. 3 v 4).

These staves present us with yet another problem. Exodus twenty-five and verse fifteen tells us that "The staves shall be in the rings of the ark: they shall not be taken from it." We can see the sense of this in the tabernacle. The ark had to be portable the same as the rest of the furniture, and Moses had to obey every instruction explicitly. All is well until we come to Numbers 4 v 6 where Aaron and his two sons (Nadab and Abihu being dead) have to cover the ark ready for the Kohathites to carry it and here we read "and shall put in the staves thereof." How could Aaron and his sons have put in the staves if they were never to be removed? Think of what has just happened (Num. 4 vv 5 & 6). Aaron and his two sons, just three men, had to unfasten the veil which was a heavy curtain measuring ten cubits by ten cubits (15' x 15') and take this veil and cover the ark with it. Then they must put on a covering of badgers skins, a heavy covering and difficult for just three men (and Aaron could not have been a young man). On top of that a cloth wholly of blue had to be spread. Now the chances are that in dragging these coverings over the ark, especially the stiffish badgers skins, the staves would be dislodged from their central position without actually being removed from the ark and therefore the last operation to be performed by Aaron and his sons was to see that everything was back to normal and "put in (place) the staves thereof".

CHAPTER TWENTY-TWO

# The Contents of the Ark

During the wilderness journey the ark contained three things; the tables of the law, the golden pot of manna and Aaron's rod that budded. The tables of the law speak to us of the righteous requirements of Jehovah from men, showing what man ought to be and is not. These tables must be contained in the ark for they condemn every man, except one, for the Lord was perfect, fulfilling every jot and tittle of the law and, as it were, containing it within Himself and this could only be accomplished by the placing of the blood-stained mercy seat as a lid upon the ark. All of the children of Israel knew what was in the ark but they had to accept it by faith for to look upon the tables of the law spelt condemnation and death.

We can now understand the lesson of 1 Sam. 6 vv 15-21 when fifty thousand and seventy men were slain. These men were not Philistines but men of Judah. They should have known what was in the ark without having to look, for "the just shall live by faith". Follow the picture through. If we take the lid off the ark we only have condemnation. We see the perfection of the Lord, we see what man should be, offending in neither word nor deed and the result? We have come short, hence condemnation. All have sinned, all are guilty.

Replace the lid of the ark, the blood-stained mercy seat. Accept the contents by faith and look upon that blood and see that "there is therefore now no condemnation to them which are in Christ Jesus." (Rom. 8 v 1).

Let us now consider the golden pot of manna. The account is given to us in Exodus 16 vv 33-end and in particular do not forget the last verse, "Now an omer is the tenth part of an ephah".

The manna was God's bread for His earthly people and Moses tells the children of Israel in Deuteronomy 8 v 3 that the Lord "fed thee with manna, which thou knewest not, neither did thy fathers know; that He might make thee know that man doth not live by bread only, but by every word that proceedeth out of the mouth of the Lord doth man live." The Lord Jesus endorsed this statement by using it to confound Satan in the wilderness of temptation. From this scripture we can clearly see that the manna is a picture of the word of God which should be the daily food of His people.

What did the children of Israel do to earn or merit this food? Nothing – almost less than nothing for they grumbled and murmured against God and His servant Moses. It is therefore apparent that the word of God is not given to us because we deserve it but that this provision is entirely of God's love and grace. Furthermore it was while the people slept that God provided the next day's food. What a wonderful thought this is. While we are asleep and unconscious God is preparing our food and sustenance for the work and trials of the morrow if only we will get up early and gather God's provision. The supply of manna did not fail for the whole of the forty years of Israel's wanderings. They were a rebellious and oftentimes stiffnecked people, yet their daily provision was always there. God was committed to bring them home to Canaan. How glorious is the thought that the Lord is committed to bring us safe to our journey's end and that in spite of ourselves "He which hath begun a good work in you will perfect it until the day of Jesus Christ." (Phil. 1 v 6-margin).

The word 'manna' conveys the meaning 'what is it?' and this is evidenced by the children of Israel "for they wist not what it was" (Exod. 16 v 15). So is the word of God to unbelieving man. He cannot see or understand how the word of God can be bread to anyone. Indeed it is a mystery even to believers, yet we know by experience that this book, the word of God, is unlike any other book. It lives and gives life and sustenance.

The manna had to be gathered early, the first thing in the morning. Now look at Mark 1 v 35, "And in the morning, rising up a great while before day, He went out, and departed into a solitary place, and there prayed." One of those little glimpses into the private life of the Son of God when He was here upon earth. If He needed to rise early and get alone with His Father, how about you and me? We shall not be able to face the day successfully without our supply of manna. This injunction applies not only to the sheep in the 'little flock' but even more so to the 'under shepherds'. The low state of many assemblies cannot be attributed to the sheep but to those who have the oversight. If they are not grounded in the word of God how can they be 'apt to teach'? Do not take the position of an elder lightly for we must all appear before the judgment seat of Christ.

Now consider what the manna was like, and in reading Exod. 16 v 31 compare it with Num. 11 vv 4-9. In Exodus the manna is pure and white, unsullied. Its taste is sweet as honey and the children of Israel gather it and perform the simple operations of cooking (v 23). In Numbers the manna is no longer pure white but is the colour of bdellium, cloudy, off white as either a pearl or amber, and its taste is no longer sweet as honey but is that of fresh oil and the people gather it, grind it in mills, beat it in a mortar, bake it in pans and make cakes of it; no longer a simple cooking operation but they beat and bash it almost out of recognition and in the process it loses its sweetness and tastes like fresh oil. What has happened? Why the change? The 'mixed multitude' that was among them fell a-lusting after Egypt. We can read about this company in Exod. 12 v 38. Brethren, beware of the 'mixed multitude', in our assemblies. They are those who travel with us, look like us, speak like us, and often act like us, but at heart they are not one with us. Perhaps it would be true to say that every assembly has its 'mixed multitude' and as soon as the way gets tough, or even before, they start to lust after the things of the world. Call to mind the words of the apostle John in his first epistle, "Love not the world, neither the things that are in the world. If any man love the world, the love of the Father is not in him." (1 Jno. 2 v 15), and do not take these words out of context but read the rest of the chapter. As soon as we start lusting after the things of the world we begin to grind and beat the word of God, trying to tell ourselves that portions of scripture that do not encourage us in our wayward actions are irrelevant under today's conditions or that they were just the personal opinions of Paul or John. Brethren, the manna has become tarnished. It is no longer pure white. It is still the word of God, we cannot dispute that, the taste of fresh oil is still there but it is no longer sweet as honey and before long the cry will go up "our soul loatheth this light food". Do not listen to, or follow after the 'mixed multitude', remember "that the friendship of the world is enmity with God, whosoever therefore will be a friend of the world is the enemy of God." (Jas. 4 v 4). Guard against joining the 'mixed multitude' with one foot in the assembly and one in the world. As such you will be a danger to yourself and, more important still, a danger to the people of God. The manna was to be collected fresh every day and there was a set portion for each Israelite. When the daily gathering was measured with an omer "he that gathered much had nothing over, and he that gathered little had no lack." (Exod. 16 v 18). How meticulous are these Old Testament types. The Christian lives a day at a time and should "Take no anxious thought for the morrow: for the morrow shall take thought for the things of itself. Sufficient unto the day is the evil thereof." (Matt. 6 v 34-margin – Newberry), and remember that the Lord, in teaching His disciples to pray, encouraged them to make this request, "Give us this day our daily bread" (Matt. 6 v 11) Every saint should gather his daily portion and it will be sufficient for the needs of the day. It is useless for us to point to gifted brethren and bemoan the fact that we could never see the things that they see in the word of God. That gifted brother can only make good to his soul his meted omer of food and if we feel that we are numbered among that company who 'gather little', provided we do it diligently, early in the morning, before the heat of the day, then the Lord will ensure that we have our omer of manna.

Now Moses issues an instruction to the children of Israel, an instruction that did not originate with Moses but was a direct command of the Lord. The Israelites were to take an omer of manna to be kept for future generations to "see the bread wherewith I (the Lord) have fed you in the wilderness" (Exod. 16 v 32). There are several wonderful things about this command especially when we consider the manna as a type of the living bread which came down from heaven. (Jno. 6). It rested on the desert floor and was the daily portion of God's people, yet one measured portion was to be taken up as a memorial. There would be no corruption in it with the passing of time and it was never to be eaten but was there as a memorial for the people to see. The Living Bread, the Lord himself, came from heaven right down to the desert floor. He humbled himself, taking the form of a servant, mingling with the dust of humanity the He might be the food for His people but God has taken that same One and raised Him to the heights of glory. It is not a mistake that Moses does not record that the omer of manna was put in a golden pot and that it was subsequently placed inside the ark of the covenant. These facts were left for Paul in the ninth chapter of the epistle to the Hebrews. Why? The full facts of the wonder of the manna could not be revealed in the Old Testament. No Israelite could in any wise have appreciated that in eating manna in the wilderness he was prefiguring the advent of the Messiah, the feeding on the Son of God or the significance of laying up a pot of manna before the Lord, but when we come to the New Testament we can sing,

> *"How wonderful that Thou the Son hast come*
> *And here for us as Son of Man hast died."*

Now consider the impact of Hebrews chapter nine. The Lord of Glory has come down to earth and provided His flesh as meat and His blood as drink for His people - what manna, what costly manna. "Wherefore God also hath highly exalted Him, and given Him a name that is above every name: that at the name of Jesus every knee should bow." (Phil. 2 vv 9 & 10). Here is the omer of manna in the golden pot, the risen Lord glorified in the presence of the Father – "Behold, I am alive for evermore" (Rev. 1 v 18), the incorruptible manna, "Thou wilt not leave my soul in hell neither wilt Thou suffer Thine Holy One to see corruption" (Acts 2 v 27). There was only one item of shittim wood (a picture of humanity) that went from the tabernacle of the desert into the glory of the temple in Jerusalem and that was the ark; surely a wonderful picture of the Lord, the only perfect humanity that could go unchanged into glory. The Lord is there in the glory for us to see but we cannot see Him. If only we could how our faith would be strengthened. Oh my brother, my sister, if faith gives place to sight it ceases to be faith, and the just shall live by faith. We must see the Lord in glory in the same way that the children of Israel saw the pot of manna for this was God's intention in commanding them to lay up an omer of manna, for it was "to be kept for your generations; that they may SEE the bread wherewith I have fed you in the wilderness" (Exod. 16 v 32). But according to Hebrews chapter nine that pot of manna was placed inside the ark and there was only one person (apart from the occasions when it was being transported) who could approach the ark and that was the High Priest on the day of atonement and even then his vision was clouded by the smoke of the incense and no one, not even the High Priest, dare look inside that ark. How then could the children of Israel possibly know that the omer of manna was laid up before the Lord? Only one way. They had the daily evidence that God fed them in a miraculous and wonderful way every morning, and because they had the practical experience of eating the daily manna they had no difficulty in knowing that the golden pot was in the sanctuary. How about us? Have a look at John 6 v 53, "Except ye eat the flesh of the Son of Man, and drink His blood, ye have no life in you." Now the Lord is not saying that eating His flesh and drinking His blood gives life. He has already told us how to obtain that life, "He that believeth on Me hath everlasting life" (Jno. 6 v 47). There are no strings attached. Life comes from believing in Him, but the evidence that we have that life is that we feed upon the manna. If we eat and feed upon that Living Bread "we shall live for ever" (v 51), because we are a redeemed people. Eating the manna in the wilderness did not make a man an Israelite. It was because a man was an Israelite, because he had been redeemed, that God provided him with his daily bread. If you and I find that we must read the word of God – the portion that we gather may be large or small but God will turn it into an omer sufficient for our daily needs – then this is the evidence that we have life and are the redeemed of the Lord, and because we eat our daily manna we can look upwards and "we see Jesus, who was made a little lower than the angels for the suffering of death, crowned with glory and honour" (Heb. 2 v 9) and we see Him just as clearly as the Israelites saw the pot of manna that was laid up for them in the sanctuary.

This omer of manna in the most Holy Place was never intended to be eaten as food and it was never intended as a permanent reminder, for when the ark was set in Jerusalem and Solomon, the King of Peace, was established on his throne we read, "There was nothing in the ark save the two tables of stone, which Moses put there at Horeb." (1 Kings 8 v 9). What a wonderful picture. When we partake of the memorial bread and wine it is not to feed upon Him but to remember Him. The omer of manna in the golden pot speaks to us of the glorified Lord, and we remember the living Lord who died but it will not always be so. He is coming again, not as the rejected Messiah but as the king in His glory and strength. No need for us to see by faith the 'golden pot of manna' in the sanctuary for in reality "Thine eyes shall see the king in His beauty" (Isa. 33 v 17). How glorious is our remembrance of Him down here, but how transient, for "ye do show the Lord's death till He come". Let us value our wonderful privilege for very soon, "He that shall come, will come".

"Now an omer is the tenth part of an ephah" (Exod. 16 v 36). We read a verse like this and wonder why God has included it in His word. Does God wish to teach us the Jewish dry measure table? Surely it seems so irrelevant. Moses clearly taught the children of Israel the lesson of the manna, "man doth not live by bread only, but by every word that proceedeth out of the mouth of the Lord doth man live" (Deut. 8 v 3). Here in Exodus 16 where we have the literal account of the giving of the manna we have this incongruous, tough verse, yet Moses is saying in Deuteronomy 8 v 3 that this is food by which we may live. Take the analogy of eating and feeding. Some food, and often the most tasty and succulent, needs a lot of chewing in order to extract the sweetness and goodness, Exodus 16 v 36 is just such a morsel of food. Let us start chewing and see what sweetness there is in this verse.

A literal translation of the word OMER is a 'sheaf'. It is exactly the same word as is used in Leviticus 23 of the wave sheaf or the firstfruits of the harvest. Bear in mind the picture that is given, a golden pot of manna measuring one omer is laid up in the sanctuary, speaking to us of the risen Lord. Now give attention to what Paul says in 1 Cor. 15 v 20, "Now is Christ risen from the dead, and become the firstfruits of them that slept." The firstfruits, the wave sheaf, the OMER, the risen Lord is now in glory. We see Him there as the Israelites saw the golden pot of manna in the ark . . . by faith. "We see Jesus . . . crowned with glory and honour" (Heb. 2 v 9). Now we must ask ourselves why does the Spirit of God take the trouble to record that an omer is the tenth part of an ephah? Most Bible students agree that numbers play an important part in our understanding of the scriptures. Many and various have been the meanings assigned to the number ten. Now just consider the number as it stands. Of all the numbers, ten is the easiest multiplier. In our modern decimal system to multiply by ten is to add a nought to the end of the multiplicand. The number ten is often used in this way in scripture to help to signify a great host, a multiplication of people. In describing the scene where the Ancient of days sits in judgment Daniel records "thousand thousands ministered unto him, and ten thousand times ten thousand stood before him:" (Dan. 7 v 10). There are many other instances in the Old Testament, perhaps the best known is in the Song of Songs, "My beloved . . . is the chiefest among ten thouand . . . Yea, he is altogether lovely." (Cant. 5 vv 10 & 16). In the New Testament the apostle Paul uses the number ten in conjunction with the thousand saying in effect that if we take ten, times ten, times ten, times ten, then we have some idea of what he is talking about in 1 Cor. 4 v 15 and again in 1 Cor. 14 v 19. We have already seen that the golden pot containing an omer of manna speaks to us of the risen Lord. If He is the firstfruits then the harvest must surely follow, "Christ the firstfruits; afterwards they that are Christ's at His coming", a great harvest, an enormous multitude that no man can number. What better way to signify it than by employing the easiest multiplier. Multiply the omer by ten . . . and may we echo by ten, by ten, by ten ad infinitum. "Now an omer is the tenth part of an ephah."

## AARON'S ROD

To understand something of the import of Aaron's rod that budded we must briefly consider the events that led up to this incident. In Numbers 16 we read that two hundred and fifty princes led by Korah challenged the priesthood as ordained of God. This was not so much a challenge to the High Priest but to the priestly system as such. It seems strange that the leader of this rebellion was of the tribe of Levi but he was a Levite and not a priest, the latter office being reserved for the sons of Aaron. The lesson here is twofold. Firstly we must not fall into the error of saying that all believers are priests of the sanctuary (see chapter on Priesthood). Secondly we must not fall into the error of appointing a separate superior priestly order, a lesson typified by the Nicolaitans which, twice over, the Lord says He hates.

The censers of the rebels who perished with Korah were beaten into broad plates to cover the altar. Why should anyone want to cover the altar? More important still, why should Jehovah want the altar covered when He took delight in the fragrance of the ascending burnt offering?

May we suggest that these broad bronze plates were used when the altar was being carried. The fire of the altar must never go out yet the altar had to be covered with a purple cloth, then on it was placed "all the vessels thereof, wherewith they minister about it, even the censers, the fleshhooks, and the shovels, and the basons, all the vessels of the altar; and they shall spread upon it a covering of badgers' skins," (Num. 4 v 14). If we ignore the broad bronze plates for a moment and imagine the above procedure taking place we shall find that the purple cloth would lie over the horns of the altar and hang down, possibly clear of the sides. As we then place all the vessels and instruments of the altar upon this purple cloth it will be carried down so that it rests on the grate in the midst of the altar. Even although the ashes had been removed, this grate would still be red hot in the centre for the fire must never go out. What happens to the purple cloth? If however broad bronze plates were first of all laid over the top of the altar, not only would they hold the coverings clear of the sides, for great emphasis is laid on the fact that they were BROAD plates, but they would form a platform on which the altar utensils could rest and be covered over by the badgers' skins. The plates would also act as a heat sink and this combined with the fact that some of the boards of the altar could be removed, this time from the top of the altar, would enable porterage to be successfully accomplished and the perpetual fire maintained.

If this be so, are there any lessons? The broad plates were "to be a memorial unto the children of Israel, that no stranger, which is not of the seed of Aaron, come near to offer incense before the Lord" (Num. 16 v 40). Might it not be that we are to understand that the whole basis of the tabernacle function, the brazen altar, will only operate correctly if holy, God-appointed men serve as dedicated priests, but don't forget that the plates were beaten very thin. Selah!!!

So much for Aaron's sons. What about Aaron himself? The priesthood of the tribe of Levi having been established in such a positive and dramatic maner, the people now turn on Moses and Aaron blaming them for killing some of the Lord's people. What we have in both of these instances, the rebellion of Korah and the people crying against Moses and Aaron, is virtually the voice of democracy. In the first instance the cry is for equality with the Levites and the priesthood. In the second the challenge is to the leadership. God gives a similar answer in both cases. To Korah the word was "Even tomorrow the Lord will show who are His, . . . even him whom He hath chosen" (Num. 16 v 5), while to the rebellious Israelites God says, ". . . that the man's rod, whom I shall choose, shall blossom:" (Num. 17 v 5). The choice is Jehovah's.

It was thus with the advent of the Son of God. Men challenged His authority and rejected Him, but His appointment as Son and High Priest was not of His choosing but of God's for Hebrews 5 vv 5 & 6 states "So also Christ glorified not Himself to be made an high priest;". It was not a self-appointed office, "but he that said unto him, Thou art my Son, today have I begotten thee.", also said in Psalm 110 v 4 "Thou art a priest for ever after the order of Melchizedek.", showing that both of these appointments came from God Himself.

J

The fact that Aaron's rod budded suggests a life from the dead, a resurrection. The other rods furnished by the eleven tribes were doubtless good rods, serviceable and practical but lifeless. So are all the other religions of the world. Many contain a good moral ethic and set out a commendable way of life, pointing to a road but lacking the power, having no life. The Lord sets Himself up as being the Way; and not only the Way but the Truth and the Life (Jno. 14 v 6) telling men that none can come to the Father but by Him (Jno. 14 v 6), not only showing the one way to the Father but also giving the life and the power for men to tread that way.

Aaron's rod was also remarkable in that it also brought forth leaves, that whereby the plant breathes, taking in that part of the atmosphere that is for the healthy growth of the plant. So the Lord not only rose from the dead but He comes to indwell the disciple so that man can breathe the breath of heaven and absorb into his soul that vital life which shall in time make him fruitful.

Almonds also were produced on Aaron's rod. The Hebrew root from which the word almond is derived suggests sleeplessness, to wake or watch for, the implication being that the almond was so called because it was the earliest to bloom. What does Paul say about the resurrection? "Christ the firstfruits; afterward they that are Christ's at his coming." (1 Cor. 15 v 23).

The content of the ark shows the fulness of God's provision for us in Christ. First of all the tables of the law, holy, just and good but speaking condemnation to men. Secondly Aaron's rod, the dead being raised to life and justification from the law, and finally the golden pot of manna, the food and sustenance for the pathway.

# CHAPTER TWENTY-THREE

# The Cherubim of Glory

An aura of mystery seems to overhang the cherubim. Some view them as the executors of God's judgement, others as God's attributes. One well-known Bible dictionary describes them as "mythical creatures". This we cannot accept as the Bible contains no myths but consists of past history, present truth, and unerring prophecy. In its revelation of the last, the Word of God often uses symbols and signs, never myths. It likens empires to various metals expressed in the form of a human statue in Daniel chapter two and kingdoms are described as animals in Daniel seven. Years are alluded to as thin or fat kine as in Pharaoh's dream and the False Prophets are alluded to as wild beasts in the Revelation. In this manner the Spirit of God brings before us the future of mankind, its various rulers and governments and by depicting these symbolically He gives us an insight into the characters, aims and desires of these mighty forces that shape human destiny.

What do the cherubim represent? They keep cropping up throughout the Bible, they are there in Genesis and it looks as though they are in the Revelation. Our only hope of finding their significance is to trace them from beginning to end. First we must realise that "cherubims" is a double plural, the singular is cherub and the plural cherubim; so in our search we must look at cherub as well as cherubim and not visualise the cherub as some cuddly little baby boy with inadequate wings sprouting from his back, flying round some heathen goddess of the Venus variety or even around a halo-encircled Virgin Mary. Such creatures are myths and do not exist. The cherub of scripture is full grown and awesome in its majesty.

The cherub is not presented to us in Scripture in chronological order and for convenience we will endeavour to consider it in terms of time so that we can see the development. Sufficient to say that the cherubim present us with the first enigmatic characters in scripture. We know who Adam was, God's first created man. We know who Eve was, created out of Adam as a helpmeet for him. We know who the serpent was, the instrument used by Satan to deceive Eve. We know who Satan was, God's arch enemy (and ours also) but who were the cherubim in the Garden of Eden? They present us with one of the last enigmatic characters in scripture for it is only by conjecture that we can identify the "Living Ones" or Living Creatures of the Revelation as being cherubim.

Chronologically the first mention that we have of a cherub is in Ezekiel 28 vv 14-19. Under the guise of addressing a lamentation over the King of Tyrus, the Lord God gives us a description of the downfall of Satan. Most commentators agree that this is so for many of the statements could not apply specifically to the King of Tyrus. It would appear that direct accusations and allusions to Satan's downfall are not allowed in the Old Testament. The archangel Michael dared not bring a railing accusation against him (Jude 9) and even in the Garden of Eden no direct allusion is made to Satan, all is addressed through the serpent. Surely this raises yet another enormous "why?" in our hearts and minds. We may get a glimpse of the reason when we consider that the Lord's anointed was always placed in a very special and sanctified position. David would not lift up his hand against Saul because he was the Lord's anointed. In Ezekiel 28 v 14 we read these words, "Thou art the anointed cherub that covereth; and I have set thee so." Even although Satan was fallen, God himself seems to restrict His condemnation and almost to lament his fall in Isaiah 14 v 12, "How art thou fallen from heaven, O Lucifer, son of the morning" etc. Yet after his fall Satan was still vested with immense power and commanded a certain presence before God as is evidenced in Job 1 v 6, "Now there was a day when the sons of God came to present themselves before the Lord, and Satan came also among them." Maybe this power and privilege was not finally curtailed until he lifted up his hand against the One who was anointed above all, the Lord himself, thus we read that Satan entered into Judas Iscariot (Jno. 13 v 27) and once again he takes the guise of another (in the Garden of Eden he uses the serpent, here he uses Judas) this time to attack, not the first Adam, but the last Adam, the Lord from heaven. The Lord had anticipated this for in the previous chapter He said to the people, ". . . now shall the prince of this world be cast out." No longer is there a restriction in God's publicising Satan's downfall, no longer is he referred to euphemistically as "the covering cherub" or "Lucifer", the curtains are fully drawn back, for he in turn has lifted up his hand against the Lord's anointed. There is no hiding behind the serpent or Judas, for the same apostle John is instructed by the Holy Spirit to write "And the great dragon was cast out, that old serpent, called the Devil, and Satan, which deceiveth the whole world." (Rev. 12 v 9). What a railing accusation.

From Ezekiel chapter 28 we therefore learn that Satan was a cherub. It may well be that he was the only cherub, that this was his exclusive rank for we read of no other cherubim at this time. That Satan was perfect in beauty and excellence we learn from this passage, that his dwelling place was upon the holy mountain of God, almost as though he stood supreme above all the hosts of heaven. Isaiah tells us that his sin was his ambition saying in his heart, "I will be like the Most High." (Isa. 14 v 14) and because of this sin God says, "I will destroy thee, O covering cherub, from the midst of the stones of fire" (Ezek. 28 v 16). How wonderful Satan must have been, the covering cherub. How great was his fall, it tore at heaven itself. Some have thought that Satan's fall was responsible for this earth being reduced to a state of "without form and void". We canot enter into this subject now, sufficient to say that Satan is cast out. The cherub's place is vacant, never to be filled again by Satan. Having set this background let us return to the first mention of the cherubim in the Bible, at the east of the Garden of Eden. How big was the Garden of Eden? A little tiny plot such as some of us have on a modern housing estate, or a vast area in which Adam and Eve could roam and explore the wonders of nature? The garden was at least big enough to have a river flowing through it which divided into four heads (Gen. 2 v 10) which makes it the largest garden that we know. Now God planted a tree, the tree of life in the midst of the garden (Gen. 2 v 9). After Adam's fall God set a "flaming sword which turned every way, to keep the way of the tree of life", so that, as the tree of life was in the midst of the garden then the flaming sword must also have been placed in the midst of the garden, but the cherubim were placed at the east of the Garden of Eden, a long way away from the centre, so we find that most of the artists' impressions of this scene contain at least two errors. Firstly there was more than one cherub. Secondly the cherubim did not hold the flaming sword. What does the scripture say? "And he placed at the east of the Garden of Eden, cherubims, AND a flaming sword which turned every way, to keep the way of the tree of life." (Gen. 3 v 24).

Pause a moment at this dramatic scene. Why was the tree of life in the Garden of Eden at all? Adam was not going to die unless he ate of the fruit of the tree of the knowledge of good and evil. God had not told him that once a day he had to eat of the fruit of the tree of life, neither were there any other conditions laid down concerning that tree. So again we ask the question, "Why was it there?".

Our conception of God is so limited. Indeed it must be, for we are finite and He is infinite. His ways are past finding out. (Rom. 11 v 33). We cannot fathom the omniscience of God. With God there are no problems, only answers and solutions. The fall did not take God by surprise, how could it when "He hath chosen us in Him before the foundation of the world". (Eph. 1 v 4)? God did not engineer the fall, but He knew that sooner or later circumstances must arise where Adam would have need of the tree of life. God also knew that He must bar Adam from eating of its fruit and also that, in the divine wisdom, the fruit of that tree would ultimately be made available to fallen man. The only thing that stood between Adam and Eve and the tree of life was the flaming sword which turned every way. There was no way past this weapon, it turned every way, and it effectively guarded the way to eternal life for Adam. Access could only be gained to that tree if the flaming sword was sheathed. Centuries later the prophet Zechariah wrote, "Awake,

O sword, against my shepherd, and against the man that is my fellow, saith the Lord of hosts." (Zech.13v7). What insight the hymnwriter had when he wrote:

> *Jehovah bade His sword awake,*
> *Oh Christ it woke 'gainst Thee,*
> *Thy blood its flaming blade must slake,*
> *Thy breast its sheath must be. Selah!*

How precious does this scene become. The sword has been sheathed. The way to the tree of life is open to all. Satan's victory is turned into a smashing defeat. Truly, "The Lord has triumphed gloriously". But what of the cherubim, why are they there? No description is given of them, no indication as to how many were present.

Look a little closer. Satan, the serpent, Eve and Adam had all been involved in the greatest tragedy of mankind's existence. God addresses a direct punishment to Adam (Gen. 3 vv 17-19). He inflicts a direct punishment on Eve (v 16). He pronounces a direct curse on the serpent (v 14) but what about Satan? No immediate punishment, no railing accusation against him. A veiled punishment in the cursing of the serpent and a prophecy concerning his future (vv 14 & 15) but no direct punishment and yet he was the instigator of the whole miserable affair, the prime mover, the real villain of the piece. Should he escape without any immediate action? Remember, Satan has lost his position as the anointed cherub, so God puts at the east of the Garden of Eden, in the direction where the sun rises, where there is the hope of a new dawn, whence the "glory of the God of Israel" will come (Ezek. 43 vv 1-6 – a scripture closely linked with the vision of the cherubim by the river Chebar, v 3), a cherub. No that's not right; God places cherubim, telling Satan in no uncertain terms that although he thinks he has gained the victory by causing man's fall, God will be the final victor and bring victory out of defeat. That God is going to bring forth, not one cherub, but cherubim to take that high and lofty place vacated by Satan because of his sin againt God. How bitter Satan's victory must have turned to him. Without a word God says to Satan, "I'm going to fill that glorious position that you once held, I'm going to set someone in the vacant seat of the cherub, and not just someone but many for they shall be cherubim". Wonder what they looked like and how many there were?

Let us press on with the trail of these cherubim. We shall purposely leave the tabernacle cherubim until later so that having come to a conclusion as to their significance we might be able to appreciate their position on the mercy seat in the Holy of Holies.

Once again we must turn to that most difficult of books in the Old Testament, Ezekiel chapter one. In this chapter the prophet is among the captives by the river Chebar and the Word of the Lord comes specifically to him describing, among other things, four living ones. These living ones were first of all like a man (v 5), they had men's hands (v 8). Each one had four faces, the face of a man, a lion, an ox and an eagle. They had four wings (v 6). Now if we compare these four living ones with those described in Revelation chapter four, we see some remarkble similarities but also some marked differences. In both cases there were four living ones, both sets are intimately associated with eyes. Animals' faces characterise both although in Ezekiel each living one has four faces whereas in Revelation it appears that each living one has only one face and they are all different. The faces in both groups are identical except for the ox and the calf although we could view the calf as a young ox. Ezekiel's creatures have four wings whereas John's have six. All of the creatures appear to be in the closest proximity to the throne of God. That there is a connection between the two sets seems quite apparent but to say that they are the same or represent the same picture or type is rather difficult until we come to Ezekiel chapter ten. In this chapter we are introduced once again to the cherubim and in verse fourteen they bear a marked resemblance to the living ones of chapter one except that one of the faces is different and again it is the ox that is changed into a cherub – wonder what a cherub's face is like? Read on a little and in verse fifteen the prophet declares emphatically, "This is the living creature that I saw by the river Chebar.", and in order that there should be no doubt about it he declares in verses 20-22 "This is the living creature that I saw under the God of Israel by the river of Chebar; and I knew that they were the cherubim. Every one had four faces apiece, and every one four wings; and the likeness of the hands of a man under their wings. And the likeness of their faces was the same faces which I saw by the river of Chebar, their appearances and themselves:". Just a moment, Ezekiel, one of the faces was different. "No", says Ezekiel, "they were the same". Gets a bit awkward doesn't it?

That the cherubim are being slowly unfolded in scripture seems obvious. In Genesis chapter three we do not know how many cherubim there were, nor do we know how many wings they had or faces, indeed we know nothing at all about them, they were just cherubim. In the tabernacle and the temple we are given more detail. Here it would appear the cherubim have only one face each and just two wings. Ezekiel gives a much more explicit and complicated picture and identifies them with four living ones. Wonder why he did this?, unless it is to identify the living ones in Revelation with the cherubim for we do not read of cherubim as such in that book. The last reference we have of them in the New Testament is in Hebrews 9 v 5 where they are referred to as the "Cherubim of Glory". What a wonderful title.

Is God changing the picture and the meaning of the cherubim as the scriptures proceed? God does not usually change His types. Leaven in scripture is a picture of sin. It does not change in the New Testament and become a picture of the gospel permeating the whole world. If we interpret it as such then we have our understanding of the types and parables completely wrong. But leaven is always leaven - it does not change in character or appearance whereas the cherubim do. Is this a constantly changing type? Could they be the executors of God's judgments in one instance and His attributes in another and something else on another occasion? This type of understanding is contrary to a right dividing of the word of truth, "Knowing this first, that no prophecy of the scripture is of any private interpretation" (2 Pet. 1 v 20), the difficulty in this case being the way the cherubim keep changing.

In the United Kingdom we have a class structure that includes peers of the realm. Some of these peers rank next in title to the monarch. One such duke decides one day to go to the races at Ascot and he dons grey topper and morning dress for the occasion. The next day he decides to take his seat in the House of Lords, and for this he wears an ordinary lounge suit. On another occasion he must attend a coronation in Westminster Abbey and then his dress will be crimson robes with ermine trimmings and a ducal coronet on his head. How do we describe a duke? As clothed in morning dress, or a lounge suit or in ducal splendour? Surely it all depends on where the peer is and what his function is on that occasion. May not the cherubim be something like that? They represent one group, one class, one order, whose appearance changes with the circumstances and the functions that they must undertake. Consider the original cherub, the anointed cherub of Ezekiel 28 v 14, Satan himself, what does he look like? No, forget the old artists and illustrations, horns, hooves and all that. What does the Word say? As the covering cherub he was perfect in beauty (Ezek. 28 vv 12-17) but he is also described as "a roaring lion" (1 Pet. 5 v 8) and as opposed to that as "an angel of light" (2 Cor. 11 v 14), or in even greater detail, "the great dragon", "the old serpent", and "the Devil" (Rev. 12 v 9). Now what does Satan look like? Surely his description varies with the circumstances and conditions prevailing at the time.

Assuming that our reasoning and deductions thus far are correct let us recap. Satan was the first and anointed cherub, second only to the Godhead itself. He committed an unpardonable sin by aspiring to be equal with God. How unlike the Lord himself, "Who, being in the form of God, thought it not a thing to be grasped at to be equal with God: but made himself of no reputation, and took upon Him the form of a servant, and was made in the likeness of men: and being found in fashion as a man He humbled himself, and became obedient unto death, even the death of the cross" (Phil. 2 vv 6-8) (Newberry). Satan is banished, the cherub's seat is vacant. As God's arch enemy, Satan engineers the fall of Adam and Eve, and God, as part of Satan's punishment, shows him that his exalted position is to be occupied by others, but by whom? Who could be raised to such heights of glory? Could 1 Cor. 6 v 3 help? "Know ye not that we shall judge angels".

We next find the cherubim on the mercy seat in the tabernacle, with their eyes ever gazing on the sacrificial blood, the covering blood, the blood of atonement, that stood between them and the condemnation of the law contained in the ark. These cherubim only had one face each, God had come down to dwell among men, they were in the Holy of Holies and their only right there was the blood of atonement. Are these a picture of the ones who ceaselessly cry, "Thou wast slain, and has redeemed us to God by thy blood" (Rev. 5 v 9)?

Why were there two cherubim on the mercy seat? Why were they made out of one beaten piece (Exod. 37 v 7) and one with the mercy seat (Exod. 25 v 19 and especially margin in Newberry, and Exod. 37 v 8)? Can Ephesians chapter two have a bearing on this? The apostle points out how far we Gentiles were alienated from the commonwealth of Israel (v 12) but now have been made nigh by the blood of Christ (v 13) and he says in verse fifteen "for to make in himself of twain one new man, so making peace". Perhaps we do not fully appreciate the greatness and importance of what God has done in uniting Jew and Gentile as one in the church. The New Testament pays a lot of attention to it, notably in Romans, Galatians and Ephesians. Jew and Gentile joined together and made one in Christ through His blood – two cherubim joined together by their wings, a heavenly union, and made one with the propitiatory, the blood-sprinkled mercy seat. Selah!!! Neither were these two cherubim alone in the Holy of Holies. The ceiling, the heavenly character of the saints, was embroidered with them. How many? Perhaps a great company that no man can number, and by the way, notice how the greatest number of these cherubim were hidden from view behind the boards of the tabernacle. Does this suggest to us that great company of saints, no longer visible in the world, who have been gathered home to glory since Pentecost?

We must pass on to Solomon's temple. Once again we have a picture of two cherubim (1 Kings 6 v 23-28). The ark has come to rest. The staves have been withdrawn (1 Kings 8 v 8). The wanderings in the desert are over and Zion has been reached. The two larger cherubim in the temple have been waiting for the smaller cherubim on the ark to arrive so that the most holy place might be complete. Could it possibly be a picture telling us that the bulk of the church is already in the glory (the two large cherubim) awaiting the arrival of those from the wilderness, "then we which are alive and remain shall be caught up . . . so shall we ever be with the Lord." (1 Thess. 4 v 17). Notice also that the walls of the holy place were decorated with cherubim again suggesting a great number. Ezekiel now comes on the scene and blows everything sky high, for he says cherubim are not like that. His cherubim are no longer static, no longer statues, they are "living ones". This appears to be a watershed in the story of the cherubim, changing them from images to living realities. Prior to Ezekiel the cherubim are not referred to as "living ones", but when we come to the next great description of these creatures we find that they are referred to as "living ones" and not cherubim (Rev. 4). It is interesting therefore to note the characteristics presented by Ezekiel. First of all they are earthly and have the characteristics of a man, they had the "appearance of a man" (Ezek. 1 v 5), "the hands of a man under their wings" (1 v 8) and their first face was "the face of a man" (1 v 10). Wonder what man these cherubim were like? Did they look like Ezekiel the prophet or perhaps more like the man described in chapter one verse twenty-six? – "And above the firmament that was over their heads was the likeness of a throne, as the appearance of a sapphire stone: and upon the likeness of the throne was the likeness as the appearance of a man above upon it". That must have shaken Ezekiel to see a man in the glory.

To enumerate all of the characteristics of Ezekiel's cherubim both in chapter one and also in chapter ten would take a volume in itself. Let the reader settle down with his Bible and a prayer. Read the two chapters concerned, and it matters little who you are or how erudite you are, you will not understand nor comprehend all of its symbolism but certain things seem absolutely clear. These creatures are changing from statues to "living ones" frighteningly majestic, characterised over and over again by the number four yet linked with a great company, "And when they went, I heard the noise of their wings, like the noise of great waters, as the voice of the Almighty, the voice of speech, as the noise of an host:" (Ezek. 1 v 24), four, the earthly number, looking like men yet connected with the glory of the God of Israel, having wings and halting at the east gate of the Lord's house as they ascended. (Ezek. 10 vv 14-end). What company, other than the church, can be identified with these characteristics? True we may not be able to identify every detail, we do not know it all yet, we are learning, but taking the overall picture the type appears to be clear. Surely our guide book, the New Testament, will make things abundantly plain.

There is only one reference to cherubim in the New Testament, Hebrews 9 v 5. Oh well, one reference is better than none. What does it say? Talking of the ark it declares "and over it the cherubim of glory shadowing the mercy-seat". Yes! Yes! – and what else? "of which we cannot now speak in detail" (Newberry margin). What a let-down. Just a moment. This scripture has at least furnished us with a wonderful title, "The Cherubim of Glory". What a superlative. What a pity the apostle could not talk more about them. Wonder why he couldn't?

One reason must surely be found in the fifth chapter where the apostle bemoans the fact that the Hebrew Christians were still babes in the things of the Lord. He had to feed them on milk and not with meat, telling them in the first verse of the next chapter that their salvation and all the basic principles that went with it were only the start of their redemption, the milk which even the youngest believer can drink, but he wants these Hebrew Christians to go on, past that, to "full growth" (Heb. 6 v 1 – Newberry margin). Perhaps we should not blame the Hebrews too harshly for their lack of appetite. Pentecost had only occurred some twenty years earlier and out of these twenty years the apostle Paul had to be converted, have his revelation of the Lord which lasted about three years (Gal. 1 v 18) and the various churches had to be established and instructed. No wonder the apostle found it difficult to tell these immature Christians about a great company, the "living ones". Not until some twenty-five years later when the aged apostle John wrote his enigmatic Patmos revelation could the truth be expounded – The Cherubim of Glory, the Living Ones. What does the word of God tell us through John?

First of all their number was four. Although they are now in the glory they are still branded as those that came from earth. Then we are told that they are full of eyes before and behind (Rev. 4 v 6) and also within (Rev. 4 v 8 cf Ezek. 1 v 18 & 10 v 12). Next we are told that their faces correspond with those of Ezekiel's cherubim except for the calf. The old ox has been laid aside, his work on earth done, and now the young calf takes his place, the eternal servant who never grows old. These "living ones" were each equipped with six wings, perhaps speaking to us of fulfilment and completeness for the most oft used reference to six in scripture is that in six days the Lord made heaven and earth, complete. Maybe the man of sin with his triple six number tends to knock us off balance, but whatever other meanings we might like to give to this number, one thing is certain about him, he will be the very embodiment of evil, the complete culmination of all that is satanic, the anti-christ, the beast – no, the wild beast. Our living ones rest not day or night (Rev. 4 v 8) ascribing glory, honour and power to Him that sits on the throne for He has "created all things" and for His "pleasure they are and were created" (Rev. 4 v 11). What a wealth of truth there is in the scriptures as we chew on its meat. How often in our egocentricity we imagine that salvation was entirely for us, that we might be saved, that we might go to heaven, that we might have eternal life, all of which is perfectly true but these living ones, with their internal and external eyes see things in a fuller and deeper manner. Our creation, our redemption, our eternity were not only for us, that is a secondary matter, the prime object and reason is "for thy pleasure they are (new creation) and were (natural creation) created" (Rev. 4 v 11).

Having looked briefly at the character of these living ones, what is their position in glory? Revelation chapter four and verse six tells us precisely, "And in the midst of the throne, and round about the throne, were four living ones". Where! In the midst of the throne? – but someone is already there "And I beheld, and lo, in the midst of the throne . . . stood a Lamb as it had been slain". (Rev. 5 v 6). Whatever our understanding and interpretation of the Revelation may be, and the interpreters are legion, there can surely be no doubt as to the one in the midst of the throne, the Lamb slain from the foundation of the world (Rev. 13 v 8), the Lord himself. And these living ones are to be with Him in the midst of the throne? That's what it says. Selah! Now listen again to the Lord's prayer in the seventeenth chapter of John's gospel, "Father, I will that they also, whom Thou has given Me, be with me where I am; that they may behold My glory, which Thou has given Me: (John. 17 v 24) – the Cherubim of Glory, with Him and like Him for all eternity, God's initial purpose fulfilled. "Let us make man in our own image." It matters not if you read no further, just revel in this scene, Glory, Glory, everlasting! Selah!

We have not quite finished with the living ones of John's divine revelation, for they are not only in the midst of the throne but they are also round about the throne (Rev. 4 v 6). What, just four living creatures? Once again we have this thought that although they are characterised by the number four yet neverthless they represent a vast company. Why are they not all in the midst of the throne? Isn't there room? Surely a great truth is being taught to us here, a thought expressed in Romans 8 v 17 ". . . heirs of God, and joint-heirs with Christ; if so be that we suffer with Him, that we may be also glorified together". Does this mean that if we do not suffer, or as some translators have it, endure with Him, then we shall not be saved or see the glory? No, may we suggest that what it does mean is that if we endure to the end, then there is a place in the "midst of the throne". If we falter then we must settle for a place "round about the throne". You must still decide your eternal position. The apostle Paul makes this abundantly clear, "For I reckon that the sufferings of this present time are not worthy to be compared with the glory which shall be revealed in us" (Rom. 8 v 18). Selah! Much, much more could be written about these "living ones" but we must needs return to our cherubim in the tabernacle.

Two golden cherubim made one with the mercy-seat, no one saw them but God alone. True there were cherubim embroidered on the ceiling and the vail in the Holy Place and the priests could look on these, flat images of the real thing. They helped the priest to understand what a cherub was like but were only pictures, the golden cherubim were inside the Holiest of Holies and surpassed the embroidery as a subject does the picture, and the two golden cherubim themselves were but images of the true, foreshadowings of the Cherubim of Glory, the Living Ones. Here on the wilderness journey, they are placed at each end of the mercy-seat gazing on the blood of atonement, seeing the blood from God's point of view. Oftentimes, when thinking of the Passover and the salvation of the children of Israel we think of them sheltering beneath the blood and rejoice that we have the same position, hearing the words of Jehovah, "When I see the blood I will pass over you.", words which speak life to the believer and death to those who reject. Wonderful words of life indeed, but also terrible words of death. We remind ourselves that the blood was sprinkled on the lintel and on the two door posts of the houses, not on the step for the blood must never be trodden underfoot by the believer. Wonderful, glorious truths, the blood seen from man's viewpoint. How about in the tabernacle? More blood was sprinkled on the ground than anywhere else, gallons of it soaked into the ground around the brazen altar. When a priest or the whole congregation sinned through ignorance blood was sprinkled before the vail in the Holy Place (Lev. 4 vv 6 & 17) and on the day of atonement the blood was sprinkled before the mercy-seat seven times. All that blood on to the earth, why? The tabernacle is not a picture of God bringing His people out of bondage in Egypt. The tabernacle is a picture of the things that must obtain if God is to dwell among His people. "Let them make me a sanctuary: that I may dwell among them" (Exod. 25 v 8). This was the objective of the tabernacle. Not only must the blood be seen upon the mercy-seat but the earth must be cleansed from its double curse. This is dealt with more fully in chapter twenty-one.

The cherubim look constantly upon that sprinkled blood of atonement. Beneath that mercy-seat there was the Mosaic covenant, the tables of the law, which, although holy, just and good (Rom. 7 v 12) spelt condemnation and death to every sinner, to every man, but as they look upon that blood they see "Jesus the mediator of the new covenant" (Heb. 12 v 24).

No originality is claimed for the thought that when the

tabernacle description specifies "pure gold" the article thus specified refers to the Lord. When the description is just "gold" it refers to the believer. This is exemplified in the boards of the tabernacle which, as we have seen, represent the believers and they are described as overlaid with gold, not pure gold. This is the sort of little quirk that stamps the scriptures as the Word of God, to the casual gold is gold, to the one whose eyes the Spirit has opened, a wondrous and marvellous detail. Look at the descriptions in Exodus 37 "And Bezaleel made the ark of shittim wood . . . and he overlaid it with PURE GOLD, within and without" (vv 1 & 2). Not much doubt about that one, the shittim wood speaking to us of the Lord's spotless humanity and the pure gold of His glorious deity. The only wooden artifact to go from the tabernacle into the temple unchanged. Our humanity although covered with gold cannot go into the temple, it must be changed. Three woods were used in the temple, the cedar, the incorruptible wood, the fir, the strong wood, the olive, the oil wood. What does 1 Cor. 15 vv 42-44 say about the change and the resurrection? "It is sown in corruption; it is raised in incorruption:" – the cedar wood. "It is sown in weakness; it is raised in power." – the fir wood. "It is sown a natural body; it is raised a spiritual body." – the olive tree (oil being a picture of the Spirit) and to crown it all, "It is sown in dishonour; it is raised in glory." All is overlaid with gold.

The next item of PURE GOLD is the mercy-seat (Exod. 37 v 6), the covering of the ark which contained the pot of manna, Aaron's rod that budded, and the tables of the law. When the wilderness is past the manna is no longer needed for the Israelites had first of all the old corn of the land and then the fruits of their own harvest. Aaron's rod is no longer needed in the ark for, "We have such an High Priest, who is set on the right hand of the throne of the Majesty in the heavens" (Heb. 8 v 1), but the tables of the law, what of those? When Solomon had finished his temple ". . . the priests brought in the ark of the covenant of the Lord unto his place, into the oracle of the house . . . There was nothing in the ark save the two tables of stone, which Moses put there at Horeb" (1 Kings 8 vv 6-9). But why cover them with the mercy-seat? How astonishing, God wrote upon these tables of stone with His own finger, yet no one was allowed to see them. The Israelites only knew that God had written them and that they were in the ark because Moses told them. "The just shall live by faith". But surely the faith of the children of Israel would have been strengthened if they could have looked upon that writing. No! It must not be, for those stones spell condemnation. Surely this was why Moses broke the first two stones when he came down from the mount and heard them singing and dancing in the camp. He knew that if he took them into the camp he was taking in God's judgment without an atonement. The mercy-seat must stay on the ark. Jehovah looks, and the cherubim look and see the blood-stained mercy-seat. The ark contained the law, so the Lord met every requirement and fulfilled the law, as it were encompassing it about, rendering its legitimate claims powerless, for, having fulfilled the law and standing pure and sinless death had no claim upon Him, He laid down that life as a ransom for the many. The law is contained, covered by the mercy-seat and the mercy-seat only made effective by the blood of atonement. Oftentimes, mayhap, we think of the perfections of the Lord, His spotless walk, always doing those things that pleased the Father. Pilate's testimony, "I find no fault in Him" (Jno. 19 v 6), the testimony of the malefactor "This man has done nothing amiss" and many other facets of His perfect character. But whatever we do we must not stop there for this only condemns us. This is what we should be, never a false step, never a wrong word. It spells CONDEMNATION in capital letters. Even although we view these things by faith, we are looking inside the ark. True we marvel at His person, and worship at His glory, but the more we ponder Him the more our hearts condemn us, until, as it were, the mercy-seat is in position. The Lord is just as glorious, just as wonderful – perhaps we'll rewrite that. The Lord becomes more glorious, more wonderful for the blood-stained mercy-seat brings us into the good of that perfect life, "and the blood of Jesus Christ His Son, cleanseth us from all sin" (1 Jno. 1 v 7). "For as by one man's disobedience many were made sinners, so by the obedience of one shall many be made righteous" (Rom. 5 v 19). No wonder those cherubim gaze constantly on that blood-stained mercy-seat of pure gold.

The next item of PURE GOLD is the table (Exod. 37 vv 10 & 11) and the instruments thereof (v 16). Here are the twelve pierced cakes of unleavened bread sprinkled with frankincense that the priests alone could eat. Whatever other significance may attach to the loaves being twelve in number it surely reminds us of the fact that the Levites were taken in place of the firstborn from every tribe, teaching us that all may become priests but few do. The loaves presented on the pure gold table set forth the person of the Lord, upon which only priests can feed. The children of Israel were given the manna in the wilderness. It satisfied their temporal needs while in the wilderness and as John six points out this is like feeding on the Lord day by day for everything on the wilderness pathway. It lies upon the ground ready for collection each day of our lives. The priests' food is different. It is fine flour, ground to perfection, it has been mixed and kneaded, it has been pierced and cooked in the heat of the oven, then sprinkled with frankincense and placed in order on the pure golden table, speaking to us of an appreciation of the Lord, unknown by the multitude and fed on only by the priests. The difference between the manna and the shewbread is rather like the difference between 1 Cor. 10 and 1 Cor. 11. The Lord's Table and the Lord's Supper. The Lord's Table is that which is provided for us every day, our food, our drink, our clothing, all the promises of scripture that help us on the wilderness journey, our daily food and sustenance both physical and spiritual. But the shewbread. Only the priests know the flavour of this. It is offered entirely on the pure golden table and administered with pure golden instruments, it speaks entirely of Him. Forget ourselves and the wilderness journey. We are now in an atmosphere that is closed completely to all of that, except for the earth floor to remind us that we are still yet mortal. All earthly sound is blotted out, all earthly light is excluded and the priest feeds on Christ and Christ alone.

Pure gold next features in the golden lampstand (Exod. 37 vv 17-24). The fact that this speaks of the Lord must be patent to all. And finally we come to that little gem, the altar of incense. No worship, no praise can be acceptable unless it is presented on the pure gold of this altar, the Lord himself.

Let us look at the lesser glories, the articles just of gold. No doubt about it they are wonderful but they lack that quality of "pure gold". The Lord must always be supreme, unique. Even although some of us may, in that future day, be in the midst of that throne with Him, we shall never be there as the newly slain young lamb. Only one can fill that role.

The first golden artefacts in Exodus 37 are the two cherubim (v 7), made one with the mercy seat but distinct from it in that the mercy seat is described as pure gold whereas the cherubim are only gold. Did we write "only" gold, isn't that glorious enough? Certainly it is but if our conclusions are correct concerning the cherubim how it emphasises the uniqueness of the Lord. He has brought many sons to glory but there is still only one begotten Son.

The other things made of gold are the rings and staves for carrying the ark, the table, and the altar of incense. The picture is surely correct for the rings and staves are the earthly means of carrying these things that are most holy during the wilderness journey.

And is that the lot? No. We've got a problem. Not another? 'Fraid so. Our type is falling to pieces for the last things that were of gold and not pure gold were the retaining crowns on the ark, the table and the altar of incense (Exod. 37 vv 2, 11 & 26). Cannot be much doubt about that. In all three instances the crown is simply of gold. But, we may argue, the rest is all of pure gold. It must be an oversight not to mention that the little strip running round the top of each article was just gold and not pure gold. If it's an oversight then we can scrap the idea that pure gold speaks of the Lord and just gold of the things relative to His people. Either the word of God is perfect in every detail or it's not the word of God. It is a truism to say that the only errors allowed in the scriptures are printing errors, translating errors, or copying errors. Now this omission of "pure" can be none of these for it is repeated three times over. Instead of abandoning the type, think it through. These crowns were not crowns of glory but were retaining edges, put there to prevent things from falling off, or to hold them secure. How often in the epistles there are exhortations encouraging us to hold fast, not to let things slip, to remain steadfast, and many another. The provision is there, in all its glory, pure gold, but there is that little bit that is required of the saints if they are to enter into the full blessing of the ark, the table and the altar of incense – "give the more earnest heed to the things which we have heard, lest at any time we should let them slip" (Heb. 2 v 1).

# CHAPTER TWENTY-FOUR

# Porterage

The next series of lessons concerns the transport of the tabernacle through the wilderness. The fourth chapter of Numbers gives us most of the details.

Initially a heavy work load fell on Aaron and his sons. Nadab and Abihu had died childless before the Lord and this left only Aaron, Eleazar and Ithamar. The Levites were specifically forbidden from helping. Indeed, on penalty of death they were forbidden even to look upon the holy things while they were being covered by Aaron and his sons (Num. 4 vv 15 & 20). Three men must unbutton the vail from the fifty taches of gold, and that at a height of ten cubits (fifteen feet) from the ground. This large, heavy curtain must be folded and then draped over the ark in order to cover it. Over this must be placed a covering of badgers' skins and then one of blue (vv 5 & 6). They must then proceed to the table of shewbread and cover it first of all with a cloth of blue then "put thereon the dishes, and the spoons, and the bowls, and covers to cover withal: and the continual bread shall be thereon" (Num. 4 v 7), then they must cover this with a cloth of scarlet. No one is going to see this cloth. Well may Aaron and his sons have contended that it was a waste of time and they were too busy, or perhaps the lesson of Nadab and Abihu had taught them that "to obey is better than sacrifice, and to hearken than the fat of rams" (1 Sam. 15 v 22). Over this scarlet cloth a covering of badgers' skins was to be placed, then the lampstand, the altar of incense and all the instruments were each to be covered, first of all with a cloth of blue and then with badgers' skins.

After the things of the holy places Aaron and his sons must

go out to the brazen altar and cover it with a purple cloth, then they must put on top all of the vessels and instruments connected with the altar and finally cover it with a covering of badgers' skins, then the tabernacle is ready to be dismantled. The sons of Kohath must carry the things of the sanctuary. The sons of Gershon were appointed to the curtains and coverings, while the sons of Merari had the burden of the boards and the pillars and all that pertained to them. Who'd belong to the tribe of Merari? True they were more numerous than the Kohathites and the Gershonites but think of their burden. Besides the pillars for the tabernacle perimeter and the gate and the door, they had twenty-eight boards or baulks of gold-covered timber, each of which would possibly weigh a ton. However did they take them down let alone put them up again, and when they were down however did they get enough men under each board to be able to carry it and keep pace with the rest of the camp? Comes to that, who built the pyramids and temples in Egypt? These men were civil engineers of some quality, besides the skills that God had given them. Don't worry, Merari, help is at hand. Just note that the heaviest, most awkward and difficult things that the priests, the Levites had to carry were the boards, and what did we conclude that the boards represented – individual believers? Oh well, perhaps some saints are a bit weighty.

Perhaps we've been a bit harsh on the saints. Here's something to cheer them up. Merari is given the charge of the boards and pillars and all that pertains to them, speaking to us of the various aspects of the individual believers. Now notice another little quirk in the word of God. Of Merari's burden alone it is written, "and by name ye shall reckon the instruments of the charge of their burden:" (Num. 4 v 32). How lovely! Here was the tabernacle being broken down into its individual components and of the burden of Merari alone, that burden that spoke of the individual believers, it is recorded that they were to be reckoned by name. Do we not recall the words of Isaiah the prophet concerning Jacob? "Fear not: for I have redeemed thee, I have called thee by thy name; thou art mine." (Isa. 43 v 1). What a progression of thrilling words. Don't be afraid, fear not. Why shouldn't we be afraid, we're surrounded by sinners and hell is the sinners' reward. The Lord tells us why. "For I have redeemed thee". All the Lord's people have clean passed through the Red Sea. True, but it's more than that. "I have called thee by thy name", each one of us personally, the boards and the pillars, each one with an individual name, wonderful! But it's not finished yet, "Thou art mine". Just think of that. We, no, here we must use the singular pronoun, I, I belong to God. Listen attentively to the voice of the apostle John and don't you dare doubt your salvation again. The Lord Jesus is speaking, "I give unto them eternal life; and they shall never perish, neither shall any man pluck them out of my hand. My Father, which gave them me, is greater than all; and no man is able to pluck them out of my Father's hand. I and my Father are one." (Jno. 10 vv 28-30).

Let us take up our song that we belong to the Lord and say with the Shulamite, "I am my beloved's, and my beloved is mine:" (Cant. 6 v 3).

Let us consider a little more detail. All of the articles of the holy places were covered in blue, proclaiming that these were heavenly things, most holy and all except one were covered on the outside with badgers' skins. Theirs was a hidden holiness, never to be appreciated, even by the Levites, only by Jehovah and the priests. The exception was the ark, for on the ark the badgers' skins and the blue cloth were reversed. Think again about this ark. This was the centre-piece, the only item of furniture in the Holy of Holies. All the wonders and glories of the Lord are crystallised here and the crowning feature is that it must be wrapped first of all in the vail. There can be no mistake about the vail for we are told that this represented His flesh (Heb. 10 v 20), God manifest in flesh (1 Tim. 3 v 16). Jehovah appreciated this and so did the priests, Aaron's sons, and so did the apostle John – "And the Word was made flesh and tabernacled among us, (and we beheld his glory, the glory as of the only begotten of the Father,) full of grace and truth." (Jno. 1 v 14). The ark is next wrapped in the badgers' skins and then in a cloth of blue. Why this reversed order of the coverings? Everything else had a covering of badgers' skins on the outside.

Imagine the camp on the move – the thousands of Israel headed by Judah and right in the middle of this immense army the tabernacle being carried all drab, just bundles upon poles except for one item, the ark, bright blue amidst all the hosts of Israel. For four thousand years God looked upon this earth and beheld its darkness and its iniquity, then one night in Bethlehem shepherds were abiding in the field, keeping watch over their flock and the glory of the Lord shone round about them and the angel of the Lord told them that a Saviour which is Christ the Lord had been born. The fulfilment of all the Old Testament types was to unfold from a manger in a wayside inn, and nigh two thousand years later the poet wrote those wonderful words concerning Bethlehem:

*"The hopes and fears of all the years are met in thee tonight."*

For the first time since Adam's fall God could look down and see amidst the drabness and unattractiveness of even the best of men, one in whom He could find His delight. One who shone out as perfect, holy, undefiled and separate from sinners, one spot of heavenly blue in the whole of mankind's existence.

One other item of the sanctuary furniture had an extra covering beside the blue cloths and the badgers' skins and that was the table of shewbread. Here Aaron was instructed firstly to cover the table with blue (Num. 4 v 7), then he was to place the instruments and the "continual bread" thereon (v 7), and spread over it a cloth of scarlet, then a covering of badgers' skins. Once again, no one except Jehovah and the priests would know of, or see, the blue and the scarlet. Well, why put them there? The blue, as we have already seen, depicts the heavenly character. The table itself, covered with pure gold, was wholly divine, but the loaves and the instruments which were separated from the table by the blue cloth and then covered with the scarlet one, what of these? We have already seen that the loaves, made of fine meal with no leaven in them and pierced so that they should not rise as they passed through the oven speak to us of the wonder, purity and fineness of the Lord's life. There was no sin in Him, no leaven; and no pride, the piercing that even when the loaf passed through the fire it did not rise up in rebellion. Jehovah says, "Cover these loaves and everything to deal with them, in a scarlet cloth". This was Jehovah's obedient servant, the one who was meek and lowly in heart. Clothe Him in the "worm scarlet", the kingship of this world. What does Matthew say as he gives the charter for that Kingdom, "Blessed are the meek: for they shall inherit the earth" (Matt. 5 v 5).

So much for the things of the sanctuaries. We now come to the court and Aaron and his sons have to remove the ashes from the brazen altar and cover it with a cloth of purple, then they have to replace the instruments used on the altar and cover all in badgers' skins. We are not told how this was accomplished when the fire must be ever burning in the altar (Lev. 6 v 13). Maybe this was the purpose of the broad plates made from Korah's censers (Num. 16) that they might act as an additional heat-sink in order to protect the coverings. After all, the covers could have been stretched over the horns of the altar and thus clear of the sides. Once again the same principle applies. God and the priests alone see anything of the purple covering. Why not a blue covering? The brazen altar was essentially of the earth. There was nothing heavenly about Calvary (except the one who hung there). It was the place of a curse. A terrible place. No covering of blue for that altar. Then why purple? This was the place where the lamb was sacrificed morning and evening, a continual offering – the lamb slain in weakness and apparent defeat, wholly acceptable to God. Now join John on the Isle of Patmos, "And one of the elders said . . . "behold, the Lion of the tribe of Juda, the Root of David, hath prevailed . . ." (Rev. 5 v 5) and John says in effect, "Lion? I can see no lion", "I beheld, and lo, in the midst of the throne . . . stood a Lamb as it had been slain," (Rev. 5 v 6). Where was it, John? "In the midst of the throne." Whose throne? "and, behold, a throne was set in heaven, and one sat on the throne" (Rev. 4 v 2). The very throne of God and in the very midst of that throne. Aaron! bring out that purple cloth. Not scarlet this time, the symbol of earthly kingship, but the Emperor's purple. The King of Kings and Lord of Lords. Seated in the heavens, Hallelujah! What a lovely picture that is in the fifth chapter of the Revelation. The elder could only see the Lord as the Lion of Juda, great David's greater Son. John knew his Saviour deeper than that, as the slain Lamb. How it reminds us of the hymn which speaks of the angels in heaven and says,

*"They know not Christ as Saviour, but worship Him as king."*

# CHAPTER TWENTY-FIVE

# Transport

Earlier on we gave words of comfort for Merari and his off-spring. He was faced, not only with taking down the heavy cumbersome boards of the tabernacle but of transporting them. It is recorded that he had over three thousand men with which to do this but there was still the problem of getting a sufficient number of men under each board in order to make porterage possible. We hear no word of complaint from Merari even although his tents are on the north side of the tabernacle, the side from which any cold night or winter winds would come. Again, the lesson of Nadab and Abihu was pretty effective.

What a relief it must have been to the family of Merari when the princes of Israel made an offering to the Lord of six wagons and twelve oxen and four of these wagons and eight oxen were allocated to Merari. Doubtless they still had to do a certain amount of heaving and shoving but nothing as compared to carrying all that timber. Does it not remind us of the Lord's words in Matthew 11 verses 28-30, "Come unto me all ye that labour and are heavy laden, and I will give you rest. Take my yoke upon you, and learn of me; for I am meek and lowly in heart: and ye shall find rest unto your souls. For my yoke is easy, and my burden is light."

Notice, however, that the Kohathites still had to carry their burdens and bear them upon their shoulders (Num. 7 v 9). Egypt's transport (Gen. 45 v 19) was permissible for the generalities of the tabernacle but for those things that speak of Christ a priestly transport is necessary. They alone can lift these things up. Is there not an echo here of the wave offering, where the priests take of these things that speak of the Lord and wave them in the Father's presence? Perhaps even as we gather to remember Him we hear Him say, as Joseph of old said to his brethren, "tell my father of all my glory in Egypt," (Gen. 45 v 13). This is the priestly burden. In the sanctuary all must be sanctified, no wagons, no wheels, just priestly shoulders. It is perhaps significant to note that in the tabernacle there is no music, not even singing. This surely does not mean that we should not sing for singing is the prerogative of the redeemed (Exod. 15 v 1) but perhaps we are being taught that music and singing alone are not acceptable to the Lord. As soon as a choir or an organ takes predominance in a gathering of the Lord's people, something is wrong for "God is a Spirit: and they that worship him must worship him in spirit and in truth." (Jno. 4 v 24). This does not necessarily mean that music is wrong, but it must never lead the praise and cannot enter into the worship. The things of Egypt and the world might be legitimately used outside the sanctuary for Jehovah's service, but inside?

All is now ready to march. The tribe of Judah leads with Issachar and Zebulun, each tribe assembled in order under its standard. In the second rank (Num. 2 v 16) followed the tribe of Reuben with Simeon and Gad, then in the centre of the convoy came the tabernacle carried on the shoulders of the Kohathites and in the six wagons, and surrounded by the Levites. Next in order came Ephraim, Manasseh and Benjamin forming the third rank, and finally Dan, Asher and Naphtali brought up the rear. "They shall go hindmost with their standards" (Num. 2 v 31). "So they pitched by their standards, and so they set forward, every one after their families, according to the house of their fathers." (Num. 2 v 34). How many in this company? 603,550 able-bodied men from twenty years old and upwards that were able to go forth to war. We are not told the maximum call-up age for the armed forces but there must have been quite a company too old to fight. In addition there were all those under twenty years of age, and let us not forget the distaff side, all the women and young girls. What a company, what shall we guess at? Over two million? Rather like the sands of the sea or the stars of heaven. This was not just an ordinary rabble, this was an orderly march and these people hadn't even heard of the apostle Paul, "Let all things be done decently and in order." (1 Cor. 14 v 40). The problems and the hardships of that journey - the sick had to be carried, babies delivered and the dead buried. Seeing that none of the 603,550 fighting men who were numbered in the camp were allowed to go into the promised land (Num. 14 vv 26-35) this alone would have occasioned an average of four deaths a day. Taking into account the rest of the children of Israel there must have been an average daily death rate of between twelve and fifteen, all to be catered for by a marching army. True the two hundred and fifty of the family of Korah presented no problems for the earth opened and swallowed them up but during the forty years there must have been nigh on two million deaths. It is true that the people were rebellious and stiffnecked and brought all their trials on themselves, but even had they gone by the shortest route the journey was impossible without the provision of Jehovah. No food, no water, plenty of pestilence and privation, but as a nation God brought them through. How about our journey through the wilderness? How many of our problems and difficulties have been occasioned simply because we would not trust and obey? Ours is an impossible journey, we are just as rebellious and mistrusting as any Israelite was, but rest assured, our God will never leave us nor desert us but will complete that which He has begun. He will make man in His own image, in spite of Satan and in spite of you and me.

We've kept this mighty host hanging around too long. All are formed up and ready. The pillar of cloud has started to move, the men of Merari put their shoulders to the wagons to get them moving and the camp begins to march. Stop! Stop! We've left something behind. The Laver! The Laver! Who's got it? Kohath, you've got all the sanctuary furniture and the brazen altar; have a look on your poles – ark, table, golden altar, lampstand, instruments, brazen altar. No, it's not with Kohath. Gershon's only got the curtains and soft stuff, he won't have it. Must be with Merari – search through his wagons – boards, pillars, cords. No, no Laver. Aaron, Eleazar and Ithamar, what did you wrap it up in? You didn't? Why not? You weren't told to? Now here's a state of things. Everything packed and ready to go and God has forgotten to give any instructions concerning the Laver. God does not forget. God teaches us lessons by His omissions. What lesson is He going to teach us by leaving the Laver behind? How we jump to conclusions. It doesn't say that they left the Laver behind, it simply doesn't tell us how they carried it. What do we know about this Laver? We do not know whether it was round, square or some other shape. We do not know its height. We do not know its breadth. We do not know its width. All we know is the material from which it was made and the fact that provision was made for the cleansing of the priests before they served in the tabernacle. How nebulous – shapeless yet functional. How like the Holy Spirit – there, yet invisible. What cover shall we put on the Laver? We don't even know how big it is or what its shape is. Who's going to tie the Laver to a pole and carry it? Who's going to attempt to limit the Holy Spirit? Right from the start "the Spirit of God moved upon the face of the waters." What shall it be, scarlet cloth, or purple or goat's hair? Don't try it. "The wind bloweth where it listeth, and thou heartest the sound thereof, but canst not tell whence it cometh, and whither it goeth:" (Jno. 3 v 8). The Holy Spirit, always there, always in the background, yet working to produce results that only God can achieve. How wonderful is the word of God. A simple omission, another little quirk, but what a wealth of truth it contains.

In our little talk about the tabernacle we haven't attempted to understand or explain every little bye-way; rather regard our talk as walking through a picture gallery. After every picture there is a door, some of which we may not even see. The key to open the door is contained in the picture, a sort of combination lock if you like. Some of these doors we have endeavoured to show you, some we have left slightly ajar, others we have opened more fully. Each one leads into another gallery full of a fresh set of pictures and doors. We have been unable to enter far into any of these side galleries. Maybe at times you will think we have wandered too far. This is the danger with these wonderful pictures, we can get carried away. Ultimately we managed to get back to the main Tabernacle Gallery again.

Now it's up to you. Take your guide book, the New Testament, in your hand and go exploring. Some of the doors might be a bit difficult to open, possibly through lack of use. Try oiling the hinges with a little prayer. Sooner or later the door will give and what glories you will see inside.

CHAPTER TWENTY-SIX

# The Priest's Garments

It was not our original intention to include the garments of the High Priest in this consideration of the tabernacle. There are so many things connected with this wilderness edifice such as the various sacrifices, the journeyings of the ark and even the feasts of Jehovah that a halt has to be called somewhere.

The garb of the High Priest, however, seems to be singled out, for its description comes between the two tabernacle accounts in Exodus. We have surely learned already that God does not waste words in His book. If God gives two accounts of the tabernacle He must have a purpose in so doing. What is the difference between the two narratives? Two items omitted in the first description are the altar of incense and the laver. Ah! that laver, how elusive it is. First it's not there, then it is. Another puzzle, another problem. There are also two events that took place between the two tabernacle descriptions - the clothing of the High Priest and his false worship of the golden calf, for in this latter incident it was Aaron who played the most important role. Connect these two couplets together. The altar of incense goes with the garments of "glory and beauty" (Exod. 28 vv 2 & 40) and the laver goes with the worship of the golden calf. Let us store these two couplets in our minds, almost as though we are putting them into a computer. Put them into the Fast Access Store ready to be called upon at a moment's notice.

Now turn to our guide book and look at Hebrews 3 v 1. "Wherefore, holy brethren, partakers of the heavenly calling, consider the APOSTLE and HIGH PRIEST of our profession, Christ Jesus;" and note that once again we have a couplet. The Lord is presented to us for our consideration first of all as "the

*277*

K

apostle" and secondly as the "High Priest". Perhaps we should point out here that nowhere in Exodus is Aaron referred to as the "High Priest", drawing our attention to the fact that he was only a type.

What is the difference between an Apostle and a High Priest? Among other things an apostle was one who received his message direct from the deity. The apostle Paul in particular emphasises that "the gospel which was preached of me is not after man. For I neither received it of man, neither was I taught it, but by the revelation of Jesus Christ". (Gal. 1 vv 11 & 12). Although we like to try and get in on the act it is more than probable that Paul was referring in particular to the apostles when he wrote in 2 Cor. 5 v 20, "Now then we are ambassadors for Christ". An ambassador receives his instructions direct from his monarch. He represents that monarch personally in a foreign land having come out directly from the royal presence. Such were the apostles.

Now consider THE APOSTLE, the Lord himself. He came out from the presence of the Father, representing the Father in all His fulness, God manifest in flesh, with a message of love and reconciliation. Remember it was God who so loved that He sent His Son. What an apostle, the one who came out to man.

Now have a look at the priest for the Lord is not only the Apostle but also the High Priest of our profession (all right have it as "confession" if it helps). The High Priest was the only one who could go into the Holy of Holies into the very presence of God and he went in by way of the gate, the brazen altar, the laver, the door and the altar of incense. (We have purposely omitted the lampstand and the table of shewbread for these were on either side of the direct route. How careful God is to put the altar of incense in the middle, central to the way of approach). So that we have the Apostle coming out from God to man and the High Priest going back from His apostolic journey to man into the very presence of the Deity.

Now recall our two couplets, first of all the garments of "glory and beauty" and the altar of incense. The Apostle is coming out from God, He does not bring the sacred incense with Him for He has not come to worship man neither is He clad in all His glory but He comes forth making Himself of no reputation, taking upon Himself the form of a servant and the likeness of man and humbling Himself and becoming obedient unto death. There can be no altar of incense or glorious apparel until He returns as the great High Priest. As the Apostle coming out from God there is no laver for the question of cleansing from sin has not been dealt with until we come to the brazen altar, for He comes out sinless and undefiled until at the place of sacrifice God lays upon Him the iniquities of us all. The sin of man-made unacceptable worship typified by the golden calf cannot be expiated on the outward journey by the Apostle for no cleansing can be effected until sin is dealt with at the place of sacrifice, the brazen altar.

Consider the High Priest, for that is what the apostle asks us to do. His work as an apostle is complete .He has delivered the message direct from the throne of God to sinful man. He has issued the invitation, "Come; for all things are now ready." (Luke 14 v 17). What an apostle, what an ambassador. Now He returns from man to God, taking the route that He has PERFECTED for us, past the gate, the only way of approach, past the brazen altar, the fragrance of the burnt offering, speaking of the finished work, always ascending to the Father. On past, past what? Yes, the laver. Aaron needed the washing of the laver to cleanse him from the idolatrous worship of the golden calf, the cleansing of the Holy Spirit. The Lord was always directed by and filled with the Holy Spirit. This is why the High Priest had to put on the holy linen garments on the day of atonement, speaking to us of the perfect spotless righteousness of our great High Priest. Rather significant that there is no mention of the laver in Leviticus sixteen, on the day of atonement. Our great High Priest goes on, through the door of the tent into which none but himself and His sons dare enter and approaches the golden altar of incense, taking of that fragrant praise and worship through the vail into the very presence of I AM, ever remembering that "Christ is not entered into the holy places made with hands, which are the figures of the true; but into heaven itself, now to appear in the presence of God for us:" (Heb. 9 v 24).

Now for a tricky one. Hebrews 9 v 7 tells us that "into the

second" (i.e. the Holy of Holies) "went the high priest alone once every year, not without blood, which he offered for himself, and for the errors of the people:". How much simpler it would have been if the apostle had omitted "offered for himself" and just said, "which he offered for the sin of the people". Pretty sure that if we had been writing the Hebrew epistle that is how we would have expressed it, but the Holy Spirit directs Paul to write "which he offered for himself". Surely this cannot be right. We shall have to do a little fast talking to get around this one for the Lord was completely sinless, He committed no errors, He did not need the blood, but the Spirit of God says we have got it wrong again, He did need the blood for Himself.

Perhaps you will feel inclined to hurl these pages across the room. This is it, it must be heresy. Calm down. We trust that by now we have demonstrated that our appreciation of the Lord's sinlessness and perfection is at least as great as yours, it matters little who you are. Words cannot describe the matchless perfection and purity of which He was the embodiment. How then could He need that cleansing blood. Look closely at our text, the "blood, which he offered for himself and for the errors of the people:" Read it again carefully. It does not say "for his errors", he had none, it says "for himself". We are so very parochial in our outlook. That blood was not only for us. There were three who needed that blood. First of all God needed it for He could not "pass over" the sinner unless He could see the blood. Secondly the Lord needed that blood. As it were He presented that blood before the Father as the evidence that He had completed the work that the Father had given Him to do. As the obedient servant the Lord could take the "the blood which He offered" (to God) "for Himself" and say, "It is finished". How wonderful! How meticulous is the word of God. Finally we, as sinners, need that blood to be presented "for the sins of the people" for without that there can be no remission of sins.

Let us then consider in detail the garments of "glory and beauty". Just a moment, why glory and beauty? The glory was Godward. No man can appreciate the full glory of the Lord. John in the first chapter of his gospel says that he beheld His glory but he is to qualify it by saying, "the glory as of the only begotten of the Father, full of grace and truth". This was only one aspect of that glory. The Father only can appreciate in full the glories of the Son. But these garments did not only show the glory, they were garments of beauty. Israel looked upon their Messiah and said, "There is no beauty that we should desire him" (Isa. 53 v 2). We look upon the same Lord and say. "He is altogether lovely" (Cant. 5 v 16). Surely garments of glory Godward and beauty manward.

Look again at these garments of "glory and beauty" and note another little quirk in the sacred writings. Consider the materials that were to be used for the high priest's garments, "Gold, and blue, and purple, and scarlet, and fine linen." (Exod. 28 v 5). They were exactly the same as those used for the gate, the door and the vail. Perhaps we had better write that last sentence again. They were ALMOST the same as those used for the gate, the door and the vail. What were the differences? First of all the inclusion of gold. The priestly garments showed all the heavenly and earthly glories of which the blue and purple and scarlet and fine linen speak, but there was this additional crowning heavenly glory – gold. It is a great and wondrous truth and full of lessons, that there was no gold used in the construction of the tabernacle until we come inside the actual tent. The court was characterised by brass and silver. How true this is until we come to our first little quirk. When the High Priest walked in the court, as he must have done quite often, gold was present among the brass and the silver. For four thousand years God had looked at mankind upon this earth. He had seen some good, some bad, some indifferent but none of them reflected the heavenly glory until the Lord came and earned the accolade, "This is my beloved Son". The golden glory shone in Him and Him alone for He was "the brightness of his glory, and the express image of his person" (Heb. 1 v 3). As the High Priest, clad in his holy garments, walked among men he proclaimed the golden glory of his antitype; but, we may remonstrate, garments of glory and beauty were also made for Aaron's sons, they too would have shown forth this golden glory. Have a look at their garments in Exodus 28 vv 40-41. No mention of gold, our attention is not to be focussed on them, they are simply there to ensure the continuity of the priesthood for Aaron, unlike our great High Priest, was mortal, "for their anointing shall surely be an everlasting priesthood throughout their generations." (Exod. 40 v 15). In Exodus 39 v 3 we read "And they did beat the gold into thin plates, and cut it into wires, to work it in the midst of the blue, and in the midst of the purple, and in the midst of the scarlet, and in the midst of the fine linen, with cunning work." (Newberry), telling us clearly that this gold of glory permeated every aspect of that which the High Priest's robes stood for. We wonder how much insight the song writer had when he wrote, "And glory walked among men". Selah!

Look at the second unexpected quirk in Aaron's garments. What was the description? "Gold and blue and purple and scarlet and fine linen". This was the overall description, not the detail, and we note that it is "fine linen" not "fine twined linen", the lesson surely being that this was a picture of the righteousness that the Lord was in Himself. It did not need to be worked upon or woven for He was a priest after the order of Mechisedec, kings of Salem . . . "King of righteousness" (Heb. 7 vv 1 & 2).

We can look upon our great High Priest and see His beauty. God alone can see His full glory. "No man knoweth the Son but the Father" (Matt. 11 v 27). This is brought out in the clothing of the High Priest. We cannot with any certainty draw a picture of the high priestly garments. There are certain things in the tabernacle of which we cannot make models as we have already shown in the laver. We do not know its size and we do not know its shape, but these restrictions teach us valuable lessons and therefore we will leave the overall picture of Aaron's attire, contenting ourselves with the scriptural description of "glory and beauty" and consider each item in closer detail.

First of all there is the Ephod. Here we go again, what is an ephod? It does not matter about the modern meaning of the word as some sort of ecclesiastical garment. What does the word of God mean by an ephod?

The first mention of ephod is in Exodus 25 v 7. Jehovah is enumerating the gifts that should be taken from the children of Israel and the last items are "onyx stones, and stones to be set in the ephod, and in the breastplate".

In Judges chapter eight we read how Gideon delivered Israel from the hand of Midian (v 22) and Gideon asked for the earrings taken from the Ishmaelites (v 24), then we read, "And Gideon made an ephod thereof" (v 27), so that an ephod can be made of metal. Look at 1 Sam 2 v 18, "But Samuel ministered before the Lord, being a child, girded with a linen ephod". Hence an ephod can be made of linen, but in Exodus twenty-eight, which concerns itself with the Ephod of Aaron we read, "And they shall make the Ephod of gold, of blue, and of purple, of scarlet, and fine twined linen, with cunning work. It shall have the two shoulder-pieces thereof joined at the two edges thereof; and so it shall be joined together. And the curious girdle of the ephod, which is upon it, shall be of the same," (vv 6-8) and lower down we read, "And they shall bind the breastplate by the rings thereof unto the rings of the ephod with a lace of blue, that it may be above the curious girdle of the ephod, and that the breastplace be not loosed from the ephod." (v 28). Nothing's easy is it? Don't give up. God gives us these problems in order to occupy our hearts and minds with eternal things. God has equipped men with brains and in the same way that we can use our tongues either to bless God, even the Father, or we can use them to curse men which are made after the similitude of God (Jas. 3 v 9) so with our brains. We can occupy them puzzling over the Times crossword every morning, mentally cursing the man who made such fiendish clues; or we can meditate on God's puzzles and when He gives us the answer, bless Him for the exercise and the glories revealed to us. What is the actual meaning of the word "Ephod"? Strong in his concordance gives it as "a girdle, or high priest's shoulder piece; also an image". The latter description seems to fit Gideon's image so we can dismiss him. We know that it was not the girdle for we have that as a separate item, so we are left with the shoulder pieces of the High Priest. Why go into all these details concerning the ephod? Mainly to show that we do not and cannot know exactly what the garb of the High Priest was like, emphasising the fact that the Father is the only one who appreciates all the glories of the Son.

From the description given in Exodus twenty-eight it is

apparent that the ephod was not just a shoulder piece for Aaron but it also functioned as a harness to hold and support the breastplate (vv 22-28). Let us consider a suitable construction. Suppose we had two lengths of linen material ornamented with blue and purple and scarlet with gold thread intermingled. The length of each of these strips would be sufficient to reach from Aaron's shoulders to his waist both front and back. The reason for this length is that we read, "And the curious girdle of the ephod, WHICH IS UPON IT, shall be of the same", (Exod. 28 v 8). Visualise these ornamental linen strips as being about fifteen centimetres wide (six inches) and drape them over the High Priest's shoulders one on either side. They extend down as far as the waist where the girdle of the ephod passes over the four ends (two front and two back). Two shoulder pieces are attached to the inside edges of the two linen strips joining them together so that they do not slip off Aaron's shoulders (Exod. 28 v 7). In this way we have a very efficient shoulder harness to support the ornate breastplate. The reason for assessing the width to be about fifteen centimetres is the necessity for them to be wide enough to support the two onyx stones on which the names of the twelve tribes of Israel were to be engraved. Let us press on to these two onyx stones and a fresh problem. The problem is common to most of the stones on the high priest's dress. If we look at the meanings given for the various stones we find over and over again that it is only a possibility that this is the stone referred to. Consider the onyx panels. The Hebrew word is SHOHAM and the meaning? – "from an unused root, probably meaning to blanch; a gem, probably the beryl (from its pale green colour) – onyx". Not very positive to say the least and similar obscure definitions are given for many of the stones in the breastplace. How wary we must be in ascribing specific qualities and meanings to each of these stones when we do not really know exactly what stones we are talking about. So there are no lessons to be learned from these jewels? Of course there are. We will deal with the breastplate later; for the moment let us confine ourselves to the onyx shoulder stones engraved with the names of the twelve tribes of Israel.

Often in the scriptures God expresses Himself in terms that

we can understand. God is omnipresent, everywhere. He sees everything yet in order to focus our attention upon a certain feature God speaks of Himself as looking and seeing in a certain direction. In Genesis chapter six, "God looked upon the earth". Why? Did He not know what was going on? Of course He did but He wants to focus our attention on the fact that these things were under the direct scrutiny of God. Psalm fourteen and verse two reads. "The Lord looked down from heaven upon the children of men", a thought repeated again in Psalm 53 v 2. "God looked down from heaven upon the children of men" and yet again in Psalm 102 v 19 "For he hath looked down from the height of his sanctuary; from heaven did the Lord behold the earth."

The engraved onyx stones on the High Priest's shoulders were of little use to the children of Israel, only the very tallest would be able to see them as they were set in their ouches of gold and perhaps none would be able to read the inscriptions clearly, but what of God? He looks down from heaven and God's viewpoint is very important with regard to the garments of the High Priest. God looks upon the onyx stones engraved with the names of His people, but why onyx stones? Having just pointed out that it is only conjecture that they were onyx stones this seems a strange question, but not if we link it with the same Hebrew word in other parts of scripture. The Hebrew word is SHOHAM and it first occurs in Genesis 2 v 12 where "the Lord God" (v 8) describes the Garden of Eden saying, the "land is good: there is bdellium and the onyx stone." That does not seem to help us much. Think a little, this is a description of that land. What land? The land where Adam was going to dwell, and of Adam we read in 1 Cor. 15 v 47, "The first man is of the earth, earthy" and verse 48 goes on "As is the earthy, such are they also that are earthy:" As God looks down on the High Priest He sees that which speaks to Him of the earth, and as these stones were engraved with "the names of the children of Israel: six of their names on one stone, and the other six names of the rest on the other stone, according to their birth." (Exod. 28 vv 9-10), may we suggest that they speak of God's earthly people, Isreael. Do not begrudge the Jews their portion, our turn will come.

Before leaving the ephod we must mention the "curious girdle".

Curious expression really, yet it is no accident for it occurs six times in Exodus in connection with this girdle and the word seems to imply "a strange place" or "a curious invention". Let us note that all of the characteristics, gold, blue, purple, scarlet and fine twined linen are incorporated into this girdle. We have already dealt with these things in detail and now we have them all grouped together in a girdle. What are we to understand by this? A girdle is that which restricts or limits, and in order to become our High Priest every aspect of His effulgence had to be restricted and a limit or boundary put upon it. Gold – the veiling of His glory; blue – the Lord from heaven walked here as a man; purple – His excellences as King of Kings limited to riding into Jerusalem on an ass; scarlet – His earthly kingship limited to an accusation over His cross, "This is Jesus, the king of the Jews"; fine twined linen – the perfection of His pure life mocked by the accusation that He was a glutton and a winebibber. That curious girdle, how it limited the glories that were His, but that was the "strange plan" of the Godhead in bringing salvation; it could be accomplished in no other way. This combination of the ephod and the girdle formed the perfect harness for holding the beautiful breastplate of judgement.

Consider this breastplacte of judgment. It is referred to as being "of judgment" not because it was to be the source of punishment and condemnation but because here the issues of right and wrong were to be revealed by the URIM AND THUMMIM, the "lights and perfections". The breastplate was not a metal casket but a pouch or bag made in the same way as the ephod and of the same materials (Exod. 28 v 15). It was to be perfectly square, measuring a span either way and it was to be doubled. We suggest that it was folded at the bottom so as to form a pouch or bag into which the Urim and Thummim were to be placed. The breastplate was to be fastened to the ouches on Aaron's shoulders by golden chains (Exod. 28 v 22-25) and to the ephod with a lace or ribbon of blue. The front of this bag or pouch was to be ornamented with precious and semi-precious stones set in golden mounts (v 20).

First of all let us look at the bejewelled front of the breastplate. The nomenclature is not nearly as precise as on the onyx stones. On the shoulder plate we are told that there were to be six names on each side, that they were to be graven into the stone "with the work of an engraver in stone, like the engravings of a signet" (Exod. 28 v 11). Furthermore they were to be in a specific order "according to their birth" (v 10). We find no such clearly defined instructions with regard to the breastplate. Our text reads, "And the stones shall be with the names of the children of Israel, twelve according to their names, like the engravings of a signet" (v 21). We may find difficulty in imagining a diamond big enough to have a name engraved on it. We may conjecture that it would be difficult, even with modern equipment, to engrave on to a diamond, one of the hardest substances known to man. All right, God could have provided a diamond as big as a house if needs be and God could have given sufficient "spirit of wisdom" (v 3) for Bezaleel, Aholiab and all their assistants to engrave the whole of the law if necesary, but it is not recorded that He did. We might even be justified in thinking that the engraving was on the gold mount of each stone for the instruction is "the stones shall be with the names of the children of Israel" (v 21).

We are not saying one way or the other but just pointing out that there is not the preciseness of instruction with regard to the breastplate as that detailed on the onyx stones. By the way, where did the stones come from to put into the breastplate? As far as we know there were no deposits of sapphires, emeralds, diamonds and amethyst in the wilderness. Cast your minds back to Exodus chapter twelve when the children of Isreal were leaving Egypt. Verse thirty-five reads, "And the children of Israel did according to the word of Moses; and they borrowed of the Egyptians jewels of silver, and jewels of gold," and we read that the people found favour in Egyptian eyes and received the jewels and the silver and the gold. So the jewels on the breastplate were jewels brought out of Egypt – how interesting. Would we be unfair to say that the salient feature about the front of the breastplate was that it was ornamented with Egyptian jewels to each of which some name or other had been given? What is Aaron going to do with this breastplate? "And Aaron shall bear the names of the children of Israel in the breastplate of judgement upon his heart, when he goeth in unto the holy place," (Exod. 28 v 29). Now here is a thing! Aaron is going into the Holy Place with the names of the children of Israel and the jewels from Egypt. As yet the vail was still intact before the Holy of Holies although there are occasions when we are encouraged to view it as already rent from top to bottom. Hebrews chapter nine supports this. Suppose this is one of these occasions for we know that our High Priest is entered into the heavens. The High Priest now stands before a rent vail, face to face with the ark and mercy seat, and where is Jehovah? "And there I will meet with thee and I will commune with thee" yes, but where? "from above the mercy seat, from between the two cherubim which are upon the ark" (Exod. 25 v 22), so that (speaking as a man and from a man's point of view) God is no longer up above, looking down on Aaron and seeing just the children of Israel on the onyx stones (His earthly people), but looking from between the cherubim, just about on eye level with the breastplate and what does He see? The children of Israel and the jewels of Egypt, Jew and Gentile made one and carried on the heart of the High Priest. "And they shall be mine, saith the Lord of hosts, in that day when I make up my jewels;" (Mal. 3 v 17). Egyptian jewels, maybe, but carried on the Lord's breast, near and dear to His heart. Selah!

We cannot leave the breastplate yet for there are still lessons to learn. What of the Urim and Thummim? "Ah yes", we cry, "lights and perfections" and promptly move on because we do not know what the Urim and Thummim are. We have no positive record of their ever having been used. The nearest is in Numbers 27 v 21 where Moses is told that Joshua should stand before Eleazar the priest "who shall ask counsel for him after the judgment of Urim before the Lord" (why no Thummim? must be a lesson there) but we do not read that this was ever put into operation. Why then mention the Urim and Thummim at all? Perhaps we should bear in mind the fact that the whole of God's will concerning His people was not yet manifest. We pointed out earlier that He would meet and commune with Moses "above the mercy seat, from between the two cherubim" and tell him "of all things which I will give thee in commandment unto the children of Israel" (Exod. 25 v 22). We now have the complete word of God. There is not going to be a further revelation until the Lord takes His people home and then we shall see how right or wrong we were in understanding His word. But, some might protest, the Urim and Thummim was used in Nehemiah's day. Was it? or was that pragmatical politician telling the priests that had no genealogy that they had not a hope of serving, but it was not really his fault or his decision. If a priest could arise with Urim and Thummim to declare their worthiness then he would be more than delighted that they should serve. As far as we can see he had not even got the original garments of the High Priest, let alone the breastplate containing the Urim and Thummim.

What then is the lesson for us? Surely this, that the wisdom and counsels of God are enshrined in the breastplate and as we have seen the breastplate shows forth the glories of both Jew (the names) and gentile (the Egyptian jewels), united into one company. As the apostle Paul puts it when writing to Timothy, "which is the church of the living God, the pillar and ground of the truth" (1 Tim. 3 v 15). No one has a special hot line to the Lord claiming special guidance or revelation from Him. If we have a problem, and who hasn't, then the answer and the only answer we shall get is through the Urim and Thummim, in other words through the revealed word of truth vested in His church.

Considering that the breastplate was made of blue and purple and scarlet and fine twined linen interspersed with gold and was therefore like a highly ornamented linen pouch, being, from what we can understand, not a terribly heavy object, the method of fastening it to the ephod seems rather elaborate. Someone was making very sure that the breastplace could not become detached therefrom. First of all there were "chains ...of wreathen work of pure gold" (Exod. 28 v 22) and these were evidently attached to two rings on the breastplate and their other ends fastened to the ouches of gold which contained the onyx stones on the High Priest's shoulders. In addition there were four other rings (vv 26 & 27) through which laces of blue were threaded in order to hold the breastplate secure "that the breastplate be not loosed from the ephod" (v 28). Wreathen chains, many stranded, plaited and entwined, not just ordinary chains but chains of exquisite workmanship. Wonder what they represent. The field is very wide and doubtless many thoughts flood into our minds. Perhaps we can give some sort of expression to them by referring to John chapter 17. The Lord is finishing the discourse given to His disciples and He directs His prayer to His Father. Space will not permit us to write the whole of the chapter here even although it would be profitable so to do. If you would understand what we are trying to express read the whole chapter and see some of the strands of the wreathen work. Let us turn over in our minds some of the wonderful truths of salvation. We shall never see the full glories of that stranded wreathen work that binds us to the breast of our Great High Priest, but meditate upon a few that even now we might "behold His glory". The apostle Paul tells us in the Ephesian epistle that "He hath chosen us in Him before the foundation of the world" (Eph. 1 v 4). Just think of that. Scientists tell us that the foundations of this world are very old indeed, running into millions of years, how many who can say. No two sources agree and after all what is a million or so either way among the world's scientists? Maybe they are right, maybe they are wrong, it does not really matter. We are still surrounded by a complex and beautiful world, but what does matter is that whether the years of this world are few or many, before ever it came into existence we were chosen in Him. That truly is a pretty strong, intricate and beautiful strand in the chains that bind us to Him.

"Before the foundation of the world" is only the beginning of the bond. It's a good beginning and goes back a long way but see some of the other strands in these chains. All of the Old Testament types and prophecies, laborious, meticulous workings on these chains until one glorious night the Saviour of the world was born. Trace the strands of that perfect life, ever fulfilling the prophecies. Think of that last supper when the Lord asked His disciples to remember Him. Onward into Gesthsemane's garden, the sweat as it were great drops of blood; the betrayal, through the judgement hallls, the spitting, the scourging, the plucking of the hair from his cheeks, the crown of thorns. Ah, wreathen work indeed. How strong were the pure golden strands that were being worked. Hear the Lord's prayer on the way to Gethsemane's garden and the culmination of all of this "That they all may be one; as thou, Father, art in me, and I in thee, that they also may be one in us" (Jno. 17 v 21). Strong words, strong chains, marvellously wrought.

Come forward into the epistles and we read "the head, even Christ: from whom the whole body fitly joined together and compacted by that which every joint supplieth, acording to the effectual working in the measure of every part, maketh increase of the body unto the edifying of itself in love." (Eph. 4 vv 15 & 16). Could we be closer to Him? The breastplate is held firm by wreathen chains and these chains are fastened to the golden ouches on the High Priest's shoulder, the place of strength and power, yet the breastplate still rests on His breast, near His heart, for "Christ also loved the church, and gave Himself for it" (Eph. 5 v 25).

But the wreathen chains are not alone in holding the breastplate for there are another four rings attached to it through which laces of blue bind it firmly to the ephod. Laces of blue; heavenly ties. Four rings; earthly anchors. This is no longer the picture of the golden crowns holding secure the mercy seat, the incense and the shewbread. Our High Priest is risen and entered into heaven itself, the wilderness is past, the ties are heavenly for He "hath raised us up together, and made us sit together in heavenly places in Christ Jesus: that in the ages to come He might shew the exceeding riches of his grace in his kindness toward us through Christ Jesus." (Eph. 2 vv 6 & 7). What heavenly laces! Safe and secure through all eternity. Selah! The next adornment of the High Priest was the robe "all of blue" referred to in Exodus 28 v 31 as "the robe of the ephod". From this we may conclude that it has to be in close proximity to the ephod and was therefore worn underneath the breastplate and possibly underneath the ephod. This robe was to have "a hole in the top of it in the midst thereof" (v 32) and this hole was to have bound edges so that the robe would not be torn at any time. In Leviticus 21 v 10 we are told that the High Priest "shall not uncover his head, nor rend his clothes". How far had Caiaphas the high priest fallen in the execution of his office when we read "Then the high priest rent his clothes" (Matt. 26 v 65) and accused the Lord of blasphemy. Who was the guilty party?

The blue suggests to us that which is heavenly not only in the character and person of the High Priest but it furnishes us with further evidence that the breastplate speaks to us of His "heavenly people" (we use this expression in order to differentiate them from His "earthly people", not forgetting that Israel has a portion in the glory for Jehovah constantly refers to Himself as "the God of Abraham, Isaac and Jacob") for the breastplate rests directly on this robe of blue, whereas the onyx stones rested directly on the ephod.

Our first impression of the robe might be a circular piece of blue material with a hole cut in the middle through which the High Priest's head could go, this hole to be bound to prevent any tearing. The reason for this impression is the location of the hole for it is described as being "in the midst thereof". Upon reflection, however, we can see that this could not be so. Were we to place the circular robe over the head of the High Priest and then place the ephod and breastplate into position over this and finally tie the curiously wrought girdle into position we should have trussed the High Priest like a chicken, unable to move his arms for they would be securely fastened to his sides by the robe, held in position by the girdle.

Another concept of the robe of the ephod seems to fit the description. If we had a strip of blue material about fifty centimetres (20") wide and at least two metres (just over two yards) long, we could cut and bind a hole for the head of the High Priest central in the fifty centimetre width and central in the two metre length. This would meet the specification that the hole must be "in the midst". If we now drape this robe of blue over the head of the High Priest we shall find that it reaches to his middle thigh front and back. The robe may have been longer than this but it could not have been much shorter for when the girdle was tied over it there must still have been enough loose material to move freely as the High Priest walked so that the bells and pomegranates, with which this robe was edged, could swing freely thereby causing the bells to sound which heralded the presence of Aaron. With this design of the robe the High

Priest's arms would be free to move even although the girdle, breastplate and ephod were in position.

Bells and pomegranates seem strange bedfellows to have along the edge of the robe. Bells we can perhaps understand for we are told their purpose "and his sound shall be heard when he goeth in unto the Holy Place before the Lord, and when he cometh out, that he die not" (Exod. 28 v 35), but what of pomegranates? It has often been pointed out that a pomegranate is absolutely full of seeds and must therefore represent fruitfulness. Do not dismiss this idea for there is often more than one thought behind some of God's types. The pomegranate is full of seeds, it would scarcely be possible to pack another one in, but a fruit that must contain even more seeds, size for size, is the fig; but God does not say that there is to be a fig then a bell but that the bells are to be alternated with pomegranates. Dare we look for another answer?

The Hebrew word for pomegranate is RIMMON. This word is surely associated with Naaman the Syrian, that incident that so many of us use at times to justify a shady religious act. Naaman had already expressed his complete faith in Jehovah, a faith that we can well understand in a man who has just been cured miraculously of leprosy. He had asked for two mules' burdens of Israel's earth to be given to him, obviously having learned the lesson of Exodus 20 v 24 "An altar of earth thou shalt make unto me, and shalt sacrifice thereon thy burnt offerings," and he now turns to Elisha with his problem about bowing in the house of Rimmon when his master goes in to worship. The prophet tells him to "Go in peace" (2 Kings 5 v 19). Surely Naaman was justified in this action because of the faith that the had already expressed. Justification by faith was to take place in the house of Rimmon, the pomegranate.

The only garment in the attire of the High Priest that is said to have a hem is the robe, where the pomegranates were. The only other places in scripture where we read of a hem are in Matthew 9 v 20 and Matthew 14 v 36, both of which scriptures refer to people being healed by touching the hem of the Lord's garment. They "besought Him that they might only touch the hem of His garment: and as many as touched were made perfectly whole." (Matt. 14 v 36) – a simple act of faith in which they were justified by being healed. The hem of His garment and the pomegranates are both connected with justification by faith.

Hebrews chapter eleven begins, "Now faith is the substance of things hoped for, the evidence of things not seen." What a pomegranate! The outside of the pomegranate is among the hardest of all fruits, just like a bit of leather, but we know that if we can penetrate this rind we have a many compartmented beautiful fruit. The leathery exterior is "the substance of things hoped for, the evidence of things not seen". What about the fruits inside the pomegranate? Read down the list in Hebrews eleven, all the patriarchs and Old Testament saints, a host of others too numerous to name and finally including all the saints right up until now for "they without us should not be made perfect" (Heb. 11 v 40), each one an individual tasty cell. Some pomegranate!

Let us return to the tabernacle. What happened there? On the day of atonement the High Priest went into the Holy Place alone. There he changed his garments and in doing so he caused the pomegranates to hit against the golden bells bordering his robe so that the sound thereof could be heard outside the Holy Place. The children of Israel did not see Aaron, they did not see him change his clothes, they did not see him take a censer of incense from the altar, they did not see him go into the Holy of Holies but they did hear the ringing of the bells as Aaron changed into the linen garments and believing the evidence of their ears they knew that their High Priest was presenting the blood of atonement before Jehovah. The noise of the bells and pomegranates was the evidence of things not seen. "The just shall live by faith", one of the most oft repeated texts in the word of God. (Hab. 2 v 4, Rom. 1 v 17. Gal. 3 v 11, Heb. 10 v 38). It is worth noting that Aaron had an alternative set of garments entirely of linen. Their exact design is difficult to ascertain although from Leviticus chapter sixteen we know that he was to have "linen breeches upon his flesh, and shall be girded with a linen girdle, and with the linen mitre shall he be attired" (v 4) and he was to put them on in the holy place (v 3). After completing the offices of the atonement he "shall put off the linen garments, which he put on when he went into the holy place, and shall leave them there . . . and put on his garments, and come forth," (vv 23 & 24). We shall deal with the linen garments in greater detail later but we mention them here because of their connection with the bells and pomegranates. Exodus twenty-eight verse thirty-five reads "and his sound shall be heard when he goeth in unto the holy place before the Lord, and when he cometh out, that he die not." It was not so much that the bells were heard as Aaron was walking about, but when he went into and came out from the Holy of Holies, in other words, when he was changing from his garments of glory and beauty into those of linen. Take note of the veiled warning in the first verse of Leviticus sixteen, "And the Lord spake unto Moses after the death of the two sons of Aaron, when they offered before the Lord, and died;". What was the admonition to Aaron? The sound of the bells must be heard when he was changing "that he die not". Perhaps we can understand something of the iniquity (or perverseness) of the holy things (Exod. 28 v 38). After all, Aaron was a man of like passions as we are. How he must have shaken that robe as he took it off and put it on. His very life depended on the sound being heard outside. We will refer to this later when we consider the linen garments.

Before leaving the robe of the ephod we would remind ourselves that men clothed the Lord in a scarlet, or purple, or gorgeous robe, earthly colours and description. God clothes the High Priest in a robe "all of blue". This High Priest, although a man, is a picture of the heavenly.

Returning to Aaron's ceremonial clothes we are next introduced to his headgear. The word translated "mitre" means "a tiara, a mitre or a turban". We feel that the latter is most likely in the case of the High Priest but we are not told exactly. What we are told in detail is the fact that there was to be a "plate of pure gold" and engraved upon it the words "HOLINESS TO THE LORD" (Exod. 28 v 36). It was to be put on a lace of blue and worn on the forefront of the mitre (v 37). Later on we are told that the blue lace was used to tie the golden plate to the mitre, "And they tied unto it a lace of blue, to fasten it ON HIGH upon the mitre". (Exod. 39 v 31).

When dealing with the onyx stones we pointed out that this was Jehovah's view of the High Priest. He sees all of the promises and prophecies concerning His earthly people made yea and amen. He sees the golden panel, so placed that it can be read by God and man, high up on the forefront of the mitre, proclaiming that this was the Holy One of Israel, and look at the glories portrayed in the mitre. What glories? No detailed description is given of the mitre for "no man knoweth the Son, but the Father;" (Matt. 11 v 27). We can see and understand something of His glories but,

> *"The Father only – glorious claim!*
> *The Son can comprehend."*

Finally we come to the coat that was designed for Aaron, possibly the largest garment of his attire yet once again very little is said about it, simply "And thou shalt embroider the coat of fine linen" (Exos. 28 v 39). Wonder what that coat was like? Did it have short or long sleeves? Did it have a hem? Did it have a collar or lapels? We shall have to wait until we get to the glory. All we are told is that it was embroidered presumably with gold and blue and purple and scarlet. Must have been a gorgeous coat, a coat of many colours – what was that? A coat of many colours. Who else had a coat of many colours? "Now Israel loved Joseph more than all his children, because he was the son of his old age: and he made him a coat of many colours." (Gen. 37 v 3). The father's appreciation of his son. Selah! Far be it from us to suggest that God is getting old. That cannot be true for He is the I AM, ageless and eternal, although He does describe Himself in His book as the "Ancient of days" (Dan. 7 v 22) but compare our reference in Genesis 37 v 3 with the first two verses of Hebrews. "God who at sundry times and in divers manners spake in time past unto the fathers by the prophets, hath in these last days spoken unto us by His Son". Selah!

We must leave the garments of glory and beauty. Not that we have exhausted all of their symbolism. We have given the bare bones. Sit back with the word of God and clothe them with flesh, but just notice another little quirk before we close. The High Priest's sumptuous robes were described as garments of "glory and beauty". This word 'beauty' is sometimes translated as 'honour' (Deut. 26 v 19, Jud. 4 v 9, Psa. 71 v 8, Jer. 33 v 9). "Garments of glory and honour". Look at the sequence of events concerning the Lord's death. John 13 v 4 tells us that He "laid aside His garments;", the cloak woven from the top throughout, the clothing in which John the baptist had seen Him as "The Lamb of God", garments that the apostle John had looked at when he beheld His glory, maybe just ordinary clothes in the eyes of the natural man but if our eyes have been opened as John's were then they must be "garments of glory and honour". Turn onwards in John's gospel to chapter 19 v 40, "Then took they the body of Jesus, and wound it in linen clothes". Behind all of the surface events and suffering is there not the echo of the High Priest whose garments of "glory and honour" were changed for those of linen on the great "Day of Atonement"? The Lord has gone into death, presented the blood of atonement to Jehovah and now what? Look at Heb. 2 v 9, "We see Jesus, who was made a little lower than the angels for the suffering of death, crowned with GLORY and HONOUR; that he by the grace of God should taste death for every man." The High Priest has been re-invested with His garments of Glory and Honour, or if you prefer the description, garments of "Glory and Beauty". Selah!

We will pass no further comment. Just ponder and let the scriptures speak for themselves. "Then took they the body of Jesus, and wound it in linen clothes" (Jno. 19 v 40). "Simon Peter . . . went into the sepulchre, and seeth the linen clothes lie, and the napkin, that was about his head, not lying with the linen clothes, but wrapped together in a place by itself." (Jno. 20 vv 6 & 7). The High Priest, gone into the most Holy Place with the blood of atonment? And the head covering lying in a place by itself, God's appreciation of His Son, distinct, separate, perfect (wrapped together)? Selah! Selah! Selah! The Spanish have a marvellous farewell saying,

> *"Vaya con Dios" "Go with God".*

not, *"God go with you"* but *"You go with God"* – He must take the lead. As you tread this wilderness pathway or fight the battles in the land, Vaya con Dios. As you open the pages of Holy Writ and seek to tread that way of righteousness, Vaya con Dios. Such is the prayer of an old man who is

> *Yours, because His.*

# General Index

The aim has been to make this index as comprehensive as possible. Words such as "Tabernacle" and "Moses" have been omitted for they occur so often that practically every page would have to be listed. Should there be any slight omissions or inclusions that you may consider unnecessary, put these down to human fallability.

Although the gender is changed, the author feels like the woman in Mark 14 v 8. "She hath done what she could". His only prayer is that this work may have added, in some very small measure, to that same workship of that same Lord.

| | |
|---|---|
| Gershon | 44, 267, 274 |
| Gethsemane | 38, 178, 208, 290, 291 |
| Gideon | 283 |
| Gift(s) | 11, 12, 138 |
| Girdle | 283, 284, 285, 286, 292, 293, 294 |
| Giving | 43, 45 |
| Glory | 42, 46, 53, 54, 120, 132, 163, 183, 210, 224, 229, 240, 241, 242, 243, 251, 253, 254, 256, 257, 258, 259, 262, 264, 265, 268, 273, 280, 281, 282, 286, 290, 292, 295, 296, 297 |
| Goat(s) | 118, 146, 147, 227, 231, 232, 233 |
| Goat's hair | 41, 146, 147, 152, 156, 275 |
| Goblets | 172, 188, 189, 191 |
| Godhead | 43, 125, 254 |
| Gold | 41, 53, 54, 158, 171, 175, 177, 178, 185, 225, 226, 232, 261, 263, 264, 265, 266, 281-287, 289, 295, 296 |
| Golden | 7, 30, 53, 236, 240, 241, 243, 260, 274, 277, 279, 281, 291, 296 |
| Gospel(s) | 65, 82, 92, 129, 213, 217, 253, 278 |
| Grace | 32, 42, 44, 46, 52, 54, 132, 163, 200, 208, 210, 214, 217, 218, 224, 237, 268, 281, 291 |
| Grate | 44, 108, 109, 110, 111, 116, 184, 203, 205, 209, 244 |
| Grating | 109, 115, 117 |
| Greece | 41 |
| Grief(s) | 228 |
| Grind | 238 |
| Ground | 230, 260, 263 |
| Guide book | 42, 43, 50, 99, 112 |
| Guilt(y) | 236 |
| | |
| Hair | 28, 33, 177 |
| Hand(s) | 112, 252, 256, 268 |
| Hangings | 50 |
| Harvest | 242, 243, 261 |
| Head(s) | 11, 12, 33, 106, 256, 291 |
| Healed | 228 |
| Heart | 227, 288, 291 |
| Heat | 44, 109, 111, 112 |
| Heaven(s) | 39, 40, 51, 131, 210, 222, 226, 228, 231, 246, 248, 249, 258, 270, 271, 279, 285, 286, 291 |
| Hebrews | 129 |
| Heifer | 86 |
| Height | 108 |
| Heirs | 259 |
| Hell | 56, 80, 81, 210, 240, 268 |
| Helpmeet | 248 |
| Hem | 293, 294 |
| Heresy | 280 |
| Herod | 19, 38, 101 |
| High Priest | 16, 23, 31, 41, 71, 127, 153, 158, 169, 170, 183, 190, 200, 202, 213, 217, 222, 226, 227, 229, 230, 232, 233, 234, 241, |

L

# INDEX

# Scriptural Index

| | | | |
|---|---|---|---|
| JOHN (*cont.*) | 16 | 24 | 24 |
| | 17 | — | 290 |
| | 17 | 12 | 232 |
| | 17 | 21 | 74, 291 |
| | 17 | 21-22 | 60 |
| | 17 | 24 | 259 |
| | 18 | 1 | 178 |
| | 18 | 4 | 37 |
| | 18 | 5 | 211 |
| | 19 | 2 | 88 |
| | 19 | 5 | 27 |
| | 19 | 6 | 262 |
| | 19 | 15 | 101 |
| | 19 | 23 | 88 |
| | 19 | 24 | 232 |
| | 19 | 26-27 | 116 |
| | 19 | 28 | 117, 232 |
| | 19 | 30 | 113, 117 |
| | 19 | 33 | 84 |
| | 19 | 33-37 | 212 |
| | 19 | 34 | 128 |
| | 19 | 40 | 297 |
| | 20 | 6 & 7 | 297 |
| | 20 | 19 | 68 |
| | 20 | 31 | 87 |
| | | | |
| 1 JOHN | 1 | 7 | 262 |
| | 2 | 12 | 181 |
| | 2 | 15 | 238 |
| | 3 | 2 | 25, 26, 80, 146, 152, 163 |
| | 3 | 5 | 227 |
| | 4 | 8 | 37 |
| | | | |
| JOSHUA | 2 | 18 | 85 |
| | 3 | 3 | 89 |
| | 3 | 4 | 222, 234 |
| | 3 | 15 | 219 |
| | 3 | 16 | 219 |
| | 3 | 17 | 219 |
| | 4 | 2 | 222 |
| | 4 | 3 | 222 |
| | 4 | 5 | 219 |
| | 4 | 8 | 219 |
| | 4 | 9 | 219, 223 |
| | 4 | 10 | 219 |
| | 4 | 16-19 | 219 |
| | 5 | 2 | 223 |
| | 8 | 30 | 119 |
| | | | |
| JUDE | — | 9 | 248 |

# INDEX

| | | | |
|---|---|---|---|
| NUMBERS (*cont.*) | 31 | 22 | 44 |
| | 35 | 16 | 44 |
| 1 PETER | 1 | 10-12 | 83 |
| | 2 | 2 | 102 |
| | 2 | 5 | 51, 206 |
| | 2 | 9 | 12, 13, 17, 21 |
| | 2 | 22 | 227 |
| | 2 | 24-25 | 228 |
| | 3 | 3 | 28 |
| | 5 | 1-6 | 74 |
| | 5 | 2 | 70 |
| | 5 | 3 | 12 |
| | 5 | 8 | 254 |
| 2 PETER | 1 | 20 | 253 |
| | 3 | 17-18 | 130 |
| PHILIPPIANS | 1 | 6 | 232, 237 |
| | 1 | 16 | 165 |
| | 2 | 6-8 | 254 |
| | 2 | 8 | 175 |
| | 2 | 8-11 | 87 |
| | 2 | 9-10 | 80, 240 |
| | 2 | 17 | 205 |
| | 3 | 10 | 21, 132, 187 |
| | 3 | 10-12 | 102 |
| | 3 | 19 | 29 |
| | 4 | 18 | 205 |
| PROVERBS | 1 | 26 | 165 |
| | 20 | 1 | 192 |
| | 21 | 4 | 81 |
| | 29 | 18 | 147 |
| PSALMS | 1 | 2 | 130 |
| | 2 | 7 | 164, 165 |
| | 14 | 2 | 285 |
| | 22 | — | 165 |
| | 22 | 14 | 213 |
| | 22 | 16 | 84 |
| | 22 | 17 | 213 |
| | 24 | 7-8 | 154 |
| | 24 | 9-10 | 154 |
| | 34 | 20 | 212 |
| | 37 | 13 | 165 |
| | 49 | 7 | 25, 78 |
| | 51 | 5 | 79 |
| | 53 | 2 | 285 |

# GOD'S SANCTUARY

ISBN 0 946351 31 7

Typeset by Newtext Composition Ltd., Glasgow
Printed by Bell & Bain Ltd., Glasgow